YOU ARE A THEOLOGIAN

THINKING RIGHT ABOUT SALVATION

BEN GISELBACH

plain**simple**faith.com
faith that just makes sense

Published by PlainSimpleFaith
www.plainsimplefaith.com

To order additional copies of *Thinking Right About Salvation (You Are A Theologian series)*
visit www.plainsimplefaith.com.

ISBN: 978-0-9911139-3-4
Library of Congress Control Number: 2018952512

Cover design & interior layout by Ben Giselbach

To my wife and best friend:
a woman who fears God,
walks in His light,
and brings so much joy to my life.
Thank you for teaching me about God's grace.

ACKNOWLEDGMENTS

G.K. Chesterton once dedicated a book to his secretary, "Without whose help this book would have been published upside down." I feel the same way about what I have written. While this book falls short in many areas, it would be a supreme embarrasment without the help of the following people, all of whom are smarter and godlier than myself. I am deeply grateful for the time, knowledge, and wisdom contributed to this book by Caleb Colley, Ted Garner, Hannah Giselbach, Brian Giselbach, Glenn Colley, Jacob Rutledge, Tony Clay, Kevin Rhodes, Don Blackwell, Tonja McRady, Rick Brumback, Jared Jackson, Hiram Kemp, Edwin Jones, Mike Vestal, Allen Webster, and Westley Hazel. I am also deeply appreciative for the layout, proofing, and design expertise of Brandon Edwards, Shane Robinson, and Tonja McRady. Some of you sacrificed a great deal of time for this project. Without your help, this book would be upside down. Thank you.

TABLE OF CONTENTS

Note to teachers: If using this book in a class situation, it is recommended that you plan on devoting at least two or three class periods for each chapter.

PREFACE

THEOLOGY is not for wimps. God expects Christians to move from the "basic principles" of the Bible to the meat of His word (Heb. 5:11-14). The goal of this book is help Christians *think*. We want to graduate from "milk" and move on to "solid food." While many of the concepts in this book are elementary, you may find others to be quite challenging. Hopefully, *challenging* is what you are looking for. Though I wrote this book as accessibly as I could, not every part is a "light read" exactly. On the other hand, I didn't write this book primarily for academics and well-educated preachers—I wrote it for average, faithful Christians who simply have a desire to go *deeper*. Take your time with this book; chew on a section at a time.

We sometimes call the study of salvation *soteriology*. We get this from the combination of two Greek words, *sōtēr* ("savior, preserver") and *logos* ("study" or "word"). Thus, *soteriology* is the study of doctrines that directly relate to salvation. Next time someone asks you what you are studying right now, just tell them *soteriology*. You are bound to impress.

Many books dealing with the subject of salvation have emphasized what must initially be done in order to find salvation. They emphasize what is popularly called the "plan of salvation" or the "5 steps of salvation," summarized in the words *hear* (Rom. 10:17), *believe* (John 3:16), *repent* (Acts 2:38), *confess* (Rom. 10:10), and be *baptized* (Rom. 6:3-4; Gal. 3:27; 1 Pet. 3:21). As important as these steps are, by themselves they do not adequately communicate the essence of salvation. These steps presuppose at least a basic, prior understanding of the human soul, the problem of sin, our desperate need for grace, and Christ's work of atonement.

Furthermore, many books dealing with the subject of salvation have stressed what one must do to be saved *at the neglect* of adequately teaching what one must to do *stay* saved. To what degree have Christians been saved from sin? Can Christians have any kind of assurance of salvation? What does the Christian walk look like? How does God keep Christians saved? You will find that I have given a great deal of attention to these subjects in this book.

Pay careful attention to the footnotes, as there are some important comments to be found. You may notice that this book cites works by Christians (who may range from faithful and unfaithful) and non-Christians alike. I reference them when I feel they bring value to a particular study. Please consider each citation based upon its own merit, and not as an endorsement of everything the individual teaches. Above all, be like the noble Bereans by studying everything you read in light of the Scriptures (cf. Acts 17:11). After all, even this book is only true to the degree that it accurately communicates what is found in God's word.

In keeping with my custom with every book in the *You Are A Theologian* series, the last chapter is designed to be more practical. I've chosen to conclude our study of salvation with an examination of the fear of God, as salvation can only be received in the context of godly fear. I am indebted to Albert N. Martin's book *The Forgotten Fear* for inspiring much of that material. Additionally, right before publishing this book, I also decided to include a critique of the phrase "salvation issue" as it is popularly used in our brotherhood. I felt such an addendum would be a good application of the principles contained in this book, challenging us to rethink our terminology. Salvation is a result of our right standing with God, not so much the satisfaction of a man-made checklist of "salvation issues."

If you are a Bible class teacher, this is a good book to use in a class setting. Don't just recite it in class; study the content ahead of time and summarize it for the audience. Make sure each student has a copy, and challenge them to study it throughout the week. You may want to spend two or three weeks on each chapter.

My hope is that you will find some of the issues discussed in this volume interesting and valuable. One of best compliments you can give me is, "Ben, you really made me think." Perhaps this book will make you think, hopefully in a way that is right.

In the hope of eternity
with Him,

Ben Giselbach
July 30, 2018

FOREWORD

BY ALLEN WEBSTER

BEN Giselbach is a young man who, like David, stands out from the crowd (1 Samuel 17:56). Like Jehu, it is easy to see his zeal for the Lord (2 Kings 10:16). Like Timothy, older men trust him (Philippians 2:20). Like Jesus, he is about his Father's business (Luke 2:49). He has untethered enthusiasm for the kingdom, undaunted optimism for the future, and an unbounded work ethic when he puts his mind to something. Few men of any age write a book a year, as he has set his heart to do.

This volume may be the most important Giselbach writes regardless of the years that may come and the books that yet remain percolating in his mind. For its theme is the most important contemplatable: **salvation**.

Giselbach takes the reader through the necessary topics to appreciate a comprehensive view of salvation. Beginning with man's composition, he demonstrates that man differs from—and will ultimately outlive—all other creatures. He turns the spotlight to the dark side of human behavior by discussing sin and its consequences. This chapter is important for no one is interested in a Savior until he realizes he is lost. Ben logically proceeds from sin to the atonement showing its development from Old Testament types, shadows, prophecies, and precepts to the beautiful completion of God's plan on the cross, at the empty tomb, and in the open door of the church.

Giselbach next turns the reader to grace and conversion, beautifully showing how grace connects to each gospel requirement—belief, repentance, confession, and baptism. He takes on easy-believeism in the chapter on sanctification—a much-needed study in our culture—and Calvinism in discussing freedom from sin. He gives the reader valuable insights in the in-depth lesson on sin from several prospectives. These two chapters alone are worth the book's price.

The section on assurance will help faithful readers sleep better at night as it gives a reasonable basis for Christian hope. It may keep nominal Christians awake at night as it gives them ample reason to pause and consider their ways. The chapter on authority shows how pivotable it is to clear the field of false standards and simply follow the Bible. Concluding with a look at the fear of the Lord, Giselbach shows how to stay motivated for the long haul—even until those sweet words, "Well done, good and faithful servant" become the most wonderful sounds ever heard.

After reading this book, do not put in on a shelf. Gift it to someone who needs it.

INTRODUCTION

SALVATION is the central theme of the Bible. The Hebrews author calls it "great" (Heb. 2:3), and a list of some of the Bible's synonyms helps us see why. Salvation means *justification* (Rom. 5:1), *regeneration* (Titus 3:5), *redemption* (Rom. 3:24), *forgiveness* (Eph. 1:7), *reconciliation* (2 Cor. 5:18–20), and *life* (1 John 3:14). What refreshing, beautiful words!

Yet as positive as salvation is, it carries with it the implication of danger. Salvation, after all, implies salvation *from something*. Thus, the Israelites were saved from Egyptian slavery (Exo. 3:7-8), Noah and his family were saved from the flood (Gen. 7), Jesus saved His apostles from a storm in Galilee (Matt. 8:25), and Christians are saved from their sins. The angel told Joseph, "[Mary] will bear a son, and you shall call His name Jesus, for He will save His people from their sins" (Matt. 1:21). We have all sinned (Rom. 3:9-10, 23), and without Jesus, we are destined to pay an unbearable price for our sins: "The wages of sin is death, but the free gift of God is eternal life in Christ Jesus our Lord" (Rom. 6:23). When Paul writes that "the wages of sin is death," he includes the "second death"—a lake that burns with fire and brimstone (Rev. 21:8). Thus, salvation for the sinner essentially means "snatching them out of the *fire*" (Jude 23, emp. added). Oh, how we should fear sin and eternal death!

Scripture highlights two basic aspects of salvation: The apostle Paul summarizes the first aspect—God's offer of salvation—in Romans 5:8: "God shows His love for us in that while we were still sinners, Christ died for us." In a word, this is God's *grace* (Eph. 2:5). We don't deserve salvation, nor can we merit it. God in His sovereignty has chosen to offer you and me salvation from our sins. But God will not save us against our will. We chose sin (Rom. 3:23), and He has invited us to now choose salvation. The fact that salvation is even an option is pure grace—we don't deserve God's invitation. Nonetheless, God still does not force anyone to be saved against their will. The incredible offer of salvation comes with a condition—*faith*.

Faith, man's response to God's grace, is the second aspect of salvation. God in His sovereignty has given man an important role in his salvation, and this role is stressed throughout the Scriptures (cf. Acts 2:40-41; Phil. 2:12). Sinners come to Christ and to God's grace by what Paul calls the "obedience of faith"—the message he was commissioned to preach to the world of sinners (Rom. 1:5; 16:26). Sinners become sons of God and heirs with Christ when, by faith, they are baptized into Christ and put on Christ (Gal. 3:26-27; Rom. 8:16-17).

Paul, in Ephesians 2:8, combines both aspects—God's grace and man's response—in one statement: "For *by grace* you have been saved *through faith*. And this is not your own doing; it is the gift of God" (emp. added). Notice that the "gift of God" (grace) is conditional; God *requires* faith. "Without faith it is impossible to please Him" (Heb. 11:6). Because pleasing God is the most important thing we can do, our study of salvation is something we cannot afford to take lightly.

We are going to study the most important—the most fascinating—the most humbling subject humanity can know. It has nothing to do with my ability (or, more accurately, my lack of ability) to express these truths. What we are going to study is the very thing the prophets of old and angels in glory longed to better understand (1 Pet. 1:10-12).

David prayed, "Restore to me the joy of your salvation" (Psa. 51:12). There is no joy like that of being saved; the saved can rejoice in the hope of eternal life (1 Pet. 1:3–6), fellowship with God (1 John 1:7), the privilege of worship (John 9:31), freedom from worry (Phil. 4:6–7), and the fellowship of other saints (John 13:35).

CHAPTER 1

THIS IS US

WHAT IS MAN?

IF one believes that mankind evolved from primordial slime over the course of millions of years, it is very difficult to argue with a straight face that mankind has any intrinsic worth. Today's secular worldview tells us that human beings are mere evolutionary flukes that now happen to infest the earth. George Gaylord Simpson, considered to be one of the most influential paleontologists[1] of the 20th century, said, "Man is the result of a purposeless and materialistic process that did not have him in mind."[2]

Such a low view of human origins results in a low view of humanity in general. Sigmund Freud, the world-renowned psychoanalyst and a fervent atheist, once quipped, "I have found little that is good about human beings. In my experience most of them are trash." He continued, "In the depths of my heart I can't help being convinced that my dear fellow men, with a few exceptions, are worthless."[3]

By accepting the evolutionary explanation of man's origin, honesty demands us to also conclude that man holds no more intrinsic value than the rest of the animal kingdom. It is from this point of view that the famous Australian secular philosopher Peter Singer rather candidly observed, "[The claim] that there is special value in the life of a member of our species [...] cannot be defended."[4] Consequently, prominent thinkers of our secular age increasingly see human population growth as a scourge upon the earth. David Attenborough, an iconic British broad-

---

1 **Paleontology** is the field of science dealing with the life forms of past geological periods as evidenced from their fossil remains.
2 George Gaylord Simpson, *The Meaning of Evolution*, p. 19
3 Ernst L. Freud, *Letters of Sigmund Freud*, 1873-1939, p. 390
4 Peter Singer, *Practical Ethics*, p. 89

caster and naturalist who has narrated some of the most well-known wildlife documentaries, says that mankind is but a "plague on the earth."[5]

The post-Christian message of secular society demands the inevitable conclusion that human beings are meaningless accidents. There is no way to rationally argue in favor of the intrinsic worth of humanity when our existence is divorced from any acknowledgment of God.[6] On the other hand, the Bible offers a much different picture of humanity. King David wrote:

> When I look at your heavens, the work of your fingers,
> The moon and the stars, which you have set in place,
> What is man that you are mindful of him,
> And the son of man that you care for him?
> Yet you have made him a little lower than the heavenly beings
> And crowned him with glory and honor. (Psalm 8:3-5)

We are not accidents. Instead, we have been intentionally *made*, held to a *moral standard*, and given a *unique, special value*. We did not come into existence out of some idle curiosity on the part of God. Rather, being fashioned in God's image (Gen. 1:26), we are just "a little lower than the heavenly beings," and thus the crowning glory of God's earthly creation.

We are not accidents. Instead, we have been intentionally made, held to a moral standard, and given a unique, special value.

The biblical worldview gives mankind a wonderfully peculiar level of dignity unequaled by any other earthly creature. God placed mankind in this position and "crowned him with glory and honor." In so doing He shared some of His sovereignty with man by granting dominion over His creation. There is a sense in which we are earth's caretakers, delegated by God to rule the natural world on His behalf. But what makes humans different from the rest of the animal kingdom?

---

5 David Attenborough, *The Telegraph*
6 In fact, all absolute and objective values are ultimately grounded in the absolute God.

WHAT MAKES A HUMAN A PERSON?

The simplest yet most profound picture of mankind is found in Genesis 1:26-28, where we read about the sixth and final day of the universe's creation. The Bible records this:

> Then God said, "Let us make man in our image, after our likeness. And let them have dominion over the fish of the sea and over the birds of the heavens and over the livestock and over all the earth and over every creeping thing that creeps on the earth." So God created man in His own image, in the image of God He created him; male and female He created them. And God blessed them. And God said to them, "Be fruitful and multiply and fill the earth and subdue it, and have dominion over the fish of the sea and over the birds of the heavens and over every living thing that moves on the earth." (Gen. 1:26-28)

In the previous days of creation, God began each day of creation with, "Let there be…" However, on the sixth day, when He created man, He used all of His creative genius. The phrase "Let us" indicates the personal involvement of every member of the Godhead.

The parallel account of man's creation in Genesis 2 gives additional information as to how man was created: "The Lord God formed man of the dust of the ground, and breathed into his nostrils the breath of life; and man became a living soul" (Gen. 2:7, KJV). That is, a living human being is a unity of dust (matter) and breath (life). The word *soul* in this passage is a general term and in this context means "person," which includes both the body and spirit. In Psalm 16:10, David wrote concerning Christ: "You will not abandon my *soul* to Sheol, or let your holy one see corruption"

Jesus taught that one man's soul is worth more than the whole world (Matt. 16:26).

(emp. added). We know the word *soul* in this context includes both the body and the spirit because both Jesus' spirit and body were resurrected—the spirit from the Hadean realm and the body from the grave (cf. Acts 2:30-31). We can see that human beings are two-fold beings.

A human person, made in the image of God, includes both the fleshly body and the spiritual soul. The precious personhood that God breathed into the nostrils of man's body is what makes humanity immeasurably valuable. Jesus taught that one man's soul is worth more than the whole world (Matt. 16:26).

PHYSICAL AND SPIRITUAL: THE DUAL NATURE OF MAN

Biblically speaking, human beings are two-dimensional; we have a physical side and a spiritual side.

The Bible presents man as being composed of two unified yet distinct states of being: physical and spiritual. This is sometimes referred to as **ontological**[7] **dualism**[8] or **dichotomy**.[9] Try not to get lost in this theological jargon; what matters most is the concept.

Biblically speaking, human beings are two-dimensional; we have a *physical* side and a *spiritual* side. Both the Old and New Testaments make this clear. As we look at the biblical terminology used in this discussion, notice there is often a degree of flexibility to the meanings of these words.[10] Thus, when we come across any of these words in Scripture, we need to pay attention to the context to know what the word means in any given instance.

BIBLICAL WORDS USED FOR THE PHYSICAL DIMENSION OF HUMAN BEINGS

Flesh. The word *flesh* (Hebrew: *basar*, Greek: *sarx*) is almost always used

---

7 **Ontology** is the philosophical the study existence. It is primarily concerned with questions such as, "What is the difference between existence and merely appearing to exist?" "Are there different categories or types of existence?" "How does one state of existence relate to another?"

8 **Dualism** teaches that man is fundamentally two parts (i.e. physical and spiritual), as opposed to monism, which teaches man is only one kind of substance (e.g. man is just a physical body).

9 **Dichotomy** is the idea that man can be divided fundamentally into two parts (i.e. body and spirit), as opposed to trichotomy, which teaches that man is composed of three distinct parts (i.e. body, soul, and spirit).

10 As we study the subject of salvation in this nine-chapter book, be impressed with the fact that many biblical words, such as *soul*, *sanctification*, *sin*, etc., have multiple definitions. This is why it is so critical to give special attention to the context of each usage. This requires us to meditate on Scripture, not just divorce individual verses from what God is actually saying.

to refer to the outer, or physical, dimension of human beings, though sometimes it is used to refer to animal or human life in general (e.g. Gen. 6:12, 17; 7:15). Naaman "went down and dipped himself seven times in the Jordan, [...] and his flesh was restored like the flesh of a little child" (2 Kings 5:14). After His resurrection, Jesus said, "Touch me, and see. For a spirit does not have flesh and bones as you see that I have" (Luke 24:39). Peter, quoting David in Psalm 16, observed that Christ's fleshly body was redeemed as well when he said Jesus was "not abandoned in Hades, nor did His flesh see corruption" (Acts 2:31).

Body. In the Bible, the word *body* (Hebrew: *basar*, Greek: *soma*) is used in reference to the outward aspect of human nature. The Hebrew language doesn't make a distinction between "body" and "flesh" (notice the same Hebrew word is used), but the Greek tongue does. The body is portrayed as being weaker than the spirit (cf. Isa. 31:3). It deteriorates and eventually dies, at which point man's spirit departs temporarily (Jas. 2:26). Paul speaks of glorifying God "in your body" (1 Cor. 6:20) and honoring Christ in the body (Phil. 1:20). We are to present the body to God "as a living sacrifice" (Rom. 12:1).

Jar of Clay. The image of a clay jar is used to illustrate the human body. "But we have this treasure [i.e. the light of the gospel—BG] in jars of clay, to show that the surpassing power belongs to God and not to us" (2 Cor. 4:7). Clay jars are made from the dirt of the earth, just as our bodies are (Gen. 2:7). And like these metaphorical clay jars, our bodies are designed to contain something inside—souls.

Earthly Tent. Similar to the jar of clay illustration, the picture of a tent is also used to illustrate the human body. Paul says that "if the tent that is our earthly home is destroyed, we have a building from God, a house not made with hands, eternal in the heavens" (2 Cor. 5:1). When the Son of God entered this physical world in a human body, John says that He "became flesh and dwelt among us" (John 1:14). The Greek word here rendered as *dwelt* is actually difficult to translate, but it literally means "pitched His tent" or "tabernacled"[11] among us. Just as a tent is a tempo-

---

11 The tabernacle was a tent that served as a temporary dwelling place of worship that the Israelites built according to God's exact specifications while traveling and wandering in the desert (cf. Exo. 39:32). They used the tabernacle until King Solomon built a more permanent

rary structure designed to house something inside, the body is a physical structure designed to house an immaterial soul, or spirit, inside.

Outer Self. There is a contrast between the outer self and the inner self. "Though our outer self is wasting away, our inner self is being renewed day by day" (2 Cor. 4:16). The outer self is visible to the eyes, tangible, able to be touched, and—as we have seen in James 2:26 as well as this passage—is apt to "waste away."

BIBLICAL WORDS USED FOR THE SPIRITUAL DIMENSION OF HUMAN BEINGS

Soul. When you read the word *pear*, you know exactly what I am talking about: a nasty, disgusting fruit that no human being should consider edible.[12] However, when you read the word *bolt*, I could be referring to any number of things. As a noun, a bolt could be a type of metal fastener or a ray of lightning (i.e. a lightning bolt); as a verb, to bolt means to run extremely fast. Only by reading the context can you know what I mean when I use the word *bolt*.

In modern times, we generally use the word *soul* synonymously with the word *spirit*. Throughout this book we will use the words interchangeably because the Bible often does this, too. Because the Bible uses the word *soul* (Hebrew: *nephesh*, Greek: *psychē*) in several different ways, we need to understand the context to know how the word *soul* is used. In fact, there are at least four major ways this word is used.[13]

First, sometimes the word for *soul* is used simply as a synonym for *person*. If we were to say, "1,503 souls perished during the sinking of the *Titanic*," we are saying that 1,503 *people* died in that tragedy. In fact, the Hebrew and Greek words for *soul* are translated *person* several times (Gen. 12:5; 46:18; Exo. 12:15; Lev. 7:20; Josh. 10:28; Jer. 52:30; Eze. 13:18; 1 Pet. 3:20). Additionally, sometimes phrases like "my soul," "your

---

temple. Since the Old Law was designed to be our schoolteacher to help us better appreciate the Christian system (cf. Gal. 3:24; Rom. 15:4), the tabernacle shows us that Jesus is our permanent avenue through which we come to worship and know God (cf. John 14:6).
12 I hate pears.
13 William Arndt, *A Greek-English Lexicon of the New Testament and Other Early Christian Literature*, p. 1098. Guy N. Woods, *Questions and Answers, Vol. II*, p. 102

soul," "his soul" are simply used in place of a pronoun, such as "I," "you," "him" (cf. Gen. 27:4; Exo. 30:16; Num. 30:5, KJV).

Second, sometimes *soul* is used in reference to the component of life that animates the bodies of humans and animals.[14] Used this way, it is the "life of the individual" and the "animating life force, sustaining earthly existence."[15] In Genesis 2:7, God assembled the body of man from the dirt of the ground and then animated it by "breathing into his nostrils the breath of life," and the man became a "living creature" (*nephesh hayyah*, literally "soul-breather" or "life-breather"). The same is said of the animals in Genesis 1:20, 24, and 30. The Law of Moses stipulated that "if there is any harm, then you shall pay life for life," or more literally, "soul for soul" (Exo. 21:23). Jesus said, "Do not be anxious about your life (literally *soul*), what you will eat or what you will drink, nor about your body, what you will put on" (Matt. 6:25). Paul and Barnabas, like countless other Christians, "risked their lives (literally *souls*) for the name of our Lord Jesus Christ" (Acts 15:26).

Third, sometimes *soul* is used in reference to man's heart or mind. In this context, the soul is the seat of mankind's moral conscience, emotions, rationality, and awareness. God commands you love Him "with all of your heart and with all your soul (*nephesh*)" (Deut. 13:3). The soul causes the body to weep (cf. Jer. 13:17; Psa. 119:28) and houses our knowledge and understanding (Psa. 139:14), thoughts, memories (Lam. 3:20), and love (1 Sam. 18:1). The soul has the capacity to remember, even when separated from the body (Luke 16:25). The soul is the source of our worship to God (Psa. 146:1). Jesus promised "rest for your souls" (Matt. 11:29) if you are faithful to Him. The early Christians "were of one heart and soul" (Acts 4:32).

Fourth, *soul* is used to refer to the part of man that lives on after death. The only difference between this usage and the third usage is the thrust of the word. Genesis 35:18 speaks of the soul leaving the body at the point of death: "As [Rachel's] soul was departing (for she was dying),

---

14   Animation, or ensoulment, is what makes something come alive in working order. Vegetation and locomotion (at the plant level) and sensation (at the animal level) are exclusive qualities of ensouled creatures.
15   Stephen D. Renn, *Expository Dictionary of Bible Words*, p. 918-919

she called his name Ben-oni." Jesus warned His disciples: "Do not fear those who kill the body but cannot kill the soul. Rather fear him who can destroy both soul and body in hell" (Matt. 10:28). Revelation 6:9 speaks of souls in heaven that have been completely separated from their bodies: "When he opened the fifth seal, I saw under the altar the souls of those who had been slain for the word of God and for the witness they had borne."

As we can see, *soul* is a general word and the context must determine what is specifically meant. So broad is the word that both the Hebrew and Greek words for *soul* are frequently translated *life* in our English Bibles. Most of the time, *soul* refers to a person—usually a person with a body, but sometimes used in reference to someone who has been disembodied.

Spirit. In contrast to the word *soul*, the word *spirit* (Hebrew: *ruach*, Greek: *pneuma*) is usually much more specific. It is used almost always in reference to "that part of us which is not susceptible of death and which survives the dissolution of the body."[16] It is used interchangeably with the word *soul* when *soul* would refer to the spiritual dimension of man (cf. Luke 1:46-47). "The body apart from the spirit is dead" (Jas. 2:26), and when Jesus died, "He bowed His head and gave up His spirit" (John 19:30). The spirit is immaterial and is different from the body. Jesus said, "A spirit does not have flesh and bones as you see that I have" (Luke 24:39).

Heart. The heart (Hebrew: *leb*, Greek, *kardia*), in a biblical sense, is what separates a person from an animal. It is used to describe the inner man with all of his or her faculties, but stressing particularly the capacity of will and intellect. The heart is the location of knowledge and memory (Eze. 3:10; Luke 2:19), has desires (2 Sam. 7:3; 1 Cor. 4:5), is where we make decisions (Deut. 15:9; Psa. 19:14; 139:23; Matt. 9:4) and can receive wisdom (2 Chron. 9:23; Matt. 12:34-35). It can be hardened (Exo. 8:15; Mark 3:5), is deceitful and can be wicked (Jer. 17:9; Rom. 1:21), and should be kept with all diligence (Prov. 4:23; Heb. 10:22).

---

16 Guy N. Woods, *Questions and Answers*, Vol. II, p. 101

Mind. The mind (Greek: *nous*) is a seldom-used New Testament word. It carries a somewhat broad meaning, but usually refers to the inner person's will or ability to be persuaded. Paul was bent on serving the law of God with his mind (Rom. 7:25). You are to "be transformed by the renewal of your mind, that by testing you may discern what is the will of God, what is good and acceptable and perfect" (Rom. 12:2). When your mind accepts something as true, the will follows suit.

Inward Self. Our spiritual dimension is summarized by the phrase "inward self." "Though our outer self is wasting away, our inner self is being renewed day by day" (2 Cor. 4:16). Because the spirit, or inward self, is immaterial, it is "unseen and eternal" (verse 18).

WE ARE A UNITY OF BODY AND SPIRIT

One of the most heinous belief systems that threatened the early church was **Gnosticism**. Though sometimes difficult to define, a central tenant of Gnosticism is the stark separation between the spiritual realm and the material realm. Gnostics taught that the physical world— including the body—is inherently evil, while the spirit is ultimately good. We see an early manifestation of Gnosticism in the 1st century in the belief that anything done in the body—even the vilest of sins—was of little consequence to the human spirit (cf. 2 Tim. 3:5-6; 2 Pet. 2:12, 18). Much of the letter of Jude is directed against this licentious teaching of early Gnosticism that permitted an unholy life (cf. Jude 4, 8, 11, 19). Another emerging Gnostic teaching in the 1st century was that of asceticism, or depriving the body of things that are good so as to achieve a higher spiritual or moral state. The Bible warns against those who taught this several times (e.g. Col. 2:21, 23; 1 Tim. 4:3).

Gnosticism is no mere ancient relic consigned to the past but a very real problem today. Many have adopted the view that when the human body is divorced from meaningful cognitive ability (i.e. the normal function of the spirit), we become somehow sub-human. When we take this Gnostic view, then those who are still in their embryonic, fetal, or early infant stages, those who suffer from advanced stages of dementia or cognitive disabilities, or those who are in a long-term comatose state are no longer persons. This modern form of Gnosticism makes it easy for even self-identified Christians to justify abortion, infanticide, and euthanasia for those with cognitive or physical disabilities. The body is seen as a mere instrument of the spirit and not part of our identity as humans. Thus some have adopted social liberalism's sexual ethic of today that human sexuality is fluid and therefore believe sexuality can be whatever we want it to be. This is what happens when people see the spirit as the sole identity of a person.

We can see that it is wrong—and dangerous—to adopt a view in mankind's dual nature that separates the body from the spirit. There is a popular quote floating around, often wrongly attributed to C.S. Lewis, that goes something like this: "You do not have a soul. You are a soul. You have a body."[17] While there is some truth to this (the soul is the location of our mind and consciousness), the body still encapsulates the mind and works in synergy with it. Humans are *incomplete* without the body. We should never make statements that imply that the body does not matter, or—worse yet—suggest that the body is somehow evil.

Our bodies are essential components of our humanity. The body was created by God and is therefore inherently good (Gen. 1:31; cf. 1 Cor. 10:23). The body is what connects us to the rest of the material creation—we dwell in a physical world. Originally, the human body was created to never die. Our bodies were not originally designed to be feeble, inclined to disease, prone to sin, and destined to die. Rather, these qualities are a consequence of sin. Our present bodies are corrupted versions of the body Adam originally had, and thus need saving—a picture of how our spirits need saving (cf. Rom. 8:23; Phil. 3:21). On the day we are literally resurrected just as Christ was resurrected, we will be given glorified bodies that will once again be perfectly suitable for our eternal home (1 Cor. 15:20-26). But do not get lost on the fact that we will nonetheless still be *bodies*.[18] God made us with bodies, and He has

---

17 None of C.S. Lewis' works contain this phrase. A 19th century Scottish minister named George MacDonald, whom Lewis knew, is the most likely originator of this quote.

18 What our glorified bodies will be like, I don't know. But Philippians 3:20-21 tells us our glorified bodies will be incorruptible and thus will live forever (1 Cor. 15:42).

promised to resurrect us with glorified bodies.

What is man? The Bible recognizes man as a unity of his two-fold nature of body and spirit. The soul divorced from the body is naked and incomplete (2 Cor. 5:1-4). Jesus told us that all human beings, both saved and lost, will be resurrected with bodies (John 5:25-29)—which wouldn't make any sense unless human beings were incomplete without *bodies*.

WHY WERE WE CREATED?

God does not need us, nor does He depend on anyone or anything for His existence. This is called God's **aseity**.[19] He did not create mankind with the primary purpose of having someone over which to rule, or to reward or punish, or to love, or to keep Him company (though there is a sense in which we are all of these things to Him).[20] There always has been, and always will be, a fellowship of relationship and love within the Trinity. God did not gain anything by creating us that He did not already have in the context of the Godhead.[21]

Why, then, did God create us? The answer: We were created to bring God glory. Isaiah 43:7 speaks of humanity, from all parts of the world, as being created "for [His] glory." See also Isaiah 43:21. Paul writes that humanity can be saved in Christ "to the praise of His glory" (Eph. 1:11-12). Therefore, the meaning of life is to "do all to the glory of God" (1 Cor. 10:31).

We may be tempted to think that we are insignificant, since God does not need or depend on us. However, the fact that God created us and made us in His image should lead us to believe the opposite. Humanity is important to God: He brought us into existence and redeemed us through the blood of His Son so we could spend eternity with Him. If God values us to this extent, what greater purpose in life could we seek than to glorify Him?

---

19 For a more detailed discussion on God's aseity, see chapter 2 of *Thinking Right About **God** (You Are A Theologian Series)*.
20 God did create us to reward us and keep company with Him, not for His benefit, but for our benefit.
21 For a more in-depth look at the Trinity, see chapter 4 of *Thinking Right About **God** (You Are A Theologian Series)*.

> *If God values us to the extent that He brought us into existence and redeemed us through the blood of His Son, what greater purpose in life could we seek than to glorify Him?*

True happiness and lasting contentment come when we live in keeping with the purpose for which we were created. David says, "In your presence there is fullness of joy; at your right hand are pleasures forevermore" (Psa. 16:11). Jesus came so that we "may have life and have it abundantly" (John 10:10). The more we know God, fear Him, and delight in His laws, the more we will know joy (cf. Ecc. 12:13). The more we delight in God, the more He rejoices in us. Isaiah writes, "As the bridegroom rejoices over the bride, so shall your God rejoice over you" (Isa. 62:5). Zephaniah prophesied that God "will rejoice over you with gladness; He will quiet you by His love; He will exult over you with loud singing" (Zeph. 3:17).

WE ARE MADE IN THE IMAGE OF GOD

As mentioned earlier, "God created man in His own image, in the image of God He created him; male and female He created them" (Gen. 1:27). What does this mean? It *does not* imply that we have a physical or material likeness to God. Scripture teaches us that God is a spirit and therefore does not have physical parts like a human (cf. John 4:24; Col. 1:15; 1 Tim. 1:17).[22] God warned mankind not to represent Him with a graven image, in part because no one had seen God and therefore no human knew what He looked like—as if anything on earth could represent God's Spirit (cf. Deut. 4:15-23).

The words *image* and *likeness*, found in Genesis 1:26-27, simply refer to the fact that we are somehow made to be like God. Like God, humanity has intellectual capacity (a capacity that exceeds all other creatures in the animal kingdom), creativity, the ability to make moral choices, the ability to communicate on a meaningful level, and immortality.

---

22 Sometimes the Bible uses **anthropomorphic** expressions to describe God, such as the "hand of God," the "throne of God," or His "face." But the Bible only does this to accommodate our human inability to think of God in ways beyond a material level. For a greater discussion on this, see chapter 1 of *Thinking Right About God (You Are A Theologian Series)*.

We would do an injustice to Genesis 1:26-27, however, if we attempt to go into more detail than these verses do. As Wayne Grudem observes, "The Text only needs to affirm that man is like God, and the rest of Scripture fills in more details to explain this."[23] The more we understand God through Scripture, the more we can better understand how we are made in His image.

In a nutshell, however, we know that being made in the image of God means man is a *person*. Humanity has personhood, just as the Father, the Son, and the Spirit all have personhood. Being a *person* is the essence of humanity's spiritual existence. Spiritual beings are personal beings. When we say the Father is a person, we mean His Spirit is the seat of His consciousness. A human is a person, meaning man's spirit is the seat of his consciousness. Additionally, as persons, we have the ability to have interpersonal relationships. We can relate not only to other people, but also to God Himself.

God has supreme knowledge and an infinite reasoning capacity and has shared some of that ability with mankind. Thus, we have an ability to contemplate things in ways unmatched by the rest of the animal world. Has your pet dog ever contemplated the question, "Is there a God?" Has your cat ever asked, "Why was I created?" Has your fish ever tried to communicate to another fish the meaning of sin or the importance of redemption?

Additionally, human beings have the luxury of free moral agency. That is, we have the ability to make choices—even choices that may not be in our immediate best interest. We are *volitional*[24] creatures. In order to be moral creatures, we must necessarily have a mind and a will just as God does.

We do not punish cats and dogs for moral failures. No one accuses the black widow spider of murder when she eats her mate. We do not put the lion before the firing squad for killing an antelope. We do not hang the raccoon for stealing food from the picnic table. Yet we hold

---

23 Wayne Grudem, *Bible Doctrine*, p. 190
24 **Volitional** means being able to choose or exercise the power of the will.

humans to a higher standard, because only humans are accountable for the choices they make. We are moral beings.

God never commanded an animal to be holy as He is holy. He never told a worm or an aardvark to reflect on His righteousness. Only humans can do this, because only humans are morally rational creatures. While Adam ultimately failed to reflect the character of God because of his decision to sin, Jesus—the second Adam—perfectly demonstrated the character of God. "He is the radiance of the glory of God and the exact imprint of His nature" (Heb. 1:3). Jesus did what Adam failed to do. We do not have to continually make the same choice Adam did. Thus, because of the example of Jesus, we better understand what it means to be made in the image of God. Human beings have a unique ability to mirror the character of God, so much so that people can look at Christians and say, "That is what God is like."

> *We have the ability to make choices—even choices that may not be in our immediate best interest.*

INCORRECT VIEWS OF MAN

"MAN IS ULTIMATELY COMPRISED OF ONE SUBSTANCE."

There are some who hold the view that man is composed exclusively of a physical body. They would argue that the human mind or spirit does not exist as a separate entity from our material flesh. Rather, the human mind is merely a product of advanced electrical connections or chemical exchanges happening within the brain. Marvin Minsky, an artificial intelligence pioneer in the 1950s, described humans as being merely "a computer made of meat."[25] This view, that man is purely one substance, is called **materialistic monism**.

Religious groups like Jehovah's Witnesses and Seventh-day Adven-

---

25 Roger Lewin, *Complexity: Life at the Edge of Chaos*, p. 160

tists hold a similar view. While they believe in a spiritual God and spiritual angels, they are **anthropological monists**—that is, they believe that mankind is only material. Groups like these do not believe in an eternal hell,[26] which would by implication have to be *eternal* if man had an immortal (indestructible) spirit. Instead, they teach that man ceases to exist when he dies outside of a saved condition. Yet the Bible teaches that the spirit is eternally conscious.

We must reject the theory that humans are only material bodies because the Bible so clearly affirms that there are two dimensions to human nature. The Bible teaches:

- The spirit survives death in a disembodied state (Ecc. 12:6-7; Luke 16:22-23; 23:43; Phil. 1:23-24; 2 Cor. 5:8). If the soul and the body were the same thing, then the spirit would die when the body dies. But the Bible demonstrates this is not the case.
- Jesus was still alive between His death and resurrection, though during those three days His body was dead (Luke 24:46; John 19:30). Jesus the Christ is the Son of God—a member of the Godhead. He did not cease to exist, though His material body was dead.
- The mind is capable of controlling the body and even operating in opposition to the body (Matt. 26:41; Rom. 7:15-20).

"MAN IS COMPRISED OF THREE DISTINCT PARTS: BODY, SOUL, AND SPIRIT."

Some hold the position that the soul is distinct from the spirit, thus making man a threefold being comprised of body, soul, and spirit. This relatively common view of man is called **trichotomy**, as opposed to **dualism**. Proponents of this view believe that the spirit and the soul are as distinct from one another as the soul and the body. The soul is seen as the basis for natural life (meaning all living creatures have a soul of sorts), where the natural faculties of consciousness are found. The spirit,

---

26 Passages like Matthew 25:46, 2 Thessalonians 1:9, and Revelation 14:11 teach that hell is, in fact, a place of eternal, conscious torment and destruction.

on the other hand, is the seat of divine communion with God (and only humans are seen as having spirits). Norman Geisler sums up this view best: "A human being is said to be *self-conscious* by virtue of her soul, *world-conscious* through her body, and *God-conscious* in her spirit."[27]

Trichotomy is further perpetuated by confusion over the flexible usage of the Bible word *soul*. It is true that nearly all forms of animal life have relative degrees of reason, consciousness, and thinking capacity. In this sense, this animating feature of the body can be called the "soul." Yet we take issue with trichotomy because when the Bible summarizes the entirety of man, Scripture portrays man as being a unity of two separate elements: body/soul, inward/outward, flesh/spirit. See passages like Matthew 10:28, 1 Corinthians 7:34, and 2 Corinthians 7:1. We must stress, however, that we can kindly disagree with people on this point. Good, faithful Christians have for generations have held differing opinions about trichotomy vs. dualism and still remained brethren.

There are a handful of passages, however, that seem to teach trichotomy at first glance. As we briefly examine these passages, we will see how these passages in reality are in harmony with dualism.

Hebrews 4:12: "The word of God is living and active, sharper than any two-edged sword, piercing to the division of soul and of spirit, of joints and of marrow, and discerning the thoughts and intentions of the heart." This is perhaps the most common proof-text used by trichotomists, who argue that this passage speaks of a division *between* the soul and spirit.

In response, however, we should note that this passage does not specifically teach a division between soul and spirit, but of a division "of soul and of spirit." We also note that the Greek word translated *division, merismos*, when used elsewhere in the Bible commonly refers to a division within a single thing, not two things (cf. Matt. 12:25-26; Luke 12:13; 1 Cor. 1:13). Hebrews 4:12 is teaching that the word of God is so powerful, it can divide the indivisible—dividing *within* the soul and *within* the spirit. Furthermore, the thrust of Hebrews 4:12 is the penetrating power

---

27 Norman Geisler, *Systematic Theology*, p. 735

of the word. It is a sword, not an ax. It is designed to puncture *into*, not *between*. Just as a sword penetrates the inner body (down to the joints and marrow), Scripture penetrates the inner spiritual man (his soul, spirit, and heart) and exposes our true thoughts and intentions.

Genesis 2:7: The King James Version renders this text: "The Lord God formed man of the dust of the ground, and breathed into his nostrils the breath of life; and man became a living soul." Only the KJV and the ASV translate here the Hebrew word *nephesh* as *soul*, which as we learned earlier in this chapter is a broad term with multiple possible meanings. Context shows that *nephesh* here represents the *entirety* of man (dust of the ground infused with life), thus translations like the NASB, NIV, CSB, NKJV, and ESV rightly render *nephesh* as "a living being" or "a living creature."

Additionally, it is assumed that the word *breath* is interchangeable with the word *spirit*. After all, the Hebrew word often translated "spirit," *ruach*, is at other times translated "breath." However, *ruach* is not used in Genesis 2:7. Another Hebrew word, *nᵉsamah*, is used, which usually refers to a "unit of air that passes in and out of the lungs through mouth and nostrils, essential to life and a causative agent for an activity of God."[28]

A careful reading of Genesis 2:7 demonstrates that it actually does not lend itself to a three-fold view of man. It contains no direct reference to the "spirit" or the spiritual nature of man. Rather, it only implies that there is an immaterial element combined with man's material body.

1 Thessalonians 5:23: "Now may the God of peace Himself sanctify you completely, and may your whole spirit and soul and body be kept blameless at the coming of our Lord Jesus Christ." In this verse, Paul is not specifically attempting to highlight a difference between the soul and spirit. The point of 1 Thessalonians 5:23 is that Christ sanctifies the *entirety* of a person. He makes the same point in 1 Corinthians 7:34 and 2 Corinthians 7:1 and makes reference only to "body and spirit."

---

28 James Swanson, *Dictionary of Biblical Languages with Semantic Domains*

Notwithstanding, 1 Thessalonians 5:23 still speaks of "spirit and soul and body." Why would Paul list both if they were not two distinct dimensions? We would reply that the Bible sometimes lists synonymous terms together to express wholeness. In Hebrews 4:12, no one attempts to separate the "heart" from the "spirit," as these refer to the same thing. In Deuteronomy 18:10-11, "a medium or a necromancer or one who inquires of the dead" refer to the same trade of spiritualism. In Mark 12:30, a person is commanded to love God with all of his "heart, soul, mind, and strength," which has reference to a person's entirety.

Without this handful of passages (Heb. 4:12; Gen. 2:7; 1 Thess. 5:23), it is difficult to conclude that man is made of three distinct parts. When you assemble all of the passages that speak about the nature of man, it is evident that two elements—the material and immaterial—represent his entirety. When *soul* and *spirit* are employed to describe a specific aspect of man's nature, they are equivalent to one another. Both words are used to describe the part of man that lives on after death (e.g. "soul," cf. Matt. 10:28; Rev. 6:9; 20:4; and "spirit," cf. Heb. 12:23). We do not hold that trichotomy is a particularly dangerous doctrine. Though, like any other faulty views, it can lend itself to greater false doctrines if not regulated by Scripture.

"MAN IS NOT UNIQUE."

An increasing number of people argue that mankind is not so different from the rest of the animal kingdom. Many proponents of the theory of evolution have set out to blur as many distinctions as possible between animals and mankind. The genetic similarities between man and beast are often pointed out, and studies in the last several decades have shown that some animals are capable of thinking and making somewhat conscious decisions. Animals are capable of learning and making decisions based upon past experiences (on a relatively basic level). In the coming years, the argument that man is not so unique from the rest of the living world will become increasingly compelling as computerized artificial intelligence becomes more and more of a reality.

Is mankind truly any different from the animal kingdom or advanced computers? Can animals be considered people? Can artificial intelligence become so advanced that robots should be given human rights?

The Bible describes only the human race as being made "in God's image," meaning humans are the only creatures in this world who can be described as "people." No matter how advanced another living organism or computer may be, only God can infuse a living material creature with an eternal spirit. Thus, only humans have the moral status accorded to them by God.

CONCLUSION

Human beings were created by God and made in His image, therefore giving each person inestimable worth. We cannot merit our value to God, as if God needs us. Instead, we were created for the purpose of bringing glory to God. The more we live in step with that purpose, the greater joy we will know.

We cannot be reduced to being purely material bodies (monism). We are dual creatures, composed of a material or fleshly dimension and an invisible or spiritual dimension. Not only that, but our dual nature is a unity. We cannot lose the body without somehow becoming less than God intended. Our bodies are an inseparable element of what makes us human. The spirit survives disembodiment from the body and still remains conscious (though incomplete and inadequate so long as it is separated from the body) between death and the resurrection, after which the spirit will be reunified with a glorified body.

DISCUSSION QUESTIONS

1. If we owe our existence to a series of meaningless, evolutionary accidents, what effect does this have on human dignity? Can there be such a thing as human ethics?

2. As it relates to the human body/spirit, define *dualism*.

3. Explain the different ways the word *soul* is used in the Bible?

4. What is *Gnosticism*?

5. In what way(s) is Gnosticism still believed or practiced today?

6. How would you explain to someone the purpose of human life?

7. What does it mean to be made in the image of God?

8. What would you say is the biggest difference between humans and animals?

9. Refute the idea of **materialistic monism**, that is, the notion that mankind is comprised of only one substance.

10. In what way do animals have a body and a soul?

CHAPTER 2

NO PERFECT PEOPLE ALLOWED

THE PROBLEM OF SIN

CHRISTIANITY is custom-made for sinners.[1] In fact, you can't become a Christian without first having at least a basic understanding of sin. All people must be brought to the point of guilt over their sin before they can truly become followers of Christ. It could even be argued that the depth of your love for Jesus is proportional to your awareness of sin and subsequent need for forgiveness.[2]

Perhaps this relationship between *recognizing sin* and *seeking salvation* explains in part why so few people obey the gospel. Western society has gone to great lengths to remove the idea of sin from society's consciousness. Karl Menninger, in his classic book *Whatever Became of Sin?*, wrote,

> The very word "sin," which seems to have disappeared, was a proud
> word. It was once a strong word, an ominous and serious word. It
> described a central point in every civilized human being's life plan
> and life style. But the word went away. It has almost disappeared—the
> word, along with the notion. Why? Doesn't anyone sin anymore?
> Doesn't anyone believe in sin?[3]

The concept of sin has been meticulously censored with more palatable words: "accident," "affair," "authenticity," "choice," "gay," "fling,"

---

1 See Luke 5:30-31. Christianity is not for those who are *innocent* (people incapable of sin, which would include infants, children under the age of accountability, and the acutely mentally disabled), those who are *in denial* (people who don't think they have a sin problem), those who are *complacent* (people who are unwilling to stop sinning), or those who *boast in their sins* (people who celebrate sin). When a sinner obeys the gospel, he/she can no longer be a slave to sin. We should note that Christianity is not a social club for active sinners but a hospital for recovering, former sinners.
2 See Luke 7:36-47; cf. 1 Tim. 1:12-16
3 Karl Menninger, *Whatever Became of Sin?*, p. 14

"heredity," "lifestyle," "mistake," "substance abuse," etc. Sin has been scrubbed from our secular vernacular.[4] A problem may even be said to be "evil, disgraceful, corrupt, prejudicial, harmful" (as true as these descriptions are), but never *sinful*.[5]

Still—as hard as we may try otherwise—no honest person can deny the reality of sin. Nearly every movie made is an indictment on our sinful human predicament in its portrayal of cruelty, disillusionment, foolishness, consequences, forgiveness, and reconciliation. The news is filled with reports of war, threats of war, drug overdoses, prostitution, rape, sexual scandals, embezzlement, terrorism, murder, legal disputes, abuse, and slander. We hear mind-boggling statistics about abortions, suicide, overcrowded prisons, and crime. History books are littered with accounts of ethnic cleansing, military sieges, world wars, holocausts, persecution, assassinations, and massacres. Even the government's enactment and enforcement of laws is an acknowledgment of the reality of wickedness and wrongdoing.

> *No honest person can deny the reality of sin.*

Clearly, mankind has a serious problem. People who have rejected the Bible have devised various theories to explain our condition. These theories claim that man's greatest problem is ultimately *ignorance* (e.g. Buddhism, Gnosticism, Hinduism), *weakness* (e.g. existentialism), *inequality*, *oppression*, or *injustice* (e.g. Marxism, liberation theology), *predetermination* (Calvinism), a remnant of our so-called former animal propensities (e.g. Evolutionary Theory), or a combination of these things (e.g. Christian liberalism, secularism). The only consistency in these theories is that they never paint sin as *the* problem. Advocates of these theories may sometimes use the word *sin* in an allegorical or figurative sense, or even in reference to offenses committed against human beings. Yet, never do they point to sin—ultimately the violation of God's will—as mankind's greatest problem. Claiming otherwise would force them to admit accountability

---

4 Even though most of the world's social and psychological problems are consequences of sin (directly or indirectly), neither the *Encyclopedia of Philosophy*, the *Encyclopedia of Psychology*, nor the *Diagnostic & Statistical Manual of Mental Disorders* (DSM-5) have any listings for sin.
5 Karl Menninger, *op. cit.*, p. 17

to a personal God.

However, to anyone who accepts the Bible as true, there is no avoiding the concept of sin. We need to understand what sin *is*. We need to know the effect sin has on us. And we especially need to see the consequences of sin. This will be our focus in this chapter.

WHAT IS SIN?

To sin, fundamentally, is to offend God. We may thus define sin as follows: *Sin is the violation of God's will in act,[6] attitude, or thought by a culpable human being whom God holds accountable.* Each part of this definition is of great importance.

THE VIOLATION OF GOD'S WILL...

To sin is the decision to do something that is contrary to God's will (1 John 5:17; Jas. 4:17). A person decides to do wrong based upon recognizing God's will (cf. Heb. 1:1-2; 2:1), then choosing to do otherwise. Today, God has revealed His will in the form of written revelation, or law (Rom. 7:7-10). This law is the expression of God's nature, rooted in His absolute holiness (1 Pet. 1:14-16).

A very basic form of this law is written on the human heart in what we call the conscience, which over time can either be trained or seared (cf. 1 Tim. 4:2). With this basic law, all human beings are given a basic sense of right and wrong, a desire for justice, a conscience that can be distressed, and an innate desire to seek God (cf. Acts 17:26-27; Rom. 2:14-16). Thus, in this way, even unbelieving heathens who have never seen a Bible are still nonetheless accountable to God's will, by the intellect and logical ability that God has placed within them, at least in a basic way (cf. Rom. 1:19-20).

A much more detailed form of the law was given by God's *special rev-*

---

6 Act, or lack thereof.

elation.[7] Scripture, as we call this law, "makes wise the simple" (Psa. 19:7), making us "wise about salvation" (2 Tim. 3:15). The Bible explains to us the sin of which our consciences are surely aware, and teaches us not only how we can be saved from the penalty of sin but how we can repair the relationship to our Father that we have severed. It teaches mankind not only the minute details of what God expects of his children but also how to obey Him with greater precision (2 Tim. 3:16-17). The more we love God, the more we will concern ourselves with the *details* of this law (John 14:15).

> *To sin,*
> *fundamentally,*
> *is to offend God.*

Thus, we sin when we do that which is contrary to God's will (a sin of *commission*), and we sin when we fail to do that which we know is God's will (a sin of *omission*; cf. Jas. 4:17). Furthermore, we sin not only when we choose to violate the clear, *explicit* commands of God's law, but also when we choose to violate the subtle, *implicit* principles found within His law. For example, Jesus rebuked the Pharisee and scribes for not caring for their elderly parents—not because they were violating an *explicit* command of the law, but because they were violating several principles *implied* in the commands of the law (cf. Matt. 15:3-9).

When we violate this law (either the portion written on the human heart or the law given by God's special revelation), we are liable to the penalty of that law. The penalty of breaking God's law is most serious (an infinite sentence of punishment) because we committed the most serious crime (a crime against an eternal, infinitely holy God). When we break God's law, we sin against Him *personally* (cf. Gen. 39:9; Lev. 6:2). We rebel against His authority, sovereignty, and wisdom. After committing adultery with Bathsheba and orchestrating the murder of her husband, David recognized his sins as being first and foremost against God, and cried, "Against you, *you only*, have I sinned and done what is evil in your sight" (Psa. 51:4, emp. added).

---

7 See chapter 2 of *Thinking Right About the* **Bible** *(You Are A Theologian Series)*

Sin consists not only of individual actions, such as stealing, lying, or committing adultery; sin is also comprised of attitudes and thoughts that are contrary to God's expectations of us. For example, the Ten Commandments not only prohibited sinful actions, but also sinful attitudes: "You shall not *covet* your neighbor's house; you shall not *covet* your neighbor's wife, or his male servant, or his female servant, or his ox, or his donkey, or anything that is your neighbor's" (Exo. 20:17, emp. added). Thus, not only is stealing wrong, but the *desire* to steal is also wrong. Other attitudes, such as envy (Gal. 5:21) and illicit anger (Matt. 5:22), are also sinful.

God doesn't merely desire our *outward* obedience to His law in action; first and foremost He wants our *inward* obedience from the heart. "You shall love the Lord your God with all your heart and with all your soul and with all your mind and with all your strength" (Mark 12:30). Thus, Christians must cultivate attitudes like gentleness and self-control (cf. Gal. 5:23) and maintain a disposition of forgiveness (Matt. 18:21-22). It is not the mere avoidance of specific sins that God desires, but a diligent pursuit of that which is virtuous.

We can also sin against God in our own thoughts. Jesus told us that lust is related to the act of adultery (Matt. 5:28). God destroyed the earth with a worldwide flood because "the wickedness of man was great on the earth, and that every intention of the thoughts of his heart was only evil continually" (Gen. 6:5). Simon was told to repent of the "intent of his heart" (cf. Acts 8:22). By not loving the truth, we will inevitably become dishonest with ourselves and disloyal to God's word over time (cf. 2 Thess. 2:10; Eph. 6:14).

The more we love God, the more we will concern ourselves with the details of His law (John 14:15).

Sin is not merely the violation of God's law, for if we stopped there, even an animal or a two-year-old child would be guilty of sinning against an infinite God. "Of course, no one not responsible for a knowledge of law and obedience to it, can be a sinner."[8] For sin to be sin, it must be committed by someone who is *culpable*. All accountable adults are culpable (making them guilty) of sin (cf. Rom. 3:23).

> *God doesn't merely desire our outward obedience to His law in action; first and foremost He wants our inward obedience from the heart.*

Culpability is defined as "meriting condemnation or blame especially as wrong or harmful."[9] The ability to account for one's actions necessitates a certain mental capacity to understand what one is doing. Jesus said, "He who has an ear, let him hear what the Spirit says to the churches" (Rev. 2:7, 11, 17, 29; 3:6, 13, 22). Said another way, Jesus expects all people who have the ability to grasp what He says to obey His words. Implied is the fact that some people do not have such an ability, thus are not accountable to these words. This would include both young children and surely the severely mentally handicapped; some human beings are not accountable to God's law and therefore not culpable when they violate God's law.

Children certainly are not born into a state of sin; they do not bear the spiritual guilt of their parents or ancestors (Eze. 18:20). As "God's offspring," humans are born into the world inherently innocent of any wrongdoing (Acts 17:29). God "forms the spirit of man" in the womb (cf. Zech. 12:1), and therefore they are created having "done nothing either good or bad" (Rom. 9:11). Jesus told His followers to become like children if they are to be saved (Matt. 18:3; cf. 19:14), implying that children are not spiritually depraved. Each child becomes account-

---

8 L.B. Wilkes, *Designs of Christian Baptism*, p. 50
9 *Merriam-Webster's Collegiate Dictionary*

able at the point when he or she discovers a "knowledge of good or evil" (cf. Deut. 1:39), which we understand varies somewhat from child to child due to variations in mental development.

Broadly speaking, it is not a human being's knowledge of right and wrong that makes one capable of sin, but one's *ability* to know right from wrong that makes one capable of sin. So we see mere ignorance of Scripture does not always excuse one from being accountable to it (Acts 17:30). When Paul explained the universal culpability of mankind, he appealed

> *Sin is not merely the violation of God's law, for if we stopped there, even an animal or a two-year-old child would be guilty of sinning against an infinite God.*

to the law of God, which included not only the written law as given to the Jews (Rom. 2:17-19), but also the *unwritten* law built into the consciences of every human being—who, by their behavior, "show that the work of the law is written on their hearts" (Rom. 2:15).

...WHOM GOD HOLDS ACCOUNTABLE

This is what further defines someone as being accountable to the law of God. We are accountable not only to *what* we know, but also to what we *are capable of* knowing but perhaps do not. *Ultimately, God alone decides this.* I may be driving a car in a foreign country and cited by a police officer for unknowingly violating a traffic law. In this case, my *ignorance* of the law did not change the fact that I still broke the law. Admittedly, I was *capable* of knowing better and I *should* have researched traffic laws before visiting the foreign country. This capability makes me responsible. Yet it is also up to the discretion of the police officer whether or not he will hold me accountable to the law I broke.

Paul was once guilty of sinning against God when he rejected the gospel and persecuted Christians, even though he "lived in all good conscience" the whole time (Acts 23:1). Paul did not intend to do wrong (cf. 1 Tim. 1:12-13), yet he still should have known better. In fact, He genuinely *thought* he was doing right the whole time, but he was nonetheless guilty of sin. To a large degree his sin was in ignorance, but it was still sin by definition.

Jesus reminded us that there will be some who apparently believed they were faithful Christians, yet they did not "do the will of the Father in heaven" (Matt. 7:21). Even though they may have been ignorant of their sins, God still considered them "workers of lawlessness" (Matt. 7:22-23)—which, not coincidentally, is a description of sin itself (1 John 3:4).

Even those in remote areas who have never been exposed to the gospel of Christ cannot claim total ignorance of God's law. God's "invisible attributes, namely, His eternal power and divine nature, have been clearly perceived, ever since the creation of the world, in the things that have been made. So they are without excuse" (Rom. 1:20). God has designed human beings in such a way that they should seek after Him (Acts 17:27), and when they fail to do so, they are betraying the law written on their hearts (Rom. 2:15-16). God will judge all men in a perfect way, including those who have never opened a Bible. God takes into account our ignorance of His law when executing judgment (Luke 12:41-48). Yet ignorance is ultimately no excuse—not even for the totally non-churched nonbeliever, who still should have sought after God.

Even Christians are faced with the unavoidable question: What part of God's will have I violated *unintentionally*? What aspect of God's will am I guilty of transgressing, perhaps even now? We will go into greater detail on this question in chapter 6. Yet, *for those who are in Christ*— those who are continually seeking Him—God in His grace has always (to some degree) made accommodation for unintentional violations of His will (cf. Lev. 4:2, 13-14, 22, 27; 5:13, 15-17; Psa. 19:12; Luke 12:48). Like a compassionate police officer or judge, God does not always charge sin to the Christian (Psa. 32:2; Acts 7:60; Rom. 4:8). This hope, however, is rather irrelevant to the alien sinner who has never obeyed the gospel. Nonetheless, it is when we fail to act in keeping with what we *know* is right that we are guilty of a sin which is most certainly charged to our account (Jas. 4:17).

The phrase, "whom God holds accountable" may make you somewhat squeamish. From our human vantage point, it allows for some situations where the exact degree of accountability in another's life is "open-ended." This is true. We find assurance in the reality that God *alone* knows the heart (Acts 1:24), and therefore knows (a) one's capacity to understand His law, and (b) whether one should have a working knowledge of His law in his or her respective point in life. It has never been mankind's job to go beyond Scripture in ascribing accountability to someone. Ultimately, only God, the sovereign Judge of mankind (Jer. 17:10; Psa. 50:6; 2 Tim. 4:8; Jas. 4:12), can determine a man's accountability. He will judge each man according to his deeds by the standard of His law in a perfect way (Rev. 20:12)—also taking into account one's *intent*, *knowledge*, and *maturity*. Yet, the fact remains that we are told to "examine ourselves" by studying our own hearts, demonstrating that we can know where we stand personally with God (1 John 5:13).

> *He will judge each man according to his deeds by the standard of His law in a perfect way (Rev. 20:12)— also taking into account one's intent, knowledge, and maturity.*

WHY IS SIN SO BAD?

Sin is the very antithesis of God's nature. Sin is created when we, with some degree of intentionality, miss the mark of God's holiness (Rom. 3:23; 1 Pet. 1:14-16). The psalmist comments, "For you are not a God who delights in wickedness; evil may not dwell with you" (Psa. 5:4). God hates sin because sin is in direct opposition to His holiness, which is the supreme description of God (cf. Isa. 6:3; Rev. 4:8). God's word holds nothing back in describing what God thinks of sin. God sees sin as a raw, putrefying sore (cf. Isa. 1:6), a heavy burden (Psa. 38:4), defiling filth (Dan. 1:8; Titus 1:15), an impossible debt to repay (Matt. 18:23-35), darkness (1 John 1:6), and a scarlet stain (Isa. 1:18). Thus, when we violate God's law, we are subject to both the *consequences* of our actions and the law's *penalty*.

OUR SIN SEVERS US FROM GOD

Because God is holy, sin creates an impassable gulf between God and us. "Your iniquities have made a separation between you and your God, and your sins have hidden His face from you so that He does not hear" (Isa. 59:2). Separation from God is, by definition, spiritual death. "They are darkened in their understanding, alienated from the life of God because of the ignorance that is in them, due to their hardness of heart" (Eph. 4:18). God created us so we could glorify Him in a loving relationship with Him. Thus, God has a supreme hatred for anything that would diminish that relationship with Him. Even immediately after the first sin, we see sin's consequence manifesting itself when Adam and Eve were found "hiding from the presence of the Lord" (Gen. 3:8) when before that, they communed with Him in the cool of the day.

When we violate God's law, we are subject to both the consequences of our actions and the law's penalty.

OUR SIN MAKES US GUILTY

When we violate God's law personally, we are guilty of breaking the law. As stated earlier, sin puts us in conflict with God on a personal level. We have rebelled against His authority and insulted His wisdom. "For the mind that is set on the flesh is hostile to God, for it does not submit to God's law; indeed, it cannot" (Rom. 8:7). So sin, first and foremost, is a legal problem in God's cosmic court. Sin against an eternal God requires sentencing by God's eternal justice. The penalty of sin is judgment, wrath, punishment, condemnation, separation, damnation, and death (Rom. 6:23; Eph. 2:1-3).

We are each accountable for our own sins. We may suffer temporal consequences of another person's sins (children suffer when a parent indulges in marital infidelity; business owners suffer when vandals steal or harm their property; etc.), but we are only *accountable* for our own personal sins. We find this principle expressed in Ezekiel 18:4: "The soul who sins shall die." We shall individually stand before the Creator and Judge of the universe and give an account of our own sins (cf. Psa. 62:12; Rom. 14:12; 2 Cor. 5:10).

OUR SIN MAKES US SLAVES

Sin turns us into slaves (John 8:34; Rom. 6:6, 17, 20). The first sin a human commits subjects him or her to the inescapable bondage of the devil. Each subsequent sin we commit sinks us deeper and deeper into an already unimaginable level of debt. The average person thinks, "I'm not enslaved to Satan; I can do whatever I want." The problem is not that sinners can't do whatever they want; the problem is that he or she doesn't *want* to do what is right (cf. Eph. 2:1-3). Satan's biggest lie is convincing people they are free while they are actually enslaved to sin.

OUR SIN MAKES US SICK

Just as drug abuse alters the brain (sometimes permanently), the more we sin the more diseased the human heart becomes (sometimes permanently, cf. Heb. 6:4-6). Thus, sin not only enslaves us and makes us guilty, but it also fundamentally changes the human heart. "The heart is deceitful above all things, and desperately sick; who can understand it?" (Jer. 17:9). The Bible often describes the effects of sin on the human heart in terms of sickness (Isa. 1:5-6; Rom. 3:10-18).

We must understand that sin is a slippery slope. The more we sin the more difficult it becomes *not* to sin. Sin weakens our resolve to fight temptation. It distorts an otherwise innocent heart and carries it into despondency and apathy. Sin has a hardening effect on the heart, putting us increasingly in rebellion to God. This biblical understanding of human sinfulness is called *depravity*.[10] Ephesians 2:1-3 describes how

---

10 We must note that the biblical concept of depravity is different than the Augustinian, or Calvinist, teaching of total depravity. According to Catholics and Augustinians, humans are born in a [more or less] totally depraved state due to Adam's sin. Those who hold this view in its

depraved we become when we personally sin (cf. Rom. 14:23). When we do not believe in God and serve Him in faith (Heb. 11:6), nothing we do can possibly make us good in God's eyes. Only at the point of baptism "through faith" can we be "raised up" from our spiritual death and our depraved heart (Col. 2:12).

WHERE DID SIN COME FROM?

No one can deny the fact that our world is full of sin. Things haven't always been this way, however. Immediately after God created the world, "God saw everything that He had made, and behold, it was very good" (Gen. 1:31). A quick glimpse at today's news headlines reveals a much different picture. Clearly, our world is no longer "very good." So what happened?

In Genesis, man was tempted by a supernatural being who took the form of a serpent (Gen. 3:1-5). This means that sin existed *prior* to its introduction to the human race (cf. 1 John 3:8). So, since sin didn't start with humanity, where did it come from? The complete picture is unclear, but the Bible seems to suggest that angels revolted against the authority of God and lost their place in the hemisphere of God (cf. 2 Pet. 2:4; Jude 6). It appears that Satan, the chief instigator and tempter among the angels, led a portion of the angels astray. It is this angel—Satan—who is portrayed as being the originator of the spiritual germ of sin. He rebelled, fell from his original state, and positioned himself as the enemy of God (cf. Rev. 12:7-9). There is not much more we can say beyond this, since the Bible does not indulge us with more details.

Sin existed prior to its introduction to the human race.

As it relates to the human race, the first sin was committed by Eve,

---

purest form believe the inevitable conclusion that because the human heart is supposedly *totally* depraved, it is impossible for someone to choose to obey the gospel by his own volition. They teach that a sinner cannot obey the gospel unless God personally chooses to regenerate an individual's totally depraved heart, thus in a way forcing someone to obey the gospel apart from the sinner's decision and faith. Read further in the chapter to see why we can know this view is wrong.

followed by Adam, in the garden of Eden (Gen. 3:1-19).[11] God told them they could eat anything in the garden except fruit from the tree of knowledge of good and evil (Gen. 2:16-17). This single tree symbolized Adam's ability to make a choice between obeying God's law and disobeying God's law.[12] Sadly, Adam and Eve deliberately disobeyed God. In many ways their sin is representative of how you and I sin today.

The story of the fall started when Satan tempted Eve. Satan, a spirit called "the tempter" (Matt. 4:3), seems to have commandeered the body of a serpent (thus earning him the nickname "serpent" in Revelation 12:9) so as to appear to Eve. His temptation appealed to three qualities of her humanity: physical nature, intellect, and pride (cf. Gen. 3:6; 1 John 2:16). Eve was tempted *physically*, for she "saw that the tree was good for food, and that it was a delight to the eyes." She was tempted *intellectually*, for she thought, "The tree was to be desired to make one wise." She was tempted *in her pride*, since she was tempted to believe that by eating the fruit she would "be like God, knowing good and evil," thus no longer having to occupy a subordinate position to a higher authority.[13]

Then, Eve—followed by Adam—transgressed the law of God. Their sin was not in being tempted, but in the *commission* of the sin itself. It is a great mystery why Adam and Eve, who both lived in a perfect environment and enjoyed an intimate relationship with God, wanted to sin. Sin is ultimately irrational. It did not make sense for Adam and Eve to think their lives could somehow be enhanced by disobeying the law of God. They made a foolish choice, and any decision we make to sin today is no less foolish. The essence of foolishness is the reckless indulgence in any kind of sins, however harmless we believe a sin to be (cf. Prov. 10:23; 12:15; 14:7, 16; 15:5; 18:2; etc.).

---

11 When the Bible refers to Adam as the first sinner, it only does so in an accommodative way. Eve was the first sinner, not Adam (cf. 1 Tim. 2:14). Yet, Adam was the head of his house and failed in keeping sin out of his dominion. Adam and Eve were one flesh, thus Eve was part of Adam's identity (Matt. 19:6).

12 Though rich in symbolism, the account of Genesis 3:1-24 is historically true. Both the Old and New Testaments assume the story of the fall of man to be a factual account. The Old Testament contains several undeniable references to the Genesis narrative of the fall (Hos. 6:7). Jesus Himself referred to the creation and fall of man indirectly (cf. Gen. 19:4-5; John 8:44), but He obviously accepted the entire Old Testament as inspired (cf. Luke 24:27; Matt. 19:4-5). Paul likewise accepted the Genesis account of man's fall as true (2 Cor. 11:3; 1 Tim. 2:13-15). Adam and Eve were literal people who existed in a *literal* Garden of Eden. They *literally* rebelled against God, they *literally* believed Satan's lie, and they were *literally* cast out of the Garden (cf. Gen. 3:24). To reject the historical account of Adam and Eve is to reject much of the foundation of the Bible's truth claims.

13 It is this attitude of liberation from any kind of authority that is the antithesis of what God desires about us. See chapter 8 for a proper understanding of the principle of submission.

Consequently, Adam and Eve died. No, they did not die *physically* (at least not immediately). They did, however, begin a process of physical degeneration. Originally, it seems the human body was designed to never die. Adam lived to be 930 years old, but he nonetheless died (Gen. 5:5). Since the day man sinned, mankind's lifespan gradually decreased to eventually last about 70 or 80 years on average (Psa. 90:10). Gareth Reese adds: "The consequences of Adam's sin to the race is this: The moment a baby is born it begins to die. Disease and sickness are the means by which physical death is finally victorious."[14] What *did* happen immediately, however, was *spiritual* death. That same day, they were separated from a familial relationship with God. Never again would God come down in the cool of the day and talk to them in the Garden. Sin severs each of us from God (Isa. 59:1-2).

When Adam and Eve sinned, God inflicted the world with a state of physical turmoil, thus giving us a vivid, physical representation of the spiritual terror of sin (Rom. 8:20-23). J.W. McGarvey comments:

> The word of God tells us that all this woe, pain, sin, sorrow and death, are the result of sin. It is a punishment that the infinite God, against whom we have sinned, has laid upon us in the present life.[15]

> All of the pain and woe and misery and death that the human race has experienced since the days of Adam to the present time, are manifestations of God's wrath against sin, and of His estimate of the enormity of the act when a man deliberately violates the law of his Maker; and this, alone, ought to teach us a great horror for sin.[16]

IMPLICATIONS OF THE FALL

First, sin is a foreign intrusion to humanity. It is not fundamentally part of what makes us human. Sometimes people excuse sin by saying, "I'm only human." Yet Adam and Eve didn't become human when they disobeyed God. In reality, when they sinned, they became less than they were intended to be. By the same token, Jesus Christ was perfectly hu-

---

14 Gareth Reese, *A Critical and Exegetical Commentary on Paul's Epistle to the Romans*, p. 243
15 J.W. McGarvey, *Sermons*, p. 17
16 p. 18

man in every respect (cf. Gal. 4:4-5; Heb. 4:15) and it could *still* be said that He was "holy, innocent, unstained, separated from sinners" (Heb. 7:26). Jesus was the most perfect human to have ever lived, and He did not sin (1 Pet. 2:22; 1 John 3:5; 2 Cor. 5:21; Heb. 4:15). Sin is not part of human nature. Rather, sin is a deadly disease that takes root after the fact, and the only cure is divine grace.

Second, when God created man, man was initially recognized as "good" (Gen. 1:31), meaning man was created innocent and holy. Thus, we see that God created mankind free of sin. This did not change the fact that there still existed within him the *possibility* to sin. When Adam and Eve surrendered to temptation, they became alienated from God and enslaved to Satan. In so doing, they also were subjected to some degree of physical corruption and moral complication.[17]

Third, God is not the author of sin. God did not sin, nor is He to blame for sin. "God cannot be tempted with evil, and He Himself tempts no one" (Jas. 1:13). He did, however, create human beings with an ability to make free moral choices. Thus, it logically follows that it is possible for sin to be committed by human beings, and thus to some degree God permits sin to occur for a season. Along these lines, we must never think that sin surprised God, caught Him off guard, or overcame His sovereign control in the universe.

A LOOK AT THE DOCTRINE OF INHERITED SIN

Many teach that in addition to introducing physical death to the human race, Adam's sin affected us in several other ways. Traditional Roman Catholicism, for example, teaches that all humans today bear responsibility for Adam's sin and therefore, even before birth, each human deserves eternal punishment. Michael Müller, a famous Catholic spokesman known for his defense of the Catholic church, explains, "We *all* have, then, sinned in Adam; His disobedience has been our disobedi-

---

17 Because of their sin, they would be subjected to a world full of new ethical dilemmas. They would have to seek God's will when making decisions, and would have to exert greater intellectual effort in conforming to God's will. God's law became more complex in response to the ever-increasing level of sin in the world. This is how they were subjected to moral complication. With sin comes *complication*. How many families have we seen with mind-boggling, complicated issues and dynamics because of the sins of individual members?

ence, his fault has been our fault"[18] (emp. added).

Like Adam, we have all sinned (Rom. 3:23), and we have nobody to blame but ourselves.

Augustinianism, also known as Calvinism, takes this view to the utmost extreme. This belief holds that not only does God holds us personally responsible for Adam's sin (thus every baby is born condemned to hell), but God has also forced upon the entire human race a host of *spiritual* problems. It is taught that humans are born with a *totally* depraved spiritual nature, meaning humans have lost their free will and thus unable to choose to do good.[19] *The Westminster Confession of Faith* states, "The guilt of Adam's first sin is imputed[20] to *all* [emp. added] his posterity. [...] The guilt of this sin is imputed, and the *corruption of nature* conveyed to *all* [emp. mine—BG] their posterity."[21] Similarly, the *1689 Baptist Confession of Faith* states, "The guilt of the *sin* was imputed, *and corrupted nature conveyed*, to *all* their posterity descending from them by ordinary generation, being now conceived in *sin*"[22] (emp. added). These two documents have not only been monumental in shaping the modern-day Presbyterian and Baptist denominations, but are also more or less representative of a majority of protestant Christendom's religious views. In other words, many churches teach that we are guilty of Adam and Eve's sin through no fault of our own. T.W. Brents succinctly states: "We are told that our natures are not only made totally corrupt by Adam's sin, but that the guilt of it was imputed to all his descendants."[23]

Did these religious groups magically pull this teaching out of thin air? No. Many point to Psalm 51:5 in support of the doctrine of inherited sin. Jesus, however, disproves this theory with the declaration that "the

---

18 Michael Müller, *God the Teacher of Mankind*, p. 205
19 This is held by many religious groups to varying degrees. Some teach we are totally unable to choose to do good ("totally depraved"), while others teach we are only inclined to do evil ("partially depraved").
20 *Impute*, used in this religious-y sort of way, means to charge to someone's account. Say my father robs a bank but is caught, and the authorities decide to impute his crime to his otherwise innocent relatives. The police would then unjustly arrest my children and me for a crime we did not commit personally. It is in this sense that many religious people today say that God *imputed* Adam's sin to us. Sometimes this is called the *doctrine of original sin*. You would be right in thinking this is unfair. If even unbelievers can recognize the supreme injustice of imputing guilt to someone who is otherwise innocent of that particular sin, how much more so does the Father understand this matter of injustice (cf. Matt. 7:9-11)?
21 *The Westminster Confession of Faith*, p. 540
22 W. J. McGlothlin, *Baptist Confessions of Faith*, p. 238
23 T.W. Brents, *The Gospel Plan of Salvation*, p. 119

kingdom of heaven belongs" to little children (Matt. 19:14). In the text in question, the psalmist is using a hyperbolic expression, similar to what is found in Psalm 58:3. Acknowledging the universal sinfulness of all accountable human beings, including his mother, David here is recognizing the fact that he was born into a world of sin. Overwhelmed with his own guilt, he sees the totality of his life as being marred by sin. Thus, it is as if he has fallen short of God's law all of his life.

However, the one text used to support the doctrine of inherited sin more than any other is Romans 5:12-21. In this passage, Paul says that "sin came into the world through one man, and death through sin, so death spread to all men because all sinned" (vs. 12). Paul continues, "One trespass led to condemnation for all men" (vs. 18) and "by one man's disobedience the many were made sinners" (vs. 19).

A misunderstanding of this text lies at the very heart of the doctrine of inherited sin. At the very least, Romans 5:12-21 does in fact teach that Adam's sin is the reason why all humans eventually die. But does this passage also teach that Adam's sin imputed guilt upon the rest of humanity? Certainly not.[24] It seems that Paul is speaking of Adam's sin in a *representative* way, bringing into focus mankind's *shared sin experience* with Adam.[25] J.D. Thomas comments, "Although Adam died spiritually as well as physically for his original sin, the death that 'passed unto all men' was not spiritual death and the 'all sinned' does not refer to our own personal sins but to our sharing representatively in Adam's sin."[26]

> *Whatever we inherited before birth from Adam's "one trespass" was totally erased before birth by Christ's "one act of righteousness" on the cross.*

---

24 Adam and Eve were created by God without being morally depraved or inclined to sin. They were given a free moral choice and chose to sin. They alone were guilty of their sin. Whatever we inherit from Adam and Eve is purely physical in nature. We did not receive our spiritual nature from Adam, but from God. Hebrews 12:9 makes a distinction between "earthly fathers" and the "Father of spirits." We inherit bodies from our earthly parents, along with whatever genetic predispositions we may be fortunate or unfortunate to inherit. Diseases and addictions can be transmitted from parent to child. But your physical body is not the spirit, which is the seat of the mind. Our earthly fathers did not give us our spirit. "God forms the spirit" (Zech. 12:1; Ecc. 12:7). If God forms man's spirit, it is unlikely that man inherits anything *spiritual* from Adam, since Adam didn't give us our spirit.
25 F. LaGard Smith, *Troubling Questions for Calvinists*, p. 71
26 J.D. Thomas, *Romans*, p. 39

Like Adam, we have all sinned (Rom. 3:23), and we have nobody to blame but ourselves. Adam passed sin to us in that he opened sin's floodgate. Paul never intended to teach that men inherited a fallen nature from Adam personally. Rather, Adam's sin is not the means by which human nature was infected, but it was the initial means through which sin achieved a sort of *footing* in the world, where each man—one by one—becomes entangled in Adam's sin and death through his or her own personal sins.

While we can be certain that we did not inherit the sin of Adam (as sin *cannot* be literally inherited), nor are we condemned to hell from birth because of Adam's sin, it ultimately does not matter whether Adam actually did this. The thrust of Romans 5:12-21 is that *whatever* mankind did receive from Adam, Christ has undone all spiritual effects of Adam's fall. Read verses 15-19:

> But the free gift is not like the trespass. For if many died through one man's trespass, *much more have the grace of God and the free gift by the grace of that one man Jesus Christ abounded for many.* And the free gift is not like the result of that one man's sin. For the judgment following one trespass brought condemnation, but the free gift following many trespasses brought justification. For if, because of one man's trespass, death reigned through that one man, much more will those who receive the abundance of grace and the free gift of righteousness reign in life through the one man Jesus Christ. *Therefore, as one trespass led to condemnation for all men, so one act of righteousness leads to justification and life for all men. For as by the one man's disobedience the many were made sinners, so by the one man's obedience the many will be made righteous.* (emp. added)

James Boyd puts it plainly: "What one lost unconditionally in Adam, he gains unconditionally in Christ. So even if we are guilty of Adam's sin (which we are not), we are relieved of that guilt in Christ just as unconditionally as we are supposed to have become guilty."[27]

Do we die because of Adam's sin? Even if we do, it does not matter, because "in Christ shall all be made alive" (1 Cor. 15:22). Did we inherit a sinful nature or inclination to sin because of Adam's sin? Even if we

---

27 James William Boyd, *System of Salvation*, p. 80

do (which we don't), it does not matter, because whatever we inherited before birth from Adam's "one trespass" was totally erased before birth by Christ's "one act of righteousness" on the cross (Rom. 5:18). In Jack Cottrell's comforting words: "Christ's redemptive work matches Adam's sin point for point, canceling its sting. Whatever guilt and depravity we possess now are ours because of our own personal sin, not Adam's."[28]

However, let us never get so lost in refuting the false theory of inherited depravity that we somehow minimize the depravity that we brought on ourselves by our own sin. Sin is the epitome of terror, and only God on a wooden cross could save us.

THE UNIVERSALITY OF SIN

All accountable human beings are guilty of sin. The Bible clearly bears out this fact in many verses. "There is no one who does not sin" (1 Kings 8:46); "No one living is righteous before you" (Psa. 143:2); "Who can say, 'I have made my heart pure; I am clean from my sin'?" (Prov. 20:9); "Surely there is not a righteous man on earth who does good and never sins" (Eccl. 7:20); "No one is good except God alone" (Mark 10:18); "If you then, who are evil" (Luke 11:13); "None is righteous, no, not one" (Rom. 3:10); "For all have sinned and fall short of the glory of God" (Rom. 3:23); "Scripture imprisoned everything under sin" (Gal. 3:22); "For we all stumble in many ways" (Jas. 3:2); "If we say we have no sin, we deceive ourselves, and the truth is not in us" (1 John 1:8).

Likewise, we also see the universality of sin by the fact that condemnation rests upon all who have not submitted to Christ in faith and obedience (John 3:18, 36; 1 John 5:12, 19). Atonement for sin, regeneration, and repentance are universal needs. All men everywhere are called upon to repent (Matt. 4:17; cf. John 3:3, 5, 16; 6:50; 12:47; Acts 4:12; 17:30).

Why is it a universal fact that all accountable human beings have committed sin against God? Surely the answer cannot be because of a so-called inherited sinful nature going all the way back to Adam, as we

---

28 Jack Cottrell, *His Truth*, p. 47

have already discussed. In addressing the universal depravity of man, Paul said, "*All* have turned aside; together they have become worthless; *no one* does good, not even one" (Rom. 3:12, emp. added). The point is that man's depravity is a result of his *own* personal responsibility of his sin and his own determined separation from God. Paul's statement is a quotation from Psalm 14, which begins, "The fool hath said in his heart there is no God. They are corrupt, they have *done abominable works*" (emp. added). Men become corrupted when they refuse to acknowledge God and when they do that which is evil (cf. Psa. 53). Just because we know every soul will eventually transgress the law of God doesn't mean they were born with the *desire* or *inherited inclination* to commit evil.

There are reasons for sin that naturally follow any finite being with free moral agency. Because we are created (and thus not deity), our existence is characterized by the possibility of experiencing fear, ignorance, doubt, etc.[29] These traits can be intensified by others and augmented by what we see and hear with our senses. Ultimately, fear is rooted in a lack of faith in what God has said, even though man has never lived a day without evidence or revelation from God, nor has man ever known a time when God reneged on a promise. Thus, all men will eventually choose their own solution to fear (dependence upon self) rather than depend on God. Adam's sin representatively opened the world to sin, thus requiring man to exert much more effort in knowing God's will.

> *Sin is the transgression of God's law in act, attitude, or thought by a culpable human being whom God holds accountable.*

CONCLUSION

God created the world of humanity with a moral framework, thus allowing the possibility that sin would enter in and become a cosmic cancer.

---

29 In sharp contrast to created beings, God cannot experience things such as fear, ignorance, or doubt because God is deity. His omnipotence, His omnipresence, His omniscience, His immutability, His holiness, His righteousness, etc., teaches us that God has no reason for fear, ignorance, or doubt. Humans, on the other hand, as created beings, do not possess these attributes and therefore we are dependent upon outside information to inform our thoughts, attitudes, and actions. We sin when we deviate from the source of information we know we can trust to our own human wisdom, assuming the same infinite attributes of God.

Satan abused the free moral agency with which he had been entrusted, persuaded other angels to join his rebellion, and was cast out of heaven. He tempted Eve, who in turn chose to rebel against God. Adam and Eve introduced sin to mankind, and their foolish decision represents the foolishness of the rest of mankind when we have universally chosen sin.

Sin is the transgression of God's law in act, attitude, or thought by a culpable human being whom God holds accountable. Sin brings immediate spiritual death because it separates us from God. Much like what happened in the Garden of Eden, it appears that every act of sin men commit against God is a result of submitting to the personal temptation of the devil. A strong argument could be made that it is impossible for man to sin unless first being prompted by the devil. Said differently, nowhere does the Bible teach that mankind is born with a sinful nature, pre-programmed to sin against God.

DISCUSSION QUESTIONS

1. Why do you think so few people obey the gospel?

2. How does God primarily express His will?

3. Is God concerned about outward conformity to His law or inward obedience from the heart? Explain your answer.

4. What does *culpability* mean?

5. Who does God hold accountable? Are there degrees of accountability? Explain your answer.

6. Why is sin so bad?

7. Did sin originate with humanity?

8. Are we born with sin?

9. Give a biblical critique of the doctrine of **inherited depravity**.

10. Does the Bible teach that all accountable humans have sinned? If so, *why* have all accountable humans sinned?

CHAPTER 3

BLOOD WORK

ATONEMENT OF SIN

IN 2013, the committee charged with editing the new official song-book for the Presbyterian Church (USA) *Glory to God: The Presbyterian Hymnal* voted 9 to 6 not to include the popular song "In Christ Alone." Why? Because the song's authors refused to let the committee change a small phrase referring to the wrath of God.[1] The lyrics in question were, "'Til on that cross as Jesus died, the wrath of God was satisfied." The Presbyterian Committee on Congregational Song didn't like those words, and so they requested permission to change the phrase to "the love of God was magnified." Recognizing that God's wrath was central to an understanding of the gravity of sin, the song's authors Stuart Townend and Keith Getty declined the request. Thus the committee voted to omit the song from the hymnal.

Does the cross magnify the love of God? Without a doubt! But brushing aside the reality that Christ "satisfied the wrath of God" towards sin fundamentally ignores our desperate need for atonement. If God feels no wrath toward sin, He cannot be holy, and thus we have no need for the atoning blood of Jesus.

Chris Joiner, the preacher at the First Presbyterian Church in Franklin, Tennessee, agreed with the committee's decision. He said, "That lyric comes close to saying that God killed Jesus. The cross is not an instrument of God's wrath."[2] Not only do many Presbyterians dislike the song; there are others throughout Christendom who dislike it as well.

---

1 "'Wrath of God' Keeps Popular Worship Song Out of 10,000-Plus Churches," *Christianity Today*
2 "Presbyterians' Decision to Drop Hymn Stirs Debate," *USA Today*

Jeremy Marshall, the preacher at the Central church of Christ in central California, said these words in this otherwise "luxurious hymn" are "like finding a gristle in the middle of a wedding cake." He continued, "That stuff about the wrath of God being spent on Jesus is problematic, and worse—it's not biblical."[3]

We shall see, however, that the satisfaction of God's wrath on the cross of Christ, as hard as it is to accept, is indeed biblical. Perhaps the reason why this phrase in the song "In Christ Alone" is so offensive is because the gospel, fundamentally, is offensive to the world (cf. 1 Cor. 1:18). The song communicates a truth that is central to the gospel message: "'Til on that cross, as Jesus died, the wrath of God was satisfied. For every sin on Him was laid. Here in the death of Christ, I live." These beautiful words should be defended, not deleted.

If we could summarize God with one word, it would surely be the word *holy*. The holiness of God is the only attribute expressed in a three-fold way in both the Old and New Testaments (cf. Isa. 6:3; Rev. 4:8). In a nutshell, God's holiness is His moral, infinite perfection. Thus, fundamentally, God's holiness is what prohibits sinful man from having a relationship with Him. Human language cannot adequately convey the hatred that God has towards sin. God *must* punish sin because He is holy. Ultimately, it is impossible for sin to escape God's vengeance—the punishment of sin can only be *reappropriated* to Christ, who has lovingly chosen to bear God's justice in our place. *Either we must suffer, or Christ must suffer.*

> *If we could summarize God with one word, it would surely be the word* holy.

Yes, the cross accomplished much more than the satisfaction of God's wrath toward sinful man. The death of Jesus demonstrated Christ's victory over death, paid the price to redeem us from the clutches of Satan, provided an example of obedience which inspires us to be faithful to God, and afforded us a framework by which God can forgive

---

3 Jeremy Marshall, "'In Christ Alone': Why I Won't Sing THAT Line"

sins while still being just. However, as true as these facts are, there can be no *salvation* of man without man being *saved from* God's wrath.

While the Presbyterian committee's decision is shocking, it nonetheless comes as no surprise. By the account of nearly every observer of Christendom, the Presbyterian Church (USA) denomination is becoming increasingly theologically liberal.[4,5] Liberalism and the subject of God's wrath have never mixed well, much like oil and water. The consistent witness of history tells us that every religious group within Christendom eventually must pick one or the other. Any group that minimizes God's wrath inevitably minimizes the atoning sacrifice of Christ. When that happens, within that group the cross of Jesus becomes an object of embarrassment at worst, and a mere sentimental illustration of God's love at best.

A core tenet of theological liberalism, when it reaches maturity, is the rejection of a God who holds His creation *accountable* for their sins. This is not unique to the modern-day Presbyterian Church (USA); the luster of a wrath-less God has been around since the early days of Christianity. The early Christian Tertullian, describing the teachings of Marcion, an early 2nd century heretic who attempted to sanitize the God of the Bible, wrote:

> A better God has been discovered, who never takes offence, is never angry, never inflicts punishment, who has prepared no fire in hell, no gnashing of teeth in the outer darkness. He is purely and simply good. He indeed forbids all delinquency, but only in word. He is in you, if you are willing to pay him homage, for the sake of appearances, that you may seem to honor God; for your fear he does not want. And so satisfied are the Marcionites with such pretenses, that they have no fear of God at all.[6]

Rob Bell, a popular religious figure today, argues we should never teach that somehow "Jesus rescues us from God." He goes on, "We do not need to be rescued from God. God is the one who rescues us from

---

4 Denny Burk, "PCUSA Rejects Popular Hymn 'In Christ Alone'"
5 We may define **liberalism** as the declaration of liberty from authority or jurisdiction. **Theological liberalism**, then, is the teaching that man should be liberated, in varying degrees, from any submission or subjugation to God's governing authority as expressed in Scripture.
6 Tertullian, *The Writings of Tertullian*, p. 292

death, sin, and destruction. God is the rescuer. This is crucial for our peace, because we shape our God, and then our God shapes us."[7] With these words, Bell reduces Jesus to nothing more than a type of glorified cheerleader or fancy PR spokesman for God. In sharp contrast, the Bible clearly says of those outside of Christ, "It is a fearful thing to fall into the hands of the living God" (Heb. 10:31). God is a God of absolute justice (cf. Psa. 11:6-7; Rom. 2:5). Therefore the Bible clearly tells us to turn to Jesus "who delivers us *from the wrath to come*" (1 Thess. 1:10, emp. added; cf. John 3:36). Yes, we need a Christ who is a good teacher, role model, comforter, and friend. But before God can wrap us in His loving embrace, a loving Son must rescue us from His wrath.

While mankind has a clear aversion to the subject of God's wrath, we need to remember the words, "It is not within man to direct his own steps" (Jer. 10:23). Once our relationship with God is severed, we cannot restore that fellowship through any good intentions of our own. Only *God* can provide a plan of atonement for our sins. And according to God's plan, "without the shedding of blood there is no forgiveness of sins" (Heb. 9:22). Evidently, atonement for sins necessitates the spilling of blood—either our blood or Christ's blood.

To appreciate the important subject of salvation, we must recognize our need for a solution to our problem of sin. God has given us the principle of atonement, which is our focus in this chapter. We may define atonement as follows: *the work of Christ in reestablishing our fellowship with God.*

GOD IS BOTH LOVE AND JUSTICE

We sing the words, "Why did my Savior come to earth?" What motivated Him to come to earth, live as a man, and die for our sins? The answer lies in the very character of God Himself, appealing primarily to two of His attributes: *love* and *justice*.[8]

---

7 Rob Bell, *Love Wins*, p. 182
8 See chapter 3 of *Thinking Right About **God** (You Are A Theologian Series)*

When thinking about the love of God, the passage which comes immediately to mind is John 3:16: "For God so loved the world, that He gave His only Son, that whoever believes in Him should not perish but have eternal life." Again, in 1 John 3:16: "By this we know love, that He laid down His life for us, and we ought to lay down our lives for the brothers."

God's incredible love is not the *only* reason Jesus died for us. The incredible *justice* of God necessitated the penalty for our sins be paid to God. Mankind's relationship to God could not be restored without paying the infinite penalty. Thus, we find the critical role of the Son of God, "whom God put forward as a propitiation by His blood" (Rom. 3:25a). To **propitiate** means "to gain or regain the favor or goodwill" of someone.[9] In the Bible, propitiation is never described as something man needs. We don't need God to regain our favor; we need *His* favor. It is *God* who is propitiated by the vindication of His just and righteous character through the atoning work of Jesus. Jesus made propitiation for us "to show God's

> *We don't need God to regain our favor; we need His favor.*

righteousness, because in His divine forbearance He had passed over former sins" (Rom. 3:25b). According to these words by Paul, God had been forgiving the sins of His people under the various Old Testament periods, but no lasting payment had been made—a fact that would cause us to question whether God is truly just if He could forgive our sins without a penalty once and for all. So God sent His Son to suffer and pay the penalty for our sins "to show His righteousness at the present time, so that He might be just and the justifier of the one who has faith in Jesus" (Rom. 3:26).

Because God is both love and justice, God planned for the atonement of mankind. It is pointless to ask which of these attributes is most important, since without God's love we would have never been offered salvation, and without God's justice the necessary requirement for our

---

9 *Merriam-Webster Dictionary*

salvation would never have been met. At the cross, "steadfast love and faithfulness meet; righteousness (justice) and peace kiss each other" (Psa. 85:10). Both were equally important in motivating God to orchestrate the cross.

WHY THE CROSS?

Before we go any further, we need to recognize that God was under no obligation to save humanity at all. If there was a plan of salvation for the angels after they sinned, the Bible does not give any indication. "God did not spare angels when they sinned, but cast them into hell and committed them to chains of gloomy darkness to be kept until the judgment" (2 Pet. 2:4). God would have been perfectly justified in leaving us to rot in our sins. Jesus did not have to make atonement for us in the cross. Nevertheless, God in His mercy chose to save us from the penalty of our sins. But was sending His Son to die on the cross the *only* way human beings could be saved?

In the garden of Gethsemane, Jesus prayed, "My Father, *if it be possible*, let this cup pass from me; nevertheless, not as I will, but as you will" (Matt. 26:39, emp. added). Here we see Jesus, in His human insecurity, dreading His looming crucifixion. Yet His anxiety is in the context of perfect faith; He made this request in the cocoon of His perfect trust in the will of the Father. God did not let this "cup" of suffering pass, meaning it really must have been necessary for atonement to be made this way.

Evidently, there was no other way to redeem mankind.

Similarly, after His resurrection, Jesus said to the two men on the road to Emmaus: "O foolish ones, and slow of heart to believe all that the prophets have spoken! Was it not *necessary* that the Christ should suffer these things and enter into His glory?" (Luke 24:26, emp. added). Evidently, there was no other way to redeem mankind, which Jesus believed the Old Testament Scriptures should have made clear to these two men (cf. Luke 24:27).

Christ had to pay the penalty for our sins (Rom. 3:26). The Hebrews writer emphasizes this: "He *had* to be made like His brothers in every respect, so that He might become a merciful and faithful high priest in the service of God, to make propitiation for the sins of the people" (Heb. 2:17, emp. added). The system of atonement commanded for the nation of Israel was intentionally designed to be inadequate, illustrating the need for a perfect sacrifice. "It is impossible for the blood of bulls and goats to take away sins" (Heb. 10:4), hence our need for a better sacrifice (cf. Heb. 9:23). Only the death of a sinless God-man, specifically the shedding of His blood, could permanently atone for our sins (Heb. 9:25-26). There was no other way.

PERIODS OF ATONEMENT IN THE BIBLE

God's plan for the atonement of mankind is seen in the Bible through-out every **dispensation**[10] of time. We find a glimpse of God's plan immediately after the sin of Adam and Eve (Gen. 3) when atonement was first needed. God told Satan, "I will put enmity between you and the woman, and between your offspring and her offspring; He shall bruise your head, and you shall bruise His heel" (Gen. 3:15). This is a miniature picture of what ultimately transpired at Calvary.

The plan for atonement was further seen in the law given for the Israelite people (Exo. 20). This law was only for a fraction of the worldwide human population, but accounts for most of the Old Testament. Referring to this exclusive law, which we often refer to as the Law of Moses, Paul says it "has become our tutor to lead us to Christ" (Gal. 3:24, NASB). It was designed to teach us about the importance of Christ.

When the covenant of Christ finally came into effect on the day of Pentecost, lasting atonement was available to all humanity. In each of these dispensations of law, God had a plan for the atonement of mankind (each one building on the other). Let us take a quick survey to examine

---

10 Don't run away from this big word. **Dispensation** refers to a system of law or government that spans a particular age of time. Today we live in the Christian Dispensation or Age, meaning today all human beings live under the law of Christ.

God's way of leading men back into fellowship with Him.

THE PATRIARCHAL DISPENSATION: FOR EVERY PERSON LIVING BETWEEN CREATION AND THE CROSS

In the Garden of Eden, we find both the *event* which caused our need for atonement and the subsequent *plan* which God set in motion as a solution. When God placed man in the Garden, He gave man everything he needed to live, including a law by which to live. "You may surely eat of every tree of the garden, but of the tree of the knowledge of good and evil you shall not eat, for in the day that you eat of it you shall surely die" (Gen. 2:16-17). Man had a choice as to whether he would obey God and live or disobey God and die.

Adam and Eve both knew that by violating God's law concerning the tree that they deserved death (Gen. 3:3). Death is the penalty of knowingly violating God's law and thus atonement is needed. "The soul who sins shall die" (Eze. 18:20). "The wages of sin is death" (Rom. 6:23). We see Adam and Eve following the path that leads to death as described by James, who tells us, "Each person is tempted when he is lured and enticed by his own desire. Then desire when it has conceived gives birth to sin, and sin when it is fully grown brings forth death" (Jas. 1:14-15). To choose sin is to choose lawlessness (1 John 3:4). "All wrongdoing is sin" (1 John 5:17); therefore, Adam and Eve broke trust with God, violated His will, and the penalty was enforced.

God knew man would sin before He created the world and already had a plan for man's atonement "before the ages for our glory" (1 Cor. 2:7). God has always desired to restore our fellowship with Him. When man sinned, God began the long walk to the cross.

Now, living in the 21st century and having the luxury of God's completed written revelation, we can easily see the totality of God's plan for atonement. Jesus, the Son of God, came to "taste death for everyone" (Heb. 2:9). Each individual human has the option of being reconciled to God because of Christ's death (Eph. 2:16).

This plan has not always been so clear to people. Before Jesus came, *other* blood was needed to restore man's fellowship with God. In the interim period between Adam's sin and Christ's sacrifice, God chose the blood of animals to represent mankind's need for atonement. In reality, we know "it is impossible for the blood of bulls and goats to take away sins" (Heb. 10:4) apart from any connection to the blood of Christ (Heb. 10:5-14). This blood could only make atonement for sins in an accommodative sense, until the blood of Jesus would ultimately accomplish final atonement.

The Bible does not divulge an abundance of information as to when animal sacrifices started being made. In Genesis 4, we see sacrifices being offered in response to God's command. Abel offered his sacrifice by faith (Heb. 11:4), which could only come about from understanding God's revelation (Rom. 10:17), so God must have told man how sacrifices were to be made. Abel's sacrifice seems to have been a constant practice, rather than a one-time act, since it is presented throughout the Bible as representing a lifestyle of righteousness (cf. Matt 23:35; Heb. 11:4; 12:24; 1 John 3:12).

We can speculate that a type of animal sacrifice happened even earlier. After their sin, Adam and Eve knew they were naked and made some makeshift clothes out of fig leaves (Gen. 3:7). This in a way symbolized mankind's inadequate attempt to cover our sins. Because their covering was inadequate, "God made for Adam and for his wife garments of skins and clothed them" (Gen. 3:21). While it is possible God caused these skins to miraculously materialize from nothing, it is also possible that God took these skins from animals that were already created (cf. Gen. 1:24). If God chose the latter, animal blood would have been shed to cover the shame of Adam and Eve because of their sins. In which case, a physical death had to occur as a result of their sin (animal flesh was substituted for guilty human flesh; animal blood was substituted for guilty human blood). However, this is only a hypothesis.

Similarly, in Genesis 22, we again find animal life being substituted for human life when God provided a ram for Abraham to sacrifice in place of his son Isaac (cf. Gen. 22:13). Because of this, Abraham named the location of the sacrifice, "The Lord will provide" (Gen. 22:14). God here provided a substitute to die in the place of a man, and it is not too much of a leap to see God teaching us something about the substitutionary atonement of His Son.

Before the Law of Moses even existed, we find a few glimpses of animal sacrifices and people serving in capacities reminiscent of what we know about priests. When Noah came out of the ark after the worldwide flood, he offered several animal sacrifices to the Lord (Gen. 8:20-22). Job similarly offered "burnt offerings according to the number of" his children (Job 1:5), and offered intercessory prayers on behalf of his friends in conjunction with their sacrifices for their sins (Job 42:7-10). Jethro, the father-in-law of Moses, is called the "priest of Midian" (Exo. 2:16; 3:1) and offered a "burnt offering and sacrifices to God" (Exo. 18:12).

After rescuing Lot from the pagan armies, Abraham was met by a man named Melchizedek. Scripture refers to him as the "king of Salem" and the "priest of God Most High" (Gen. 14:18). This is the first mention of the word *priest* in the Bible, which tells us that there was some sort of priesthood long before the nation of Israel existed. Hebrews tells us Melchizedek was a "high priest" (Heb. 6:20), suggesting there were other priests. Jesus, today, serves as our high priest "after the order of Melchizedek" (Heb. 5:6, 10; 6:20; Psa. 110:4).

In preparation for the Lord's appearance on Mt. Sinai, the Israelites were commanded to consecrate themselves and "wash their garments" (Exo. 19:10). It had only been three months since the Lord delivered them from Egyptian captivity; God had not yet given a special law to Moses. When Moses was with the Lord on the mountain, God told Moses to go down and tell "the priests who come near to the Lord" to "consecrate themselves" (Exo. 19:22) and "do not let the priests and the people break through to come up to the Lord" (Exo. 19:24).

In all of these examples, notice there is atonement for the sins of man, offered by people serving in the capacity of priests, before the Law of Moses was given. We see animal sacrifices serving as substitutes for sinful man, setting the stage for the coming sacrifice of God the Son.

THE MOSAIC DISPENSATION: FOR A SELECT PEOPLE—THE ISRAELITES—FROM SINAI TO THE CROSS

God gave a special covenant to the descendants of Jacob (or Israel, cf. Gen. 32:28). We call this the Law of Moses. In this special covenant, God fine-tuned the priesthood and the requirements of the law, but we find the general principles of atonement seen under the Patriarchal dispensation unchanged.

In the Law of Moses, God reiterated that human fellowship with Him is destroyed when one sins (Deut. 23:14). Thus, there is a dire need for fellowship to be restored and for sin to be covered through sacrifice (Lev. 1–7), just as we saw with the Patriarchal dispensation. With the Israelites, however, God limited the priesthood to the descendants of Levi (Num. 3:1-10), who were tasked with offering sacrifices wherever and whenever God required worship (Exo. 20:24; Lev. 17:1-7). The high priests, specifically, were to be of the bloodline of Aaron (Exo. 28; Lev. 8–9).

Almost the entire book of Leviticus is about the importance of atonement in the Mosaic covenant. The emphasis of Leviticus is *holiness*, and one cannot be holy (dedicated *to* God) while simultaneously being separated *from* God due to sin. Sin is uncleanness. And just as there are different kinds of sin, the first five chapters of Leviticus outline five different offerings to be made by the Israelites:

- **Leviticus 1: The Burnt Offering**. This was a *voluntary* offering *for God's sake* which typified the perfect and praiseworthy work of Christ. The whole offering, except the skin of the animal, was burnt upon the altar and all went up to God as a sweet aroma. It symbolized Christ, the final sacrifice "without blemish" (Lev. 1:3), who gave "Himself up for us, a fragrant offering and sacrifice to God" (Eph. 5:2). This offering was not so much about the covering of sin as it was accomplishing the will of God, glorifying Him and vindicating His holiness and majesty.

- **Leviticus 2: The Meal Offering**. This was another *voluntary* offering *for God's sake* which typified the perfect and praiseworthy work of Christ. This offering was a non-meat sacrifice, so there was no shedding of blood. The emphasis here is on the life that is offered rather than the death, symbolizing the perfection of Christ as He lived. Jesus lived a perfect life and did not sin (2 Cor. 5:21; Heb. 4:15; 1 Pet. 2:22; 1 John 3:5). Similarly, there wasn't supposed to be any leavening agent in the meal offering, perhaps because Scripture often uses leaven to symbolize sin (Matt. 16:6-12; Mark 8:15; Luke 12:1; 1 Cor. 5:6; Gal. 5:9). Instead, in the offering's fine flour we see the sinless humanity of Jesus, in the oil we see the grace that characterized His life, and in the frankincense we see the sweetness of His life. This sacrifice teaches us that we are to practice a life like that of Jesus.

- **Leviticus 3: The Peace Offering**. This was yet *another voluntary* offering *for God's sake* which typified the perfect and praiseworthy work of Christ. This is about restoring our communion or fellowship with God. The part of the offering meant for God was the blood, the fat, and the entrails of the animal, which were burnt upon the altar as "a food offering to the Lord" (Lev. 3:11). The part for man was the breast of the animal, which was given to Aaron and his sons, and the right shoulder of the animal, which was given to the priest (Lev. 7:31-32). Thus we see both God and man feeding on the same offering, emblematic today of the communion we have with God because of the cross of Christ. This offering symbolizes God's mercy in rescuing sinners and restoring us to Himself. God has been propitiated, man has been reconciled, and there is once again peace.

- **Leviticus 4: The Sin Offering**. This was a *required* offering *for the sinner* and typified the sacrifice of Christ to cover the faults and sins of humanity. This offering was specifically for sin and symbolizes Christ for us today, who was made to be sin for us (2 Cor. 5:21). Jesus endured the judgment and wrath of God against sin by serving as our substitute. Our sins were not only *covered* by Christ's sacrifice on the cross—they were *borne* by Him as typified in this sin offering. Here we see the holiness of God and the wretchedness of sin being represented in the bull, which was to be burnt up entirely outside the camp of Israel.

- **Leviticus 5: The Trespass Offering**. This was another *required* offering *for the sinner* and typified the sacrifice of Christ to cover the faults and sins of humanity. The focus of this sacrifice was humanity's trespass against the government, or sovereignty, of God. God is Lord and King, and He must keep the moral order of the universe. Thus, restitution for our sins was made. The blood of the offering made atonement, and the sinner was forgiven. Fundamentally, this offering symbolized Christ who died on the cross for our sins, restoring us to God (cf. Psa. 69:4).

What should be fascinating to us is how each of these sacrifices represents a different perspective of what Jesus accomplished on the cross. The order in which these offerings are presented in Leviticus is especially interesting, starting with the burnt offering in chapter 1 and ending with the trespass offering in chapter 5. If we take these offerings in their reverse order, they directly correspond to the order of things we realize in our salvation.

When we first approach the cross, awakened to the horror of our sins, the first thing we need is forgiveness of our many sins, or trespasses. But Jesus did not merely forgive our past sins—He also "bore our sins" (1 Pet. 2:24), thus freeing us from the slavery of sin itself. In other words, we quickly realize we need not only forgiveness but also *release* from our sinful nature[11] which we brought on ourselves (cf. Eph. 2:1-3). Beyond these two things, we see that our relationship with God

> *Jesus did not merely forgive our past sins—He also "bore our sins" (1 Pet. 2:24), thus freeing us from the slavery of sin itself.*

---

11 See chapter 2 on the biblical doctrine of man's sinful nature, in contrast to the Calvinistic doctrine of total depravity.

has been restored and we are once again at peace with Him. As we mature, we increasingly appreciate the character and perfection of Jesus as symbolized in the meal offering. Even more so, as we grow, we begin to long more and more for the glory and holiness of God as typified in the burnt offering.

THE CHRISTIAN DISPENSATION: FOR EVERY PERSON FROM THE CROSS TO PRESENT

After a brief overview of both the Patriarchal and Mosaic dispensations, we can more clearly understand why God "sent forth His Son, born of a woman, born under the law, to redeem those who were under the law, so that we might receive adoption as sons" (Gal. 4:4-5).

Jesus is God's own Son (John 3:16; 5:18; 10:38). For Him to be an adequate sacrifice for mankind, He could not remain in heaven (cf. John 3:13), but had to become flesh (John 1:14; Rom. 8:3). The Hebrews author writes:

> Since therefore the children share in flesh and blood, He himself likewise partook of the same things, that through death He might destroy the one who has the power of death, that is, the devil, and deliver all those who through fear of death were subject to lifelong slavery. (Heb. 2:14-15)

Jesus was willing to leave the realm of God to enter this world as a man (cf. Phil. 2:6-8). He did this voluntarily, as He said, "I lay down my life that I may take it up again. No one takes it from me, but I lay it down of my own accord" (John 10:17-18). This is the most precious truth to ever be told.

In the Old Testament, God commanded animals to be sacrificed in the place of man, or as a substitute for man, who deserved to die because of his/her sin. God commanded this, not because animals were adequate enough to atone for sin, but to teach mankind about the principle of atonement seen ultimately in Christ. The Old Testament, and the Law of Moses specifically, was designed to teach us about the importance of the Christian system (Rom. 15:4; Gal. 3:24). Innocent blood must be shed in order to make propitiation for human sin. Thus, we can begin to understand the breathtaking reality that Jesus substituted Himself for man who deserved to die because of sin. John tells us, "He is the propitiation for our sins, and not for ours only but also for the sins of the whole world" (1 John 2:2). God "passed over" former sins spanning the history of the world, not because of the blood of bulls and goats, but ultimately because of the sacrifice of His Son (Rom. 3:23-26; cf. Heb. 10:4).

When the new law of Christ came into effect on the day of Pentecost (Heb. 7:12; cf. Matt. 16:13-19; Acts 2:14-38), the priesthood was changed and the law of God changed. No longer were animal sacrifices to be repeatedly made by an earthly priesthood on behalf of all men.

CHRIST'S ATONEMENT ON TWO FRONTS

Christ atoned for sinful mankind in two distinct ways. First, Jesus' perfectly obedient life of following God's will serves as our representative. Second, Jesus suffered for us, taking the penalty we deserved for our sins by dying in our place.

CHRIST'S OBEDIENT LIFE

Why did Jesus die when He was an adult about thirty-three years of age? Why couldn't Jesus have died when He was a young child? The answer is that He earned not only forgiveness of our sins in His death (thus giving us a clean slate), but He also lived in such a way that *His* perfect submission to God would be counted, in a sense, in the place of *our* obedience (thus covering our unintentional human shortcomings as we submit to God).

Jesus did not merely live a sinless life. More accurately, Jesus lived a life that *abounded* in righteousness. Not only did Jesus fulfill the Old Testament prophecies about Him; He also *exceeded* the demands of God's law (Matt. 5:17-20). I am convinced that Christ's *entire life* of submission and obedience to the Father—not just His death—was an essential aspect of His atonement for us.

Jesus did not merely live a sinless life. More accurately, Jesus lived a life that abounded in righteousness.

Because of His life, "in Him we might become the righteousness of God" (2 Cor. 5:21). By His "obedience the many will be made righteous" (Rom. 5:19). His conformity and submission to the law changed how God now looks at His children, so long as they remain faithful. Even the most faithful of Christians will nonetheless be "unprofitable servants" (Luke 17:10) and all our righteousness "like filthy rags" (Isa. 64:6, NKJV). But when those who are "in Christ" stand before the Lord, God counts not their shortcomings but the righteous perfection of Christ. Paul said His chief goal in life was to "be found in Him, not having a righteousness of [his] own that comes from the law, but that which comes through faith in Christ, the righteousness from God that depends on faith" (Phil. 3:9).

Being counted as righteous requires more than the forgiveness of *past* sins. True righteousness before God requires perfect conformity to the law itself (cf. Jas. 2:10). "It will be righteousness for us, if we are careful to do all this commandment before the Lord our God, as He has commanded us" (Deut. 6:25). Thus, obedience to the law makes one righteous (cf. Rom. 6:16; 10:5). Christ has obeyed the law of God to the uttermost degree "in order that the righteous requirement of the law might be fulfilled in us, who walk not according to the flesh but according to the Spirit" (Rom. 8:4).

This should be very comforting to Christians. There is a sense in which Christ's conformity to God's law serves *representatively* in the place of my conformity to God's law. Stating it another way, when faithful Christians die, they hand their obedient lives in Christ over to God, who in turn trades their faithful yet flawed records of obedience for the perfect record of Jesus' life. Wayne Jackson comments, "Christians, therefore, are accounted as righteous, hence in this accommodative sense, they become 'partakers of the divine nature' (2 Peter 1:3-4)."[12] But this assurance is only for those who "walk according to the Spirit" (Rom. 8:4).

CHRIST'S VICARIOUS[13] SUFFERING AND DEATH

Jesus could have lived to be 100 years old, perfectly obeying God's law the entire time, but a sacrifice would *still* have been necessary to secure our salvation from sin. Thus, in addition to Christ's absolute fulfillment of the law and prophecies in His life, Christ also took on Himself the suffering that was necessary to pay the penalty for our sins.

Generally speaking, Christ's entire life was one of suffering, especially when one considers what He forfeited by leaving heaven. The Son of God voluntarily left the realm of God to become a human being, placing Himself in a world full of pain, disease, grief, sin, and death (cf. Phil. 2:6-8). "Although He was a son, He learned obedience through what He *suffered*" (Heb. 5:8, emp. added). His ministry was characterized as being under frequent verbal assault and physical threat (cf. Heb. 12:3-4). Scripture does not explicitly state that His earthly father Joseph died, but since we read nothing about him after the time Jesus is twelve, we can surmise that he died during Jesus' lifetime, meaning Jesus most likely went through a grieving process. We know Jesus experienced grief at the death of His friend Lazarus (John 11:35). We also know Jesus endured great suffering during His temptation in the wilderness (Matt. 4:1-11). Toward the end of His life, Jesus' suffering peaked as His crucifixion grew near. In the garden of Gethsemane, as He was awaiting His imminent death, He told His disciples, "My soul is very sorrowful, even to death; remain here" (Matt. 26:38). The cross was the climax of His suffering, not only because of the physical pain, but also because of the weight of the world's sin. Scripture presents four distinct kinds of pain Jesus suffered at Calvary:[14]

---

12 Wayne Jackson, "Jehovah's Righteous Branch"

13 A vicar is someone who stands in the place of, or represents, another. Thus, the vicarious role of Christ means He stood in our place and represented us. He suffered, died, and bore the penalty that only we deserved.

14 **Calvary** is one of the names of the location where Jesus was crucified. It is only found in Luke 23:33 in the King James Version; the English Standard Version translates the term more literally, "the place that is called The Skull." *Calvary* is derived from the Latin phrase, *Calvariae Locus*, for this location.

First, there is the obvious physical pain and death that accompanied crucifixion. Sometimes a well-meaning comment is made such as this: "Jesus experienced more pain than any other human." However, this assertion is unwarranted; there is no reason to believe that Jesus experienced more physical pain than any other human being who underwent crucifixion. Nonetheless, Roman crucifixion was one of the most excruciating[15] forms of execution invented by man.

Though foreign to us in modern times, the phrase, "and they crucified Him" (Mark 15:24) would have evoked painful imagery among many 1st century readers who were all too familiar with the public spectacle of crucifixion. While crucifixion involved substantial blood loss and impalement of the body, the primary cause of death was due to an agonizing process of asphyxiation. When a human is fastened to a cross by nails, traditionally through the wrists (the hands do not contain enough bone structure to support the body's weight without the nails eventually ripping through the flesh), his arms are forced to bear most of his body's weight. However, this makes it difficult to breathe, since being fastened this way restricts the chest cavity from moving in the necessary upward and outward direction. Eventually, the person who is crucified has no choice but to breathe by pushing up with his feet, which are also nailed to the cross. Thus, crucifixion is designed to force humans to thrust their weight against the nails driven through their feet in order to avoid suffocation. Adding to this unimaginable pain, this repeated up and down motion of the body causes a person's back (the skin often having being shredded by a brutal session of scourging) to continually scrape against the wooden cross.[16]

This was often a tragically slow process. Sometimes people would even survive for days on a cross, barely being able to breathe the whole time. On the rare occasion that the executioner had to expedite the dying process, he would break the legs of the person being crucified, thus prohibiting them from thrusting their weight against the nails in their feet. "Crucifracture (breaking the legs below the knees), if performed,

---

15 In fact, this is the origin of the word *excruciating*. It is a combination of two Latin words, which together literally mean "out of crucifying."
16 William D. Edwards, "On the Physical Death of Jesus," *Journal of the American Medical Association*, p. 1461

led to an asphyxic death within minutes."[17] This is what happened to the criminals being crucified next to Jesus:

> Since it was the day of Preparation, and so that the bodies would not remain on the cross on the Sabbath (for that Sabbath was a high day), the Jews asked Pilate that their legs might be broken and that they might be taken away. So the soldiers came and broke the legs of the first, and of the other who had been crucified with Him. But when they came to Jesus and saw that He was already dead, they did not break His legs. (John 19:31-33)

Second, there was the pain of bearing the world's sin. In terms of physical pain, we can easily begin to understand the horror of crucifixion. Yet, even more terrible for Jesus must have been the psychological torment of knowing the world's guilt of sin. Having a carnal nature, it is difficult for us to grasp the terror of sin. However, as we grow closer to God, the more repugnant sin becomes to us. Jesus had a perfect awareness of the evil of sin. Sin was, and still is, opposite to every aspect of His character. But when He was crucified, everything He hated was fully poured on Him.

Scripture plainly tells us that our sins were put on Jesus: "The Lord has laid on Him the iniquity of us all" and thus He "bore the sin of many" (Isa. 53:6, 12). Paul writes that Jesus became "a curse for us" (Gal. 3:13). The Hebrews writer says that Jesus has been "offered once to bear the sins of many" (Heb. 9:28). Peter reminds us that "He Himself bore our sins in His body on the tree" (1 Pet. 2:24), suffering "once for sins" (1 Pet. 3:18).

Paul again tells us that God made His Son "to be sin who knew no sin" (2 Cor. 5:21). That Jesus "became sin" is merely an idiom, pointing to the fact that Jesus became our *sin offering*. Jesus of course never sinned (1 Pet. 2:22; Heb. 4:15; 1 John 3:5; 1 Pet. 1:19) and therefore was not guilty, as one cannot be guilty of another person's sin. However, Jesus did "become sin" in the sense that He bore the *consequences* of our sin, suffering God's wrath in His death and the subsequent alienation from God. In the words of William Baker, "He experienced the accumulation

---

17 Edwards

of the haunting, lonely, terrifying separation from God humanity has felt since the first sin."[18] Many object by making the observation, "But that isn't fair!" To which we reply, that's true.

Third, there was the pain of abandonment. Admittedly, the degree to which Jesus was abandoned by the Father is difficult to grasp, since the Bible does not give us many details. Caution should be exercised on this point. Nevertheless, there was a very real sense in which Jesus as a human did believe Himself to be abandoned not only by His friends (Matt. 26:56; cf. John 13:1), but by His Father Himself. In the moment immediately before His death, Jesus cried out, "Eli, Eli, lema sabachthani?" that is, "My God, my God, why have you forsaken me?" (Matt. 27:46). What Jesus was dreading in the garden of Gethsemane (Mark 14:34), He experienced at His death. Because sin separates us from God (Isa. 59:2), the fellowship that the Son had with the Father was severed to the degree that Jesus representatively became sin (cf. 2 Cor. 5:21), since God in His holiness cannot behold evil (Hab. 1:13). Jesus therefore faced the weight of our guilt by Himself.

Fourth, there was the pain of His bearing the force of God's wrath. There are few subjects more unpopular in the modern church than the wrath of God. But, popular or not, God's wrath burns against sin (Rom. 1:18; 2:5-9; 3:9-20) and consequently the sinner himself (John 3:36; Eph. 5:6; Col. 3:6; Heb. 3:11). God, of course, wouldn't be God if He were not incensed by sin. "God is a righteous judge, and a God who feels indignation every day" (Psa. 7:11).

Drunk with delusion of cheap, sentimental love, modern people tend to ask the question, "How can a loving God send anyone to hell?" In contrast, the apostle Paul, having an accurate knowledge of God, begs us to ask a completely different question in Romans 3:21-26: How can a righteous God *not* punish people immediately and fully for their sins? The answer is that God's wrath is appeased and justice is satisfied only in the cross of Christ. In the words of Thomas R. Schreiner, "Christ as the substitute would absorb the full payment for sin."[19] God cannot forgive

---

18 William R. Baker, *2 Corinthians*, p. 241
19 Thomas R. Schreiner, *Four Views: The Nature of the Atonement*, p. 88

sin without punishing it. Since man's first sin, God has been forgiving penitent people and storing up His righteous anger against their sins. At the cross of Christ, we find God in a sense unleashing His wrath on His own Son—wrath which only humanity deserved.

The key biblical concept that best summarizes Christ's death in mankind's atonement is propitiation, which basically means "an offering that turns away wrath."[20] God's wrath is a theme that permeates Scripture. The worldwide flood was not merely a consequence of human sin but was also God's personal wrath towards human evil (cf. Gen. 6:5-8). Nadab and Abihu were consumed with fire after failing to honor God as holy by casually entering God's presence instead of following the prescribed instructions (cf. Lev. 10:1-3). Achan and his family were destroyed because they coveted and took banned material, and God's anger burned against Israel (cf. Josh. 7:1). Ananias and Sapphira dropped dead because they lied to God Himself (Acts 5:1-11). A whole book could be written detailing the examples of God's wrath against sinful man.

Four passages refer to Jesus' death as "propitiation": Romans 3:25-26, Hebrews 2:17, 1 John 2:2, and 4:10. The Greek terms that are used (verb: *haliskomai*, noun: *halismos*) communicate the imagery of a sacrifice that served to turn away the wrath of God, allowing Him to once again look upon mankind favorably. The holiness and justice of God demand the price for sin be paid. Without realizing this about God's nature, the death of Christ cannot be adequately understood. Charles B. Hodge, Jr.

> *God's wrath is a theme that permeates Scripture.*

writes: "Propitiation enforces the enormity of sin. Love without wrath is sentimentality. Divine grace satisfied divine wrath by a divine self-sacrifice."[21]

We should not confuse the propitiation of Christ as the appeasement of an angry God by a somehow more merciful being. Rather, the

---

20 Jack Cottrell, *The Faith Once for All*, p. 265
21 Charles B. Hodge, Jr., *The Agony and Glory of the Cross*, p. 129

Scriptures plainly describes God as a God of love (cf. 1 John 4:8, 16), and it was God Himself who provided the propitiation—the covering of our sins—at a great cost to Himself. Because both the Father and the Son are both one, Jesus is not separate from the Father in the sense that He more merciful, while the Father is more fearful. Our triune God, perfectly one, provided the substitute for man Himself. This much the Bible tells us; whatever else the Bible word *propitiation* entails, we are not told.

> *Our triune God, perfectly one, provided the substitute for man Himself.*

We call this perspective of Christ's death "penal substitution." His sacrifice was penal in the sense that He bore the penalty of our sins when He died. His sacrifice was also a substitution in the sense that He voluntarily became a substitute for man when He died. "The biblical gospel of atonement is of God satisfying Himself by substituting Himself for us."[22]

DIFFERENT ASPECTS OF ATONEMENT

In addition to Christ's penal substitution in relation to God's wrath, there are other perspectives of Christ's atonement that satisfy God's other attributes. The atoning work of Christ was a multifaceted event that affected us in different ways. When examining the theme of atonement in the Bible, we find Scripture describing the atonement with different words. All of these words show how Christ's death solved a different problem we had as sinners:

1. We deserve *death*, which is the penalty for sin.

2. We deserve *wrath*, which is God's response to sin.

3. We deserve *condemnation*, because we are guilty of sin.

4. We deserve *separation* from God, because we have sinned

---

22 John W. Stott, *The Cross of Christ*, p. 159

against Him.

5. We deserve *bondage* to sin and *slavery* to the power of Satan.

The death of Jesus solved each of these five problems in the following ways:

1. **Sacrifice.** "The soul who sins shall die" (Eze. 18:4; cf. Rom. 6:23; Gal. 3:10; Jas. 1:15; Rev. 21:8). To pay the penalty of our sins for us, Christ voluntarily sacrificed Himself in our place. "He has appeared once for all at the end of the ages to put away sin by the sacrifice of Himself" (Heb. 9:26).

2. **Propitiation.** We have already discussed the substitutionary nature of Jesus' sacrifice for mankind. The animal sacrifices that permeate the Old Testament were substitutionary in nature to the degree that they were connected to the blood of Jesus, which once and for all propitiated God's wrath. Therefore, to save us from the wrath we deserve, Christ died to *satisfy* God's wrath. "In this is love, not that we have loved God but that He loved us and sent His Son to be the propitiation for our sins" (1 John 4:10).

3. **Justification.** Ultimately, we have no one to blame but ourselves. We have sinned, and therefore we are guilty. Just as *guilt* is a legal term, *justification* is also a legal term wherein we are pronounced "just" by God, our Judge. Only God can justify someone (Rom. 8:33-34). Because of the atoning work of Christ, God can now "justify the ungodly" (Rom. 3:20, 24, 28; 4:5; 5:9). The atonement of Christ is so powerful that when I obey the gospel by faith, God then looks at me "just-as-if-I'd" never sinned.[23] We are no less *guilty*; we have simply been delivered from the *penalty* of our guilt. Romans 4:23-25 summarizes this idea.

---

23 This popular quip, used by many preachers and writers before me, has its shortcomings. Justification doesn't change the fact that we sinned, and does not undo the sometimes devastating consequences of our sins. The phrase also doesn't go far enough in communicating that when the Christian is justified, his sins are not just neutralized, but Christ's merit is now the Christian's merit. God has taken away the debt of our sins and has replaced it with His righteousness.

4. **Reconciliation**. Sin destroys our relationship with God (Isa. 59:2), hence our desperate need for reconciliation. As with justification, this too is accomplished by the atoning work of Christ. Through Christ, God "reconciled us to Himself and gave us the ministry of reconciliation; that is, in Christ God was reconciling the world to Himself, not counting their trespasses against them" (2 Cor. 5:18-19).

5. **Redemption**. When we sin, we immediately become slaves to sin and Satan, and therefore we need to be purchased out of slavery. At this point the word *ransom* becomes our focus. A ransom is a price paid for someone who is subjected to another. Jesus came "to give His life as a ransom for many" (Mark 10:45; 1 Tim. 2:6). However, this ransom is not completely analogous to ransom arrangements paid on earth between humans, since Jesus paid the ransom to God, not to Satan. The devil has never had the power to demand payment from God. The penalty for sin was paid by Christ and received and accepted by the Father. Jesus came to "deliver all those who through fear of death were subject to lifelong slavery" (Heb. 2:15).

CONCLUSION

We must remember that because God is perfectly and absolutely holy, He cannot overlook human sin (Hab. 1:3). It is impossible for Him to do so, otherwise He would not be God. His just and holy nature requires that wickedness be punished (Psa. 89:14). Yet, His compassionate and merciful nature (Eph. 2:4) also means that He simultaneously desires for the salvation of every human (cf. 1 Tim. 2:4; 2 Pet. 3:9). Thus, the sacrifice of His Son was not a cruel act on God's part. It was a necessary action in God's scheme of redemption for mankind, thus satisfying divine justice (Isa. 53:11; Rom. 3:26). The crucifixion was not a vindictive act on God's part, but a demonstration of unspeakable love (John 3:16). David Lipscomb writes:

The wisdom that pervades the universe is seen in this: that while the most unselfish of human beings are willing to suffer vicariously—suffer that others may be freed from just suffering—there is nothing that so touches the heart and moves the wrongdoer to repentance and a change of life like seeing an innocent one take on himself the penalties of the evil doer to save him from suffering and share his woe. The willingness to suffer for the sins of another is met by the response in the human heart that vicarious suffering moves and helps the sinner to cease to sin and be pure. There is nothing that touches the human heart to lead it to cease to sin and to do well like the sinless Jesus leaving the courts of heaven and coming to earth to suffer and die as a sinner to save the sinner from the just penalty of his sins.[24]

Our adversary, the devil, does not mind if we believe in God as long as we neglect the reality of His judgment. Despite what Satan would have us believe, God's wrath toward sin is not in disharmony with His love. The Bible speaks with unmistakable clarity about retribution for disobedience (Gen. 6; Nahum 1; 2 Thess. 1; 2 Pet. 3; Rev. 20). To neglect this and "fall into the hands of the living God" is "a terrifying thing" (Heb. 10:31).

---

24   David Lipscomb, *Salvation from Sin*, p. 190

DISCUSSION QUESTIONS

1. Why do you think theological liberalism tends to minimize the biblical theme of God's wrath and thus opposes the concept of penal substitutionary atonement?

2. Why can't God overlook sin?

3. What does *propitiate* mean?

4. Was the crucifixion of Jesus necessary in securing the salvation of man? Explain your answer.

5. As it relates to Christ's atoning work on the cross, what was the purpose of the law of Moses?

6. When do you think God chose the blood of animals to represent mankind's need for atonement? *Why* do you think God chose blood?

7. List some of things that Jesus accomplished through His death on the cross.

8. Why do you think Jesus was crucified well into His adult years, rather than as a child?

9. Why was it so important for Christ to obey the law of God to the uttermost degree?

10. What kinds of pain did Jesus experience at His crucifixion?

CHAPTER 4

THE MASTER PLAN

THE GRACE OF CONVERSION

TWO missionaries proclaiming the gospel in a foreign land were unjustly accused of a crime. They were promptly beaten and thrown in prison without any due process. Yet, because their faith could not be shaken, they prayed and sang songs throughout the night despite the weird looks they received from the other prisoners. Then, without any warning, there was a severe earthquake that jolted the prison house, shaking the stocks off their feet and knocking the doors off the hinges. The jailer was about to kill himself according to custom (he assumed the prisoners had seized the opportunity to escape) when one of the missionaries quickly shouted, "We are all here!"

Flabbergasted by the restraint of the prisoners in not escaping, the jailer called for lights and rushed in, then trembling with fear he fell down before Paul and Silas (the two missionaries). Not only had he heard the hope-filled singing of the gospel by these strange missionaries, he also witnessed a peculiar confidence about them despite their wounds. They seemed so at peace, while he—a sinner—felt so tormented. Earlier he had thought to himself, "Which of us is actually imprisoned? Them or me?" Now, trembling at their feet, it was only natural for him to ask, "Sirs, what must I do to be saved?" (Acts 16:16-30). With these words, the jailer expressed his greatest need: someone to save him from his sin.

Jesus Christ has triumphed over death, suffered God's wrath in our place, paid our ransom, and lived a life of perfect obedience. But salvation is not automatically applied to everyone. So how does an unbeliever become a believer? How does a slave become free? How does an outsider enter the kingdom? The answer: He or she must be *converted*.

GOD'S INVITATION

No one can come to God unless he is first *drawn* by God (John 6:44). Salvation is God's initiative, not ours. God desires the conversion of all men (2 Pet. 3:9), and so God invites "all men everywhere" to come to Him (Acts 17:30). Nevertheless, the process of man's conversion must be initiated by God's action, and all sinners are inclined to resist God because they are sinful (cf. Eph. 2:1-3).[1] The word *draws* (*helkō*) in John 6:44 literally means to drag; there is some sort of friction or resistance towards the one doing the pulling. Our sins drag us away from God, and if we are to be saved, God must drag us back.

How does God do this? Does God *force* people to come to Him? Is there some sort of secret switch the Holy Spirit mysteriously flips in the human heart? No, the Bible teaches nothing of the sort. Instead, the way in which God draws mankind is by the preaching of His word. Or, in the words of John 6:45, we are "taught by God." The word of God is the only thing that can penetrate the rebellious, sin-diseased human heart and plant the seed of faith (Heb. 4:12). "Faith comes from hearing, and hearing through the word of Christ" (Rom. 10:17). When we are "born again" (John 3:3-5), we are born "not of perishable seed but of imperishable, through the living and abiding word of God" (1 Pet. 1:23).[2]

How should we understand God's invitation of salvation? Note the following characteristics:

GOD'S INVITATION IS *CONDITIONAL*

Many people think that salvation is *unconditional*. That is, because many people believe that man is "totally depraved" (see chapter 2), man cannot

---

1 Because of our tender hearts, serious Christians often ask themselves why more people don't obey the gospel. "Are we not working hard enough?" "Are we not knowledgeable enough about the Bible?" "Do we need to try new methods?" "Should the church be doing anything differently?" These questions merit self-examination. But the biggest reason why more people don't obey the gospel is because they don't desire the gospel.
2 Also consider John 12:32; 20:31; Romans 1:16; James 1:18.

do anything to be saved. For example, even if Jesus Himself appeared on live TV before millions of people—pleading in the most convincing way possible for people to follow Him—no one would believe in Him because no one could (since they are all "totally depraved"). One might as well be in a morgue with an offer of a million dollars to any corpse who will simply reach up and grab it.

Therefore, those who believe in the doctrine of **total depravity** believe that God *forces* faith upon select people. If no man can respond to God's invitation, then God must nebulously choose those whom He desires to save. How God makes this decision is anyone's guess. In other words, every individual's eternal destiny was predestined unconditionally.

Thankfully, this is not what the Bible teaches. We are not born totally depraved; we can *choose* to accept God's free gift of salvation. However, His invitation is not without conditions. Scripture tells us that God has, in fact, predestined who will be saved and who will be damned (Eph. 1:5). But God has not predestined, or chosen, on an *individual* level whom to save. He does not force faith upon anyone. Instead, God in His foreknowledge knew who would submit to the gospel conditions of salvation (Rom. 8:29-30; 1 Pet. 1:1-2). He predestined that *group* of people to salvation (2 Thess. 2:13). Anyone who wants to be included in that group of saved people can join them.

God does not pick which sinners will become believers. God in His grace has allowed the sinner to make that decision. God has decided, however, who will be saved by the fact that He has given a set of conditions to which we must comply. Before we were born, He knew those who would obey these conditions by name (cf. Luke 10:20). Later in this chapter we will find God's conditions for salvation.

GOD'S INVITATION IS *UNIVERSAL*

Additionally, there is a common belief that the atoning work of Jesus is limited only to those that God supposedly chooses to save. This is called the doctrine of **limited atonement**. However, the Bible plainly said that

Jesus died for *all* men (2 Cor. 5:15), not a limited number. The reason is because God "wants *all* people to be saved" (1 Tim. 2:3-5, emp. added).

Sadly, few accept God's invitation to all men (Matt. 7:14). But the atoning work of Jesus was so powerful that His blood could save all men if all men wanted to be numbered among the group of people predestined by God. God loved "the world," and will save "whoever believes in Him" (John 3:16). God doesn't want anyone to perish (2 Pet. 3:9).

GOD'S INVITATION IS *RESISTIBLE*

Because many believe that man is totally depraved and that God must unconditionally predestine an individual to be saved, it logically follows that an individual cannot resist God's invitation (should he be one of the lucky few to receive such an invitation). The doctrine that the Spirit performs a special operation on the sinner's heart—forcing regeneration, faith, and repentance—is called **irresistible grace.** All who are invited by God have no choice but to accept.

However, the Bible does not teach *irresistible* grace. God's call is for everyone, but sadly not everyone accepts Him. All sinners have the ability to decide whether they will submit to God's drawing power or resist it. When Jesus invited people to enter the kingdom, many rejected Him, about whom He said they "were not willing" (Matt. 23:37). Stephen told the men who were about to martyr him because of his faith, "You always resist the Holy Spirit" (Acts 7:51). What a tragic state in which to find oneself. God is calling all men; will you accept His urgent invitation?

TO BE SAVED, MAN MUST RESPOND TO GOD'S INVITATION

Not all humans are saved (sadly, most die lost). **Universalism** is the doctrine that all men are automatically saved, regardless of whether or not they are believers. Yet the Bible plainly teaches that man must *respond* to God's invitation—there is something he must do to receive the gift of God's grace (cf. Eph. 2:9). A passage of Scripture that summarizes

God's plan for the salvation of mankind is Ephesians 2:8-10, which we will use in this chapter as a framework for understanding conversion.

SAVED BY *GRACE*

"For *by grace you have been saved* through faith. And it is not your own doing; *it is the gift of God*" (Eph. 2:8, emp. added). Once we have sinned against God, it would be nothing short of supreme arrogance to think we can initiate our own saving. We are spiritually dead, and dead men can't work their way back to life (Col. 2:13). To put the parable in Matthew 18:21-35 in modern terms, no middle-class American worker could pay off an $8 billion debt by himself.

Since God is the one whom we have sinned against, only God can extend the offer of forgiveness. If we are to be saved, it is purely in the context of God's grace. We "are justified by His grace as a gift, through the redemption that is in Christ Jesus" (Rom. 3:24).

God has conditions with which we must comply if we desire forgiveness, yet the basis of our salvation is God's grace. In fact, the first condition for salvation is the realization of our desperate need for God's grace. It is by God's grace that He didn't destroy us the moment we sinned, it is by God's grace that He invited us back to a relationship with Him, and it is by His grace that we have the option of responding to His invitation in trust and obedience.

Salvation is a gift, not a wage to be earned by our meritorious goodness or works of piety. Salvation comes "by grace," not by our moral excellence or how skilled we happen to be in keeping God's law (not to minimize the importance and urgency of following God's law).

The benefit of God's grace is reserved for those who truly love Him and dedicate the remainder of their lives to Him in humble obedience (Matt. 6:33; 1 John 1:9; 4:19; Rom. 8:4-6). But after all is said and done, we trust in God's power to save us through the redemptive work of His Son, not our own performance. While there are commands that must be obeyed in order to be saved, it is important that we not lose sight of the fact that our response to God's call is in the context of His grace (cf. Rom. 1:5). If it weren't for the grace of God, even the godliest Christian you've ever met couldn't enter heaven.

SAVED BY GRACE THROUGH *FAITH*

"For by grace you have been saved **through faith**. And it is not your own doing; it is the gift of God" (Eph. 2:8, emp. added). Grace is the basis of salvation, and faith is the means by which we accept salvation. The ground of our salvation is Jesus Christ and His atoning work on the cross. The condition of our salvation is how we respond in faith.

Faith is an attitude, a disposition of submission, a state of mind. Faith is a confident trust in God and a total abandonment of self-reliance. Practically speaking, this means taking God at His word. If we have faith in God, then there is nothing God could command in Scripture that we would refuse to believe and do—*even if we don't fully understand the reason behind God's command.* If God says something, we accept it as true, we trust it more than we trust our own wisdom, and we submit to it.

> *Faith is an attitude, a disposition of submission, a state of mind. Faith is a confident trust in God and a total abandonment of self-reliance. Practically speaking, this means taking God at His word.*

Salvation is never earned, deserved, or merited out of sacrifice, good deeds, or accomplishments. If we could somehow work our way into heaven with enough elbow grease, then salvation wouldn't be grace. Remember, salvation is not wages paid, but a gift freely given (Rom. 4:4-5).

When the Bible gives a summary statement of God's condition for salvation, that condition is faith (John 1:12; 3:16, 18, 36; Acts 16:31; Rom. 3:22, 28; 4:1-25; 5:1; Gal. 2:16; 3:1-18; Eph. 2:8-9; 1 John 5:13). Yet faith does not merely mean "mental assent." Even demons mentally assent to the reality of

God (Jas. 2:19). If your faith is not a repenting, obedient faith, then it is not biblical faith.

FAITH IS INSEPARABLE FROM **REPENTANCE.**

Repentance and faith are conjoined twins. In fact, so inseparable is repentance from faith that repentance is often mentioned as the sole condition of salvation (Luke 24:47; Acts 3:19; 5:31; 11:18; 17:30; 26:20; 2 Tim. 2:25; Heb. 6:6; 2 Pet. 3:9). Is this a contradiction? Are we saved by faith, or are we saved by repentance? We are saved by both, because they are each involved in each other. True repentance towards God presupposes faith in Him.

> *If we could somehow work our way into heaven with enough elbow grease, then salvation wouldn't be grace.*

The most common Greek word translated *repent* is *metanoeō* and literally means to change one's mind. When Jesus and His apostles commanded repentance (cf. Luke 13:1-5), they were commanding people to change their minds, hearts, and wills. We change our minds about sin; we start hating sin. Repentance is "an honest renunciation of all sin and a full surrender of the heart and life to God."[3] We exchange one viewpoint for another, one object of dedication for another. It goes without saying that when you change your viewpoint, a change of attitude and behavior always follows. I like how Harvey Everest puts it: "Repentance is not something to be known, nor something to be felt, but something to be done."[4]

While some passages only imply it, repentance always involves a "from" and a "to." Depending on how messy the sinner's life, the exact form of "from" may vary from person to person.[5] For example, Peter told the Jews on the Day of Pentecost to repent, meaning they were to

---

3 Harvey W. Everest, *The Old Faith Restated*, p. 171
4 p. 170
5 e.g. A liar will have to leave a life of lying (and correct whatever mistruths have been purposefully spoken); an adulterer will have to leave a life of adultery (and give up whatever adulterous or otherwise sinful relationships); a homosexual will have to leave a life of homosexuality (refusing to practice what the Bible calls "unnatural affection," cf. Rom. 1:26-27); a thief will have to leave a life of theft (and return whatever has been stolen); etc.

change *from* unbelief and start believing in Jesus Christ (Acts 2:23, 36). This meant not only a change in opinion, but also a change in behavior. In Acts 17:30, Paul told the Athenians to repent, meaning they were to change from practicing idolatry (cf. vs. 22-29), and start believing in Jesus Christ (vs. 31).

And, following the leaving "from" something must coming the going "to" something else. Notice that the "to" of repentance is largely identical to the "to" of faith. Paul speaks of "repentance *toward* God" (Acts 20:21). Elsewhere he speaks of "repentance leading *to* a knowledge of the truth" (2 Tim. 2:25, emp. added). Faith implies repentance, because faith necessitates a change from unbelief to belief. If we tell a person to repent, or if we tell a person to believe, we are essentially telling him to do the same thing. Each of these two words simply emphasizes a different aspect of the same thing. Repentance emphasizes change; faith emphasizes the object of that change. Repentance is the proper attitude toward sin; faith is the proper attitude toward God.

FAITH IS INSEPARABLE FROM **OBEDIENCE.**

Faith cannot be divorced from obedience. Where there is no obedience, there is no faith. The English Standard Version translates Jesus' words in John 3:36: "Whoever *believes* in the Son has eternal life; whoever does not *obey* the Son shall not see life, but the wrath of God remains on him" (emp. added). Notice in this text that belief in the truth (faith), and submission to the truth (obedience), are synonymous. You do not believe if you do not act on that belief. Belief and obedience are used interchangeably in the new covenant (Rom. 10:16; Gal. 5:7; Heb. 11:8). Eternal destruction is reserved for those "who do not obey the gospel of our Lord Jesus" (2 Thess. 1:8; cf. 1 Pet. 3:1; 4:17). Eternal salvation is only for those "who obey Him" (Heb. 5:9). We must be totally persuaded by His invitation to obey (cf. Acts 26:28). If you do not surrender your

> *Repentance is the proper attitude toward sin; faith is the proper attitude toward God.*

will to Jesus in submissive obedience, then any claim of belief is merely a lie (Jas. 2:26).

In our base text, Ephesians 2:8-10, Paul explicitly tells us that we are saved "by grace through faith," not by works. There is much confusion on this point. When a Christian points out the biblical imperative of obedience in order to be saved, many are quick to parrot Paul's words, "We are not saved by works!" Therefore, we must clearly differentiate faithful obedience from the "works" mentioned by Paul.

For example, there are many works that are unable to save us:

- Works done "to be seen of men" cannot save (Matt. 23:5).
- Works wherein we glory in our own ability cannot save (Acts 7:41; Rom. 4:2, 4).
- Works we boast about cannot save (Rom. 3:27; Eph. 2:9).
- Works which lead us to reject the Son of God cannot save (Rom. 9:31-33)
- Works of the Law of Moses cannot save (Gal. 2:16)
- Works of our own doing cannot save (2 Tim. 2:1-9; Titus 3:5)
- Works of the devil cannot save (1 John 3:8)

As we can see, there is no work we can do to *earn* our salvation with God. In fact, if we trust our works to save us, there is nothing good about those works. Works of merit have no place in man's salvation. On the other hand, works of obedience and submission are completely different. Faith is humble obedience to God's law. We can be saved only if we "*do* what is right and acceptable to Him" (Acts 10:35, emp. added). Christians, if they wish to be faithful, have no choice but to "*perform deeds* in keeping with their repentance" (Acts 26:20, emp. added). We will be judged in part on the works done for the glory of God (Rom. 2:6). There is a sense in which we can "save ourselves" if we *choose to obey* the gospel (Acts 2:40). All of the cases

> *Faith cannot be divorced from obedience. Where there is no obedience, there is no faith.*

> *Salvation requires the possession of works of obedience, done in faith, resting on God's grace and provision.*

of conversion in the book of Acts make it clear that faithful obedience is necessary to be saved by grace (Acts 2:38-41; 8:12, 35-39; 9:18; 16:30-33; 18:8; 22:16).

The only faith that saves is a "working faith" (Gal. 5:6). When Paul tells us we are not saved by works, he is discussing meritorious works (Eph. 2:8-9). However, salvation requires the possession of works of obedience, done in faith, resting on God's grace and provision (Rom. 1:5; 16:26).

FAITH IS INSEPARABLE FROM **CONFESSION.**

One cannot be a secret believer and simultaneously be pleasing to God (cf. John 12:42). Jesus expects His disciples to be willing to "confess Him before men" (Matt. 10:32). John wrote, "Whoever confesses that Jesus is the Son of God, God abides in him, and he in God" (1 John 4:15, cf. 4:2). Timothy "made the good confession in the presence of many witnesses" (1 Tim. 6:12). Confession is not merely a phrase to be uttered once immediately before baptism, but a *continual practice* by every follower of Christ.[6] I must be confessing the Lord daily in how I think, talk, conduct my business, and treat my neighbor. If I do not regularly communicate to others my submission to the Lordship of Jesus, I surely am not living by faith.

It is interesting how Romans 10:9-10 links faith to confession. The Spirit wants us to know that Christians cannot separate the two. Confession without faith is hypocrisy and therefore of no value for salvation (Matt. 7:21-23), and faith without confession is simply

---

6 The idea that one cannot be saved unless He makes some sort of formal "confession" immediately before immersion misses the point of the gospel. Most build this doctrine—that one's salvation depends in part on a phrase uttered before baptism—on Acts 8:37. It us unwise, however, to rely on Acts 8:37 because its inclusion in Scripture is controversial among even the most conservative of textual scholars. Metzger observes that the formula in verse 37 "may have [first] been written in the margin of a copy of Acts" centuries ago and that "the earliest known New Testament manuscript that contains these words dates from the sixth century" (p. 315). The evidence produced by the field of textual criticism suggests that scribes, as they copied the sacred text, over the years allowed a commentary about this practice of the early church (in the way people confessed their faith in Jesus before they were baptized) to creep into the text and eventually become verse 37. However, it does indeed seem unthinkable that Philip would have baptized the eunuch without first verifying that the man indeed believed in Jesus. Thus this textual discrepancy is no problem in practical terms for us today, as it will always be a universal fact that anyone learning to become a Christian will invariably confess his or her belief in Jesus to the person teaching him or her the gospel.

unthinkable. Additionally, it is important to note that in the original language of Romans 10:10, *confesses* is in the present tense, indicating continuous action. Of the Jews who refused to accept Jesus as the Messiah, Paul essentially says that if one "keeps on trusting" and "keeps up making public acknowledgment," then he or she will be saved. Christians must boldly proclaim their faith, even when faced with death.

SAVED BY GRACE THROUGH FAITH AT THE MOMENT OF *BAPTISM*

Both Ephesians and Colossians, two of Paul's letters written while in prison, have remarkably similar content. Our main text, Ephesians 2:8-10, and Colossians 2:8-13 are addressing similar themes. Both texts teach we were dead in our sins (Eph. 2:1; Col. 2:13); we once followed the world (Eph. 2:2; Col. 2:8); we were raised by God from the dead (Eph. 2:5; Col. 2:12-13); we were saved through faith (Eph. 2:8; Col. 2:12), etc. Colossians, however, adds a significant point. Our faith comes in contact with God's grace *at the point of baptism*: "...Having been buried with Him *in baptism*, in which you were also raised with Him through faith in the powerful working of God, who raised Him from the dead" (Col. 2:12, emp. added).

> *Grace is the <u>basis</u> of our salvation, faith is the <u>means</u> of our salvation, and baptism is the <u>occasion</u> of our salvation.*

Since the sum of Scripture is truth (cf. Psa. 119:160), notice what happens when we add Ephesians 2:8-10 and Colossians 2:12 together: Grace is the *basis* of our salvation, faith is the *means* of our salvation, and baptism is the *occasion* of our salvation. We are "buried with Him" and "raised with Him" when we are baptized. With almost identical wording, Paul says "we were buried with Him by baptism into death" so that we might "walk in newness of life" (Rom. 6:4).

The crowd on the day of Pentecost believed in Jesus Christ, but had not yet been forgiven of their sins. They still had to do something, namely "repent and be baptized" (Acts 2:38). Only at that point could they consider their sins forgiven and receive the "gift of the Holy Spirit."[7] Notice how clear the Bible is about the essential nature of baptism:

- Baptism is the point at which one is born again (John 3:5).
- Baptism is the point at which one's sins are washed away (Acts 22:16).
- Baptism is the point at which one is saved (1 Pet. 3:21; Titus 3:5).
- Baptism is the point at which one enters the body (the church) of Christ (1 Cor. 12:13).
- Baptism is the point at which we put on Christ (Gal. 3:27).
- Baptism is how we identify with Christ and His death (Rom. 6:3).
- Baptism marks the beginning of our walk with Christ (Rom. 6:4).

There is only one baptism for Christians today (Eph. 4:5). While there are two aspects to this baptism (physical/spiritual, water/Spirit, cf. John 3:5), it is a single occasion.

WHAT IS BAPTISM?

Before ascending into heaven, Jesus commanded the world to be baptized: "Go therefore and make disciples of all nations, baptizing them in the name of the Father and of the Son and of the Holy Spirit" (Matt. 28:19). What is interesting is the Greek word He chose to use in communicating what He wanted His disciples to do. He could have used the word *niptō*, which is found 17 times in the New Testament. It is properly translated "wash," and refers to cleaning or taking a bath, yet is never used in reference to baptism. He could have used *louō*, which also

---

7 While there is much disagreement about this, perhaps the "gift of the Holy Spirit" was the "promise of being resurrected to eternal life" (see the last mention of both the "receiving" and the "Holy Spirit" by Peter which his hearers would have remembered, in Acts 2:33, and compare to John 5:29). Alternatively, the "gift of the Holy Spirit" was the ability to perform a miraculous gift of the Holy Spirit, which was conveyed to someone by the laying on of an apostle's hands (Acts 8:18). Elsewhere in the book of Acts and the New Testament, the same Greek word for "gift" is almost always used in the context of the miraculous.

means "washing," and is always translated that way and is never translated *baptism*. He could have used *rhantizō*, which means to "sprinkle, splash liquid on something, or purify,"[8] yet is never used in the Bible to describe baptism. He could have used *cheó*, which appears in various forms to designate pouring, but is never used in connection to baptism. He could have used *brechō*, translated in the New Testament as "to rain" or "to wash," but never in connection to baptism.

The word Jesus used for baptism was *baptizō*. The same is true for all the writers of the New Testament. The common meaning of that word, as used by any ordinary person in the days of Jesus and His apostles, was to "immerse, dip, or plunge." LB. Wilkes confidently observes: "All scholars, critics, lexicographers, commentators, and church historians are agreed as to this; all, I mean, who are authority, and who have spoken on the subject, that it signifies to immerse."[9]

The Greek word for *baptism*, as used in the first century, means "immersion," and no reputable scholar denies this. Even John Calvin wrote, "The term *baptize* means to immerse, and that this was the form used by the primitive church."[10] Martin Luther wrote, "I would have the candidates for baptism completely immersed in the water, as the word says." Why? Because baptism, Luther argues, "is that immersion in water from which it derives its name, for the Greek *baptizo* means 'I immerse,' and *baptisma* means 'immersion.'"[11]

We can conclude, without apology or reservation, that when the New Testament speaks of baptism, it is referring to the physical act of momentarily submerging a person completely in water. This is the only way to baptize someone biblically. If the Bible is true and our only standard of faith, then we must firmly reject any idea that baptism can also include sprinkling or pouring a small amount of water on one's head—however popular these views are in Christendom.

Furthermore, we understand baptism means immersion because

---

8 James Swanson, *Dictionary of Biblical Languages with Semantic Domains*
9 L.B. Wilkes, *Designs of Christian Baptism*, p. 45
10 John Calvin, *Institutes*, p. 868
11 Martin Luther, *Babylonian Captivity of the Church*, p. 37

We can conclude, without apology or reservation, that when the New Testament speaks of baptism, it is referring to the physical act of momentarily submerging a person completely in water.

baptism symbolizes death, burial, and resurrection. Romans 6:4 says that "we were buried therefore with Him by baptism into death, in order that, just as Christ was raised from the dead by the glory of the Father, we too might walk in newness of life." Colossians 2:12 says we have been "buried with Him in baptism, in which [we] were also raised with Him through faith." How silly it is to picture someone burying a dead body simply by pouring a cup full of dirt over his head. Similarly, how can sprinkling water on someone's head symbolize baptism? We may confidently conclude that when Jesus commanded people to be baptized, He meant total immersion in water.

WHAT DOES ONE NEED TO *KNOW* TO BE BAPTIZED?

We have established that to be saved, God must first call him or her (John 6:44). The way in which God calls is by teaching. Therefore, no one can come to God unless he is first taught certain things (John 6:45). Far too many people do not understand this concept. Many believe that one must simply be sincere in order to be baptized. Yet a good conscience is not the only criteria (cf. Acts 23:1; 26:9).

What does one need to be taught before he can be baptized? The best answer is found by asking, "What did those in the book of Acts believe when they were baptized?" The only accounts of conversion the Spirit recorded for us in the Bible are found in the book of Acts. Therefore we must look to those conversions to discover what God expected real people to know before they were baptized. After hearing the gospel first preached on the Day of Pentecost, those in Acts 2 understood several important truths.

First, they understood that Jesus of Nazareth is the Lord and the Christ (Acts 2:36). Believing in Jesus means much more than seeing Him as an historical figure. It means knowing that He is the fulfillment of the Old Testament figures and prophecies about Him (Matt. 5:17). To confess that Jesus is the Son of God (Rom. 10:10; 1 Tim. 6:12-13) means to believe in His deity (John 5:17-18; 10:30), His virgin birth (Luke 1:35) and that He was resurrected from the dead (Rom. 1:4).

What did those in the book of Acts believe when they were baptized?

Second, they understood that they were guilty of sin and needed to repent (Acts 2:37). In other words, they understood they had to "do" something to be saved. Peter told them to repent and be baptized for the remission of their sins. Thus, they had to commit to a change in life, knowing that following Jesus means complete submission to Him (Heb. 5:9). To become a Christian, one must realize that he is in essence killing his former identity—one of sin and rebellion towards God (Eph. 2:1-3)—and assuming the identity of Christ (Gal. 2:20).

Third, they understood that their sins were not forgiven until they were baptized (Acts 2:38). It is a good indication that someone is not ready for baptism if they are content with postponing baptism. Who in their right mind can bear the thought of waiting a few days (or even a few unnecessary hours) before having their sins forgiven? Baptism is the moment when one's sins are washed away (Acts 22:16). This is why we see the Philippian jailer being baptized "at once" during that "same hour" of the night (Acts 16:33).

Fourth, they understood that Jesus now reigns over His kingdom, and they needed to be a part of that kingdom (Acts 2:30-36). Peter's whole sermon was in essence an invitation to the kingdom of God. In fact, when inspired preachers taught the gospel to lost people, they preached the "kingdom" to people (Acts 8:12; 19:8; 20:25; 28:23, 31). Evidently, it was important for people to know *something* about this kingdom—the domain of Christ—before they could be baptized.

A very interesting account is found in Acts 19:1-7. Paul arrived in Ephesus and found 12 men who claimed to be disciples of Jesus. Paul, however, wanted to be sure that they were truly disciples of Jesus, and so he asked a question that would authenticate their claim. He asked, "Did you receive the Holy Spirit when you believed?" They replied, "No, we have not even heard that there is a Holy Spirit" (Acts 19:2), thus betraying the fact that they had an inadequate grasp of the things they needed to understand prior to baptism.

We need to understand why Paul would have asked these men such a question. There have always been certain identifying marks of a true Christian, and sometimes these marks are era-specific. Today, if you encountered someone who claimed to be a faithful Christian, like Paul you would verify their claim by asking any number of basic questions. "What is the name of the church you attend?" "Do you take the Lord's Supper every first day of the week?" "Does your church utilize female preachers in the assembly?" "Do you think you were saved before you were baptized?" These are not failproof questions, but they are fairly accurate ways of assessing the credibility of one's claim of being a member of the church of Jesus.

In the first century, Christians were well aware of the miraculous gift of the Holy Spirit. In this way, the Holy Spirit (and the ability to perform some sort of miraculous function) did not automatically fall on people when they were baptized (Acts 8:16). All Scriptural evidence points to the fact that only an apostle could transfer this "gift" to Christians (1 Cor. 12:1; Rom. 1:11; Acts 8:17).[12] God gave Christians these gifts in the first century because the New Testament canon had not yet been completed and thoroughly distributed, and so the early church depended on these gifts for God's guidance. Once the New Testament was completed, however, these miraculous gifts would be no longer needed and thus would cease (cf. 1 Cor. 13:8-10). So when Paul asked these 12 men if they had "received the Holy Spirit when they believed," he was essentially asking them, "Do you have what you need

---

12 These miraculous gifts, or "manifestations of the Spirit," listed in 1 Corinthians 12:8-11, included divine wisdom not gained by human experience, knowledge not naturally learned, miraculous healing, prophecy, a super-human ability to discern falsehood, the ability to speak in a language that one hasn't studied, etc.

to instruct you as Christians?"

These men were clueless, meaning they had not been taught by an evangelist proclaiming the present kingdom of God. They were taught inaccurate information, which was enough evidence for Paul to ask, "Into what then were you baptized?" They responded, "Into John's baptism" (Acts 19:3). They *thought* they were obeying God by being baptized into John's baptism—their intentions were right—but good intentions alone are not adequate to make one a candidate for baptism.

To better appreciate this fact, consider the scope of understanding needed for John's baptism. It was a baptism of belief and submission to the Lord (cf. John 1:23; Acts 19:4); a baptism of repentance (Matt. 3:1-2, 11; Acts 19:4); a baptism of immersion in water (John 1:26; 3:23), a baptism of forgiveness of sins (Mark 1:4; Luke 3:3). Simply believing in Jesus, repenting of sin, and desiring forgiveness does not, in and of itself, make one eligible for baptism.

The one major thing John's baptism lacked compared to the "one baptism" today was that it was *preparatory* to the coming kingdom. "Repent, for the kingdom of heaven is at hand" (Matt. 3:2; 4:17) was the slogan of John's baptism, meaning the kingdom had not yet arrived. In contrast, the baptism of today is a baptism in view of the fact that the kingdom has *now arrived*. The early Christians spoke of the kingdom as something that was now here, and lost people needed to submit to that present kingdom (1 Cor. 4:20; Col. 1:13; Acts 28:23, 31). Thus, the difference between John's baptism and today's baptism was one's frame of reference concerning the kingdom of Christ.

The kingdom is built upon the bedrock truth of Jesus' death and resurrection (1 Cor. 15:14-19). The kingdom is the realm of the saved (Col. 1:13). The kingdom is the domain of Jesus, over which He rules (1 Cor. 15:27-28; Heb. 1:8). The kingdom manifests itself as the one and only church that Jesus built (Matt. 16:18-19). When early Christians proclaimed the gospel to the world, they preached about this kingdom (Acts 8:12; 19:8; 28:23, 31). Christianity is about belonging to that kingdom, and one must understand something about this kingdom before being baptized.

Though John's baptism was one of repentance and forgiveness, as it relates to the kingdom, John's baptism was merely a baptism of *anticipation*. To be baptized with John's baptism after the establishment of the kingdom meant you had a wrong understanding of the nature of that kingdom *as it now is*. When John was baptizing, Jesus was not yet on His throne. In Christian baptism, however, Jesus is now reigning on His throne. *The "one baptism" today is about accepting Christ's reign in a body governed from heaven.* That body is the church (Eph. 1:22-23), the kingdom and dominion of God (cf. Col. 1:13). *Baptism must acknowledge His governance.*

How much does one need to know to be saved? Surely not much more than what has been discussed here. Once one is in Christ (2 Cor. 5:17), he or she will begin a process of lifelong growth (1 Pet. 2:1-3). Yet, as Wayne Jackson comments, "There is a threshold level of comprehension that may (and must) be embraced confidently and happily" before someone should be allowed to be baptized.[13]

Good intentions alone never saved anyone (Matt. 7:21-23). Perhaps someone was baptized into a denomination, believing with all of his heart he was doing the right thing at the time. But if he was not baptized with an accurate, biblical understanding about what was taking place at baptism, then he can never have "a pure conscience" until he is baptized according to the biblical pattern (cf. 1 Pet. 3:21). There are things someone *must* understand before his baptism can be considered the "one baptism" (Eph. 4:4-6) into the kingdom of God.

HOW DO YOU KNOW SOMEONE IS *READY* FOR BAPTISM?

First, because baptism is a burial of the dead (Rom. 6:3-11), one must be dead enough to be buried. A person must be eager to give up everything that displeases God in order to be eligible for baptism (cf. Col. 3:1-10). Yet if someone is not heartbroken over sin, unwilling to leave behind

---

13 Wayne Jackson, "What Must I Know to Be Saved?" *ChristianCourier.com*

whatever sinful relationships and desires he has in his life, then he is not dead enough to be buried.

Second, one must be ready to leave everything behind and submit to Jesus as Lord. One must have "sanctified in his heart Christ as Lord" (1 Pet. 3:15, NKJV). Unless Jesus is Lord over one's life, then he or she will eventually leave the kingdom when persecution, pressure, or pain inevitably come. "The fleeting pleasure of sin" (Heb. 11:24-26) will eventually win back the heart of anyone who has not made Jesus Lord. There is a peculiar joy that one must have to become a Christian—a joy so strong that one is willing to put to death anything that will weaken one's ability to follow Christ (cf. Matt. 13:44-46).

If someone truly is dead enough to be buried, and if someone has truly submitted to the Lord, this removes much of the guesswork as to whether a person will remain faithful to the Lord. People might not know much about the Bible, but if they have truly made Jesus Lord, then there is no question that they will submit to the truth when they come to a better knowledge of it.

SAVED BY GRACE THROUGH FAITH AT THE MOMENT OF BAPTISM *FOR GOOD WORKS*

"For we are His workmanship, created in Christ Jesus *for good works*, which God prepared beforehand, that we should walk in them" (Eph. 2:10, emp. added). God is the divine artist—the carpenter, the architect—who created us. He made the plan to save us; He predestined for adoption all who would be in Christ (Eph. 1:5); He formed the Christian family (Eph. 1:10); He gave life to those who were spiritually dead (Eph. 2:1, 5). Now, "if anyone is in Christ, he is a new creation" (2 Cor. 5:17).

Yet, just because God (and not our works, Eph. 2:9) is the source of our salvation doesn't mean we don't have good works to do. God saved us so that we can do good works. He did not save us *by* our works (as if we somehow worked hard enough that we now deserve salvation), nor did He save us *from* works (as if God has freed Christians from any obligation to obey His will). God saved us *for* good works. The very reason God saved you was so you could serve Him.[14] God did not save us because we were good; He saved us so that we *can be* good. One of the purposes of Jesus' death was that He might "purify for Himself a people for His own possession who are zealous for good works" (Titus 2:14).

> *God did not save us because we were good; He saved us so that we can be good.*

Notice that "God prepared beforehand" the works we are to do. It is not up to *us* to determine what is good. Rather, God tells us what is good in His word. We live by every word that proceeds from the mouth of God (cf. Matt. 4:4). As we walk in the works He has prepared, we are justified—not because we have earned salvation, but because, like Abraham and Rahab,[15] we have obediently submitted to God's will. "And being made perfect, He became the source of eternal salvation to all who *obey* Him" (Heb. 5:9, emp. added). This does not give us reason to boast (cf. Eph. 2:9), for our lives are imperfect even at our best, and we are taught to continually look to the blood of Jesus for cleansing (1 John 1:6-10). But the person who submits to God's plan for making him righteous does righteousness, thus becoming righteous (see 1 John 3:7).

It seems whenever total obedience is taught that there is someone nearby who parrots something like, "But works don't save us!" Saying, "We're not saved by works" is like saying, "Samson didn't get his strength from his hair." It's a moot point. Of course Samson's hair didn't give him strength; God was the source of his strength all along. But Samson had to keep his hair long if he wished to maintain his strength.[16] Likewise, our works don't save us; the grace of God does! But by the grace of God,

---

14 If your life is not characterized primarily by your service to God, are you truly saved? 2 Cor. 13:5; Phil. 2:12.

15 Abraham, because of his great faith in God, was obedient to God's commands. "Was not Abraham our father justified by works, in that he offered up Isaac his son upon the altar?" (Jas. 2:21). Rahab, too, was justified by her faith when she took action that reflected her complete trust in the God of Israel. "And in like manner was not also Rahab the harlot justified by works, in that she received the messengers, and sent them out another way?" (Jas. 2:25). In both cases, these servants of God were justified in their Lord's eyes because their works reflected their absolute trust in God. The inverse is also true; a lack of works reflects a lack of trust. "Why do you call me 'Lord, Lord,' and not do what I tell you?" (Luke 6:46). People are saved by works today because their absolute trust/faith in God leads them to do His will. We say "saved by works" in this context in an accommodative sense, for as James says, "You see that a person is justified by works and not by faith alone" (Jas. 2:24). James is speaking of works of faith—the inevitable result of our absolute trust in God. Such works justify us because they are not actually *our* works, but *God's* works (Eph. 2:10).

16 Judges 13:5; 16:16-17

He has commanded all men do something in order to be saved. There can be no salvation apart from heartfelt works of obedience to Him, starting with the "obedience of faith" (Rom. 1:5), followed by a lifelong commitment to good works.

To continue being saved by God's grace, we must continue serving God in faithful obedience—not because this will somehow merit salvation (Luke 17:10), but because we love Him and our faithfulness to Him is God's condition for our salvation. Thus, Christians are urged to remain faithful (Acts 11:23) and continue walking in His light (1 John 1:7).

We now have a new master. Before we became Christians, we were slaves to sin and death (Rom. 6:16-17). Since God has released us, we are now slaves to God and His will (Rom. 6:18-22). While we are saved by God's grace, that face does not release us from Christianity still being a system of laws that must be obeyed (Rom. 6:14). Yet good works are not the foundation of our salvation—God's grace is the foundation. Good works are the necessary *consequence* of our salvation. Thus, salvation only belongs to those who desire to be faithful (Rev. 2:10). When we stop following God's commandments to the best of our ability, we have stopped living by faith.

CONCLUSION

We are saved by God's grace through our faith at the moment of baptism for the purpose of good works. God's grace is the *reason* we can have salvation in the first place. Faith is the *means* through which we are allowed access to God's grace. Baptism is the *occasion* at which God accomplishes our salvation. Works of obedience is the *way* by which we exercise our faith.

Consider the example of a gift card to your favorite restaurant. The reason there is food to be eaten is because of the restaurant, and the means of transferring that food from the kitchen to your plate is the gift card. However, the time in which the food actually enters your stomach is when you decide to actually visit the restaurant and eat the food. You don't receive your food the moment you receive your gift card; you must first take the gift card to the restaurant in order to be filled.

Likewise, *grace*, *faith*, *baptism*, and *good works* are all words describing the basis of our salvation from different perspectives. All must be kept in view of one another. Salvation is much too important to not get this right.

And now—those who believe that Jesus is Lord and that God wants to save you—why do you wait? "Rise and be baptized and wash away your sins, calling on His name" (Acts 22:16).

DISCUSSION QUESTIONS

1. What does our sin do to our relationship with God?

2. How does God draw us?

3. What is the doctrine of *total depravity*? What does the Bible have to say about this teaching?

4. What is the doctrine of *limited atonement*? What does the Bible have to say about this teaching?

5. What is the doctrine of *irresistible grace*? What does the Bible have to say about this teaching?

6. What can you imagine are some of the consequences of living under the delusion that we must earn our way to heaven?

7. How are repentance and faith related?

8. What are some good indications that someone is not ready to be baptized, despite claiming a desire to be baptized?

9. What is the difference between John's baptism and the "one baptism" of the New Covenant?

10. Can someone be saved today without works? Explain your answer.

CHAPTER 5

BECOMING WHAT WE HAVE BECOME

SANCTIFICATION

MILLIONS of self-identifying Christians have heard the message that salvation is free. It is a gift. It is by grace. And before this message has finished reverberating through the church building, the masses have concluded that sanctification must therefore be *optional*. But this isn't true. A half-truth is a whole lie. While salvation is free, sanctification is *mandatory*.

To be sanctified is to be *changed* from how you once were. The biggest threat to the church is not atheism, secularism, or radical Islam. The biggest threat to the church is *easy-believism*. This pseudo-Christianity only produces *indifference* instead of *transformation*. It is a plague that has left far more casualties in its wake than the bubonic plague, smallpox, and cholera combined.

Because of easy-believism, you now have many who have been baptized, but are still dead in their sins and don't know it. Dietrich Bonhoeffer calls this problem "cheap grace"—the idea that salvation doesn't come with any cost or price to be paid. He comments: "Cheap grace is the preaching of forgiveness without requiring repentance, baptism without church discipline, Communion without confession, absolution without personal confession. Cheap grace is grace without discipleship, grace without the cross, grace without Jesus Christ, living and incarnate."[1]

How many Christians have you seen firsthand who are quick to accept the benefits of Christianity while apparently forfeiting any attempt at

---

1 Dietrich Bonhoeffer, *The Cost of Discipleship*, p. 44

holiness? Bonhoeffer says further, "The essence of grace, we suppose, is that the account has been paid in advance; and, because it has been paid, everything can be had for nothing."[2] The harm this belief has done to the Lord's church is beyond estimate. Easy-believism, cheap grace, or whatever else you want to call it, is perhaps the root cause of the diminishing influence of Christianity in the Western world. On many fronts today, all that is left is a morally anemic church to confront our morally corrupt society.

But easy-believism—forgiveness without transformation—grace without cost—isn't the gospel. It is another gospel. It offers comfort to people who have never been saved. There are multitudes of preachers across our land quick to condemn the idea that we can be saved by works without grace (cf. Eph. 2:9), but how many preachers are brave enough to condemn the belief that we can be saved by grace without *change*? Yet the Bible makes this clear: Justification without sanctification is a false gospel. Paul warns about this in Romans 6:1-2; 1 Corinthians 6:9-11; Galatians 5:19-21; Ephesians 5:3-7. James denounces this in James 2:14-26. John seems fixated on addressing this problem in his first letter, as seen in 1 John 1:6; 2:3-4, 9-11; 3:3-10, 14-15; 4:20. You cannot become a Christian without dying to yourself. Unchanged Christians are not Christians.

The primary concern of God in our redemption is not merely the forgiveness of *past* sins, but a functional relationship with Him *now*. The only way God's children can walk with Him is if they pursue holiness (Rom. 14:17; Heb. 12:14; cf. Amos 3:3). Salvation is not merely a Band-Aid for our sins—it is a lifelong process of transformation so we can walk with the Lord.

THE MEANING OF SANCTIFICATION

The basic meaning of *sanctify* in both the Old and New Testaments is "to make holy, that is, to separate from the world and consecrate to

---

2 p. 43

God."[3] The concept of sanctification is found in the Hebrew word *kādhash* and the Greek word *hagiázō*, both of which are found in various forms and are usually translated "holy," "hallow," "hallowed," "holiness," "consecrate," "saint," "sanctify," etc. The most basic concept of sanctification is *separation*. It logically follows that if sanctification means dedication *to* God, it also means separation *from* sin. One writer observes, "To move toward God is to move away from sin as surely as to go north means to go away from south."[4]

> *The primary concern of God in our redemption is not merely the forgiveness of past sins, but a functional relationship with Him now.*

To be holy means more than practicing a high degree morality. Even an atheist can have a measure of morality. But morality is only one result of being holy. To be holy *primarily* refers to being in a relationship with God. Someone we consider a good, moral individual yet who is not a Christian is nonetheless unholy.

When Paul wrote his letters to the Christians in Rome, Corinth, and Ephesus, he begins by calling them *saints* (Rom. 1:7; 1 Cor. 1:2; 2 Cor. 1:1; Eph. 1:1-2). In his first letter to the Corinthians, he specifically says they have been "sanctified in Christ Jesus" (1 Cor. 1:2), meaning they had become sanctified when they obeyed the gospel of Christ (Rom. 1:5, 16-17; 6:17-18). In other words, being a *Christian* and being *sanctified* should be synonymous. In fact, the most common designation for Christians in the Bible is *saint*, a usage that occurs some 56 times in the New Testament.[5] Everyone who is a Christian is a saint and thus enjoys the blessings of sanctification. But the *extent* of our sanctification depends on our desire to obey Jesus.

God has invited all sinners to become saints and, therefore, to a state of sanctification. If you are a Christian, you are sanctified (and you must live accordingly). We understand that salvation is a free gift of God (cf.

---

3 Franklin Harris Rall, "Sanctification," *The International Standard Bible Encyclopaedia*, p. 2682
4 F. Leroy Forlines, *The Quest for Truth*, p. 222
5 Dub McClish, "The Holy Spirit, Sanctification, and Sinless Perfection," *What Do You Know About the Holy Spirit?*, p. 274

Eph. 2:8-10), but we must also understand that it is a gift God expects us to *use*. Just because a gift is free doesn't mean it will work. Salvation only works if we are sanctified, otherwise it is of no use to us—and we are then of no use to God.

THREE IMPORTANT WORDS: JUSTIFICATION, SANCTIFICATION, AND REGENERATION

Sin creates three major problems: *guilt*, *sickness*, and *death*. First, sin makes us guilty, which in turn makes us liable to punishment.[6] Second, sin makes us sick,[7] which hardens the heart, numbs the conscience, and inclines us to sin even more. Third, sin brings death by killing us spiritually.[8] It separates us from God, which is the definition of spiritual death. Hence our dire need for salvation.

Being a Christian and being sanctified should be synonymous.

Just as sin introduced three problems (guilt, sickness, and death), with salvation comes three solutions: **justification**, **sanctification**, and **regeneration**. *Justification* is the solution to our guilt, and *sanctification* is the healing of our sickness, and *regeneration* is the resurrection from our spiritual graves. These three terms are closely related. The difference between them is the perspective from which they describe a person's conversion. Consider the different thrust of each word:

JUSTIFICATION

When we are converted, we are *justified*. Justification is a legal term, referring to the acquittal of our guilt and the declaration of our righteousness in God's sight.[9] The emphasis here is on our status before God, not necessarily our character (for sometimes wicked people are justified in a

---

6 Each man will be judged according to his own works (cf. Psa. 62:12; Eze. 18:4; Rom. 14:12).
7 In His illustration involving the tree and the fruit (representing people and their deeds), He says both have been corrupted (Matt. 7:17-20; 12:33-35). Sin has a deteriorating effect on the heart (cf. Isa. 1:5-6; Jer. 17:9; Rom. 3:10-18). One cannot sin and remain unchanged.
8 Gen. 2:17; Prov. 14:12; 16:25; Rom. 5:12; 6:16, 23; 7:13; Jas. 1:15
9 Stephen D. Renn, *Expository Dictionary of Bible Words*, p. 547

corrupt human court, cf. Isa. 5:23). Thus we find that justification is not something we deserve (for we were wicked and deserved punishment); justification means that God treats us *as if* we were righteous. Don't flatter yourself here; we are not justified on the basis of our own righteousness (otherwise we wouldn't need forgiveness), but on the basis of Jesus' righteousness in place of our sinfulness (2 Cor. 5:21; Phil. 3:9).

God treats us as righteous *because* we have been forgiven. Therefore, the sweet message of justification is that God no longer charges us with sin (Psa. 32:2; Rom. 4:8). This is the same for everyone. No child of God is *more saved* than any other child of God. Justification is the same for everyone—regardless of whether you have been a Christian for five days or five decades (Matt. 20:1-16). In God's court, no one is more justified than another. Someone is either saved or he is not.

SANCTIFICATION

We are sanctified at the moment of conversion, being set apart from the world and dedicated to God's will. When we are born again, sin can no longer be a habit or pattern of life (1 John 3:9). C. Ryder Smith comments: "This is a word of the same root as *holy* and it implies that there is now through the indwelling Spirit a living link between God and the believer, and that thereby a man who had been bad becomes, or is in the process of becoming, a good man."[10, 11]

While justification takes place in God's court and is therefore *external* to us, sanctification takes place in the human heart and is therefore an *internal* change. While justification and sanctification are different words describing different things, they should

> *While justification takes place in God's court and is therefore external to us, sanctification takes place in the human heart and is therefore an internal change.*

---

10 The Holy Spirit is the agent of our sanctification (Rom. 15:16; 1 Cor. 6:11), and the word of God is the means by which the Holy Spirit convicts, converts, and sanctifies human beings (John 17:17; Eph. 5:26; Rom. 6:17-18). The Spirit does not force us to do anything; He convicts us. With that conviction, we choose a sanctified life (1 Pet. 1:15), separating ourselves from the worldly practices of non-Christians (2 Cor. 6:14-18), and dedicating ourselves to God (Rom. 12:1-2).
11 C. Ryder Smith, *The Bible Doctrine of Salvation*, p. 203

not be separated because Scripture does not separate them (1 Cor. 6:11). Not only does God justify us when we have committed ourselves to living sanctified lives before Him, but also we are to live sanctified lives because God has justified us. Sanctification and justification are two sides of the same coin. If you are not sanctified, then you are not justified.

REGENERATION

While we were still sinners, we were spiritually dead (Eph. 2:1). A dead man can't give himself life.[12] Being dead, there is no amount of good we can do to please God. We must be regenerated, otherwise we will continue to produce bad fruit (Matt. 7:16-18; 12:33-35).

Therefore a distinct change occurs in our lives at the moment of conversion, for Paul talks about "the washing of regeneration and renewal in the Holy Spirit" (Titus 3:5). When God converts us, we are released from sin's grip and are made holy. This change is called *regeneration* (Titus 3:5), *rebirth* (John 3:5), *re-creation* (2 Cor. 5:17), or *resurrection* (Eph. 2:5-6; Col. 2:12-13). Regeneration changes our nature,[13] justification changes our relationship to God, and sanctification changes our likeness.

> *When God regenerated us, He placed us on a renewed course of life—one based on a spiritual perspective.*

No longer do we operate by the world's wisdom or live by our carnal appetites. We have been *regenerated*. This is what it means to "walk by faith, not by sight" (2 Cor. 5:7). To walk by faith does not mean that we walk without knowing where we are going; it means we now walk with the assurance of God's blessings we will receive. Nor does walking by faith mean taking blind leaps into unknown directions; it just means there is

---

12 There are limits to every illustration, and here the illustration of death breaks down. Someone who is physically dead could not choose to come physically back to life even if he had the choice, because the body is no longer conscious. However, someone who is spiritually dead can choose spiritual life if God offers it, because the spirit is always conscious. God doesn't force spiritually dead people back to life, but He has given us the choice—if indeed we are willing to obey.

13 We must note that the Bible describes regeneration in a much different way than Calvinism. In the Calvinistic idea of *irresistible grace*, the Spirit enters the sinner's heart prior to the sinner having any kind of faith. But in the Bible, we find the sinner being brought to faith by the word of God, causing him to submit to the God's call of conversion. At baptism, a person is *regenerated* (or born again), thus becoming a Christian. Our nature has been changed because we have chosen to allow God to change it.

a way of seeing other than by human sight or intuition. When God regenerated us, He placed us on a renewed course of life—one based on a spiritual perspective.

SANCTIFICATION BEGINS AT CONVERSION ("PUT ON THE NEW SELF")

One of the most concise descriptions of sanctification is found in Colossians 3:10, where Paul commands, "Put on the new self, which is being renewed in knowledge after the image of its creator." In context (Col. 3:5-14), Paul is telling early Christians they are to "put to death" their worldly inclinations (vs. 5-9) and "put on" the qualities of holiness (vs. 10-14). The message is that God's children must be sanctified, otherwise we will face "the wrath of God" (vs. 6).

One of the implied truths in Colossians 3:10 is that you cannot be sanctified until you have "put on the new self." That is to say, sanctification begins at the moment God justifies us. At conversion, there is a sense in which we are fully sanctified, separated from our former selves and dedicated to God. Justification makes our sanctification possible. Justification is not dependent upon sanctification, but sanctification is dependent upon justification. Justification makes sanctification possible in two ways.

First, justification frees us from the power of sin. Sin enslaves (e.g. John 8:34; Rom. 6:20). When sin rules, sanctification is impossible. Yet because we are justified, Paul writes, "Sin will have no dominion over you, since you are not under law but under grace" (Rom. 6:14). Just a few verses earlier, he says that the "one who has died has been set free from sin" (Rom. 6:7). Here we find the way in which we are released from the slavery of sin. Obviously, when a slave dies, he or she can no longer serve his owner. The word translated "set free," *dikaioō*, should actually be translated *justified*. Thus, when we are buried in baptism, we are baptized into the penal death of Jesus and raised with Him. Christians are "no longer enslaved to sin" (Rom. 6:6). We are delivered from the domain of sin and transferred to the domain of God's grace. "As sin reigned in death, grace also might reign through righteousness leading to eternal life through Jesus Christ our Lord" (Rom. 5:21).

Second, justification opens the door to a sanctified life. Paul tells us that if we have died with Christ at baptism, we will be united with Him "in a resurrection like His" (Rom. 6:5). To be resurrected with Christ is to overcome sin. We follow in the likeness of Christ's resurrection from the dead when we "walk in newness of life" (Rom. 6:4). The justifying power of God allows us to live *changed* lives.

SANCTIFICATION IS A PROCESS ("BEING RENEWED")

"Put on the new self, which is *being renewed* in knowledge after the image of its creator" (Col. 3:10, emp. added). "Being renewed," *anakainoō*, is in the present tense, meaning an ongoing action. While sanctification begins at conversion (2 Cor. 5:17), sanctification is a *process* that produces more fruit as we mature (2 Pet. 3:18).

There is a sense in which we are sanctified at the moment of justification because the righteousness of Christ becomes ours. In another sense, we fall short of being *totally* sanctified in this life, especially when we are first converted and thus just spiritual babes in Christ (cf. 1 Pet. 2:1-3; Heb. 5:14-16). Because of our ignorance of God's will, we don't always know how God wants us to live. Some sins are simply more obvious than others. But as we learn to discern God's will over the course of our lives, we become stronger Christians and thus become more sanctified. Guy N. Woods writes, "Sanctification is thus a matter of degree and it develops as we become more and more consecrated to His service, and yield ourselves more fully to His will as expressed in His commandments."[14]

Our sanctification will not be totally complete until we are resurrected. I don't suppose a Christian can ever reach a state of sinless perfection,

---

14 Guy N. Woods, *Questions and Answers* Vol. II, p. 188

since we will always at times miss the mark of God's perfection. Scripture assumes even the most faithful of Christians will still err at times (1 John 1:8; Matt. 6:11-12). In this way, the difference between Christians and non-Christians is that faithful Christians don't *intentionally* sin.

A true Christian "cannot sin" (1 John 3:9)—not willfully, that is. This is a paradox, for we are also told, "If we say that we have no sin, we deceive ourselves" (1 John 1:8). Thus, in this earthly life, there will forever be something paradoxical about the Christian: he is both saint and sinner. C. Ryder Smith comments, "He is not yet altogether healthy, but he has passed the crisis of his disease. If one may carry the metaphor a little farther, the microbes of sin are not all gone, but they are going. 'There is a sin not unto death' (1 John 5:17)."[15]

When we die and go to be with the Lord, our sanctification will be complete. Because "nothing unclean will ever enter" into the presence of God (Rev. 21:27), we know the spirit of the Christian will be "made perfect" (Heb. 12:23) so we can be finally in His presence. When the Lord returns, He will "transform our lowly body to be like His glorious body" (Phil. 3:21). "At His coming" (1 Cor. 15:23), as Paul says, we will physically be resurrected and will fully "bear the image of the man of heaven" (1 Cor. 15:49). Both the body and the spirit will be completely sanctified when we are resurrected. There will not be anything in our character or personality that will be incompatible with God and an eternal communion with Him.

SANCTIFICATION IS THE RESTORATION OF WHO WE ARE SUPPOSED TO BE ("AFTER THE IMAGE OF HIM")

"Put on the new self, which is being renewed in knowledge *after the image of its creator*" (Col. 3:10, emp. added). God made us in His image (Gen. 1:26-27). But when we sinned, we lost some of our likeness to God. Sinners no longer think, feel, or act in keeping with God's like-

---

15 C. Ryder Smith, *The Bible Doctrine of Salvation*, p. 242

ness. So when God redeemed us, He not only intends to forgive our sins but also desires to restore our personality back to His likeness. As Paul says, we are to be "conformed to the image of His Son" (Rom. 8:29). The word translated *conformed—summorphos—*refers not to an outward change but an inward change of the heart. Gareth Reese comments that this Greek word, based on the word *morphe*, suggests "that this change into the likeness of Christ is inward and thorough, not simply an outward and superficial resemblance."[16] We don't just follow a cold list of rules; we *love* conforming to God's will.

> *We are never more true to ourselves than when we are closest to God—when our inner man is most closely conformed to His likeness.*

In Romans 12:2, Paul says not to "be conformed to this world, but be transformed by the renewal of your mind." The word *mind*, from the Greek word *nous*, refers to "the sum total of the whole mental and moral state of being."[17] This means our sanctification should spring forth fundamentally from our *inner* personality.[18]

We are never more true to ourselves than when we are closest to God—when our inner man is most closely conformed to His likeness. Sanctification then is the lifelong process of moving closer to God. If we are to be like Christ, we need to pursue His likeness down to the depths of our personality. Our words and actions must be expressions of what is happening in the inner man. We must totally surrender the heart, soul, mind, and strength to God (Mark 12:30).

Sanctification makes us better people. Our sense of self-worth is based upon the fact that we were created in the image of God. Sin disfigured and distorted this image, but sanctification is the process of restoring that image. God considered us worth (not worthy) the cost of redeeming us and adopting us back into His family. Christians are now sons of God. This is the basis of self-worth and positive self-image.

---

16 Gareth Reese, *Romans*, p. 376
17 William Arndt, *A Greek-English Lexicon of the New Testament and Other Early Christian Literature*, p. 680
18 By *personality* we mean the essence of what makes you who you are.

SCRIPTURE AND SANCTIFICATION ("IN KNOWLEDGE")

"Put on the new self, which is being renewed *in knowledge* after the image of its creator" (Col. 3:10, emp. added). With reference to the New Covenant, the law of Christ's last will and testament, God says, "I will put my laws into their minds, and write them on their hearts" (Heb. 8:10). To be a Christian means more than simply following a divine rulebook. Following Christ means truly *meditating* on His words and allowing the heart and mind to be transformed.

In His prayer in the garden, Jesus prayed about His disciples, "Sanctify them in the truth; your word is truth" (John 17:17). Earlier, with similar words, Jesus taught, "You will know the truth, and the truth will set you free" (John 8:32). Truth, when it is understood by the mind and believed by the heart, becomes knowledge. When we truly believe something, it produces the appropriate attitude and action.

Paul commands us to "think about" whatever is true, honorable, just, pure, lovely, and commendable (Phil. 4:8). He commanded us to think about these things because what we *think* about becomes *who we are*. Thinking about something means meditating on it. The Bible repeatedly commands us to mediate on God's revealed truth (Josh. 1:8; Psa. 1:2; 19:14; 63:6; 119:15; 143:5; 1 Tim. 4:15).

We continue the process of sanctification as we improve our godly lives and increase in "the knowledge of God, and of Jesus our Lord" and "through the knowledge of Him who called us to His own glory and excellence" (2 Pet. 1:2-3). Knowledge comes through understanding, believing, and practicing the truth.

BECOMING MORE DISCERNING AS WE BECOME MORE SANCTIFIED

You can often tell the maturity of a Christian by his or her level of discernment. Christians need to be people who have scruples, even if there is not a specific "book, chapter, verse" in the Bible to which they can point. The phrase "things like these" in Galatians 5:21 indicates that we shouldn't have to be told specifically how to live; those who are sanctified by the Spirit are smart enough to know how to live. As we become more sanctified, we begin sharing the traits of Christ Himself. It is interesting to me how similar in nature and disposition strong, mature Christians are to one another.

You can often tell the maturity of a Christian by his or her level of discernment. Christians need to be people who have scruples, even if there is not a specific "book, chapter, verse" in the Bible to which they can point.

Our standard is not merely avoiding what is *wrong*, but pursuing what is *right*. We should be concerned about that which is noble, beautiful, and excellent. We should never settle for cheap worship, second-rate discipleship, and bare-minimum obedience. Paul writes that we are to "approve what is excellent" (Phil. 1:10). The NIV renders his words "discern what is best." Not all cultures, lifestyles, hobbies, and pastimes are equal. God expects us to make distinctions in our conduct, in our attire, in our mannerisms, in our recreation, and in our life-decisions. We should always strive for what is best.

Our postmodern, pluralistic society has rejected the idea that some cultures and customs are better than others. As Christians, we cannot accept this. We must be like Christ in all areas of our being. We cannot excuse bad decisions as being "individual taste," "Christian liberty," "evangelism," or "influence." Nothing reflects the spirit of the age as much as people's attitude in areas of virtue, beauty, and excellence. This is reflected particularly in how people dress, what people listen to, and what people joke about. We cannot settle for what culture says is "normal." People cave in these areas before they do in moral areas. Once we let down our guard in areas of ideals, beauty, entertainment, or excellence, we will inevitably become spiritually numb. When we bow to the spirit of the age, we are set for a moral decay.

As we grow in the knowledge of the Lord, the Holy Spirit helps us be the kind of person who loves, experiences joy, peace, patience, etc. (Gal. 5:22-23). As the Spirit produces this fruit in us, these virtues begin to characterize what is in the heart and mind.

YOU CANNOT GET TO HEAVEN WITHOUT BEING SANCTIFIED

1 John 3:9 is a very clear and concise verse about the Christian and sanctification. In no uncertain terms, John says, "No one born of God makes a practice of sinning, for God's seed abides in him; and he cannot keep on sinning, because he has been born of God." In other words, true Christians *cannot* practice sin (while still being Christians), nor can they *continue* in sin. It does not mean that Christians never err, but it does mean that sin is *out of place* in the Christian's life. And as long as a Christian wants to be "born of God," sin cannot be a habit.

How do we reconcile this passage with the reality that sometimes faithful Christians sin, make bad judgments, and come to the occasional wrong conclusion about God's will? The key is found in the distinction the Bible makes between sins of ignorance and presumptuous sins—a distinction clearly seen in passages like Numbers 15:27-31 and Psalm 19:12-13. Throughout the ages, God has always provided a way of atonement for unintentional sins born out of weakness, ignorance, or involuntary lack of conformity. In 1 John 3:9, John is not referring to failures out of weakness or ignorance, but rather a deliberate or defiant decision to sin. More attention to this subject will be given in chapters 6 and 7.

Throughout the ages, God has always provided a way of atonement for unintentional sins born out of weakness, ignorance, or involuntary lack of conformity.

The New Testament makes clear that those who are characterized by gross immorality cannot be saved (1 Cor. 6:9-10; Gal. 5:9-

10; Eph. 5:3-5). Heaven is *only* for those who are actively pursuing righteousness in Christ. Paul makes it clear that salvation must result in a changed life (2 Cor. 5:17; Eph. 2:10). John rather bluntly says that those who fail to practice righteousness are not saved (1 John 2:3-4, 15-16; 3:2-3, 10; 5:4).

Because being born again means being regenerated, Christians now have a new nature. Before conversion, we experimented with, flirted with, and indulged in sin. Now, being sanctified, we no longer seek satisfaction in sin—instead we delight in righteousness. We have declared war on sin. While we may not win every battle, we are persistent solders who never give up the fight. If we do sin, it is only because we lost a battle we tried not to lose, not because we joined the enemy. Even when we have committed sin, the word of God in the human heart begins a process of conviction that will produce repentance.

Christians cannot be indifferent about sin. Faithful children of God will always have shortcomings—there will always be room for growth—but because we are sanctified, our hearts will always be cultivable soil. We have all fallen from a state of righteousness and into a state of sin (Rom. 3:10). Sanctification is the process wherein God rescues us from our state of sin and back into a state of righteousness. If there is no separation from sin, there is no sanctification and thus there is longer a sacrifice for our sins (Heb. 10:26).

SANCTIFICATION OFFERS HOPE TO EVERYONE, EVEN THE WORST OF SINNERS

The world is not getting any better. Illicit drugs, alcohol, abortion, theft, every imaginable form of sexual immorality, violence, and dishonesty are all found in abundance. While every accountable person has been stained with sin, some people have been particularly tarnished. The devil is lurking around like a lion, and he has succeeded in gaining a stronger foothold in the lives of some than he has others. By the time someone hears the gospel even at a young age, it is not uncommon for his life to be deeply destroyed by sin. There are multitudes of people all around us who are messed up, confused, scarred, and enslaved by sin.

But the gospel offers peace to even the messiest of people. Christianity is a message of hope to everyone who has been soiled by sin. God not only forgives sin (justification), but He also changes lives (sanctification). God has never met someone who was too damaged by sin to be transformed by His sanctifying grace. The gospel is powerful enough to make dishonest people honest, impure people pure, unholy people holy, and filthy people clean.

1 Corinthians 6:9-11 is one of the most encouraging verses in the Bible for people entrenched in sin. Corinth was a dark, wicked city, and from this passage we can see that many of the citizens of that city had been saved from all kinds of sin, including alcoholism, theft, homosexuality, adultery, and idolatry. But by God's grace, they repented and made sin a foreign element in their lives. "Such were some of you" (1 Cor. 6:11) will always be the hope-filled call to holiness for everyone who struggles with sin. They had not only been forgiven of their past; they had been sanctified. They had been regenerated into new creatures in Christ (2 Cor. 5:17). The way of Christ is so meaningful because you no longer have to be defined by your sins.

If you grew up in a religious environment and were protected from the worst of sins, you have a lot for which to be thankful. Many were not so blessed. If your family has been spared much of the messy consequences of sin from which countless other families are presently suffering, don't forget to praise the Lord. Incidentally, if your local church does not have people who were saved and sanctified from a life of deep sin, it is not to your credit but because the church is not effectively ministering to your surrounding society.

"Such were some of you" (1 Cor. 6:11) will always be the hope-filled call to holiness for everyone who struggles with sin.

CONCLUSION

When we compare ourselves—with our tattered past—to our perfect and holy God, our shortcomings make us want to say with Isaiah, "Woe is me! For I am lost; for I am a man of unclean lips, and I dwell in the midst of a people of unclean lips; for my eyes have seen the King, the Lord of hosts!" (Isa. 6:5). When we feel so unworthy of a relationship with God, we need to remember Christ's words, "My grace is sufficient for you" (2 Cor. 12:9). God not only forgives; He changes us. Jesus says, "Come to me, all who labor and are heavy laden, and I will give you rest" (Matt. 11:28).

DISCUSSION QUESTIONS

1. What do you think is the biggest threat to the church today?

2. What does *sanctify* mean?

3. Is a holy person merely someone who tries to avoid sin? Explain your answer.

4. What is *justification*?

5. What is *sanctification*? In what sense are Christians sanctified now, and in what sense are Christians undergoing a process of sanctification?

6. What is *regeneration*?

7. Can someone be justified without also being sanctified?

8. What effect does justification have on us?

9. Explain how sanctified people are discerning people.

10. In what ways does God save Christians *now*, and not just in prospect?

CHAPTER 6

MORE THAN A SINNER

FREEDOM FROM SIN

WE sometimes hear people excuse their faults by saying, "I'm only human," as if being human makes wrongdoing somehow, ultimately, *unavoidable*. It is not uncommon to hear even Christians make statements like, "I'm just a sinner" or "We sin daily." Sentiments like these often imply a sort of resignation to the idea expressed in the popular phrase, "to sin every day in thought, word, and deed."

Of course, Christians can relate all too well to the difficulties of being human. We *are* human—living in a broken world—faced with the daily temptation to sin. At some point in the life of a Christian, it seems inevitable that he will make mistakes. And, chances are, that likelihood is not far away from many of us.

But Jesus gives us a new way of being human. Because Jesus rose from the dead, every person alive today has the option of also being risen from spiritual death. While we await our *physical* resurrection, we can enjoy a new *spiritual* resurrection in Christ now. Today, we no longer have to be slaves to sin (Rom. 6:18; 8:2). Through the sanctifying and regenerating blood of Christ, we have been freed from the bondage of **depravity**[1] we once brought upon ourselves (cf. Eph. 2:1-3). So in a way, Jesus gives Christians a new humanity:

> For you have died, and your life is hidden with Christ in God. [...]

---

1 **Depravity** simply means *moral corruption* or *wickedness*. The decision to become a sinner in time produces moral depravity—the studied and skillful practice of sin (Eph. 2:1-3). When Paul uses the phrase, "by nature," he is not referring to something inborn, but in this case something acquired by practice—a sort of *second nature*. This is not to be confused with the false doctrine called "inherited depravity" (see chapter 2). We have not inherited any kind of depravity from Adam or God, nor have we been born with any defect in our character. Unregenerated yet accountable man is depraved because he has chosen the dark road (Rom. 3:9-10; 5:12). We do not sin because we are depraved; we are depraved because we sin.

Put to death therefore what is earthly in you: sexual immorality, impurity, passion, evil desire, and covetousness, which is idolatry. [...] In these you too once walked, when you were living in them. [...] You have put off the old self with its practices and have put on the new self, which is being renewed in knowledge after the image of its creator. (Col. 3:3, 5, 7, 9-10)

We are now ready to examine the main issue this chapter: How do we reconcile the reality that even faithful Christians fall short in perfectly conforming to God's will with the fact that God has plainly charged us not to sin (e.g. John 5:14; 8:11; Rom. 6:12-14; 1 Cor. 15:34; Heb. 12:1; 1 Pet. 2:21-22; 1 John 2:1, 6)?

On one hand, many seem to take for granted the idea that Christians are going to sin over the course of their lifetime. A quick survey of the kind of teaching popularly heard in Christendom today leaves the impression that Christians will, more or less, continually sin. Hopefully, over time, Christians will sin less frequently as they mature, but this does not change the fact that their sin is still inevitable (so it is portrayed). Do we really have to resign ourselves to the idea that Christians must always be sinners, regardless of how much they may try *not* to sin? 1 John 3:9 says: "No one born of God makes a practice of sinning, for God's seed abides in him; and he cannot keep on sinning, because he has been born of God" (cf. Rom. 6:1-2, 14-15). Isn't the phrase, "he cannot keep on sinning" a meaningless statement if it is true that even mature Christians can't help but sin (however less frequently)? Judging by how some Christians talk about this subject, many have resigned themselves to the fact that sin in the life of the Christian is still inevitable, and by implication we can't help but "keep on sinning" (just less frequently).

On the other hand, the Bible repeatedly stresses that Christians have a *choice* over sin (cf. John 5:14; 1 Cor. 15:34; Jas. 1:15; 1 John 2:1). It seems that every page of Scripture contains warnings against sin with the implication that God's children don't have to sin if they don't want to (Rom. 6:1; 1 John 3:4). Jesus has released His followers from the bondage of sin (John 8:36; Rom. 6:6, 14, 18). Why would our loving Father command us to stop sinning if He knew there would be times when we couldn't help but sin? Surely God wouldn't command Christians to stop sinning if He knew we ultimately could not (cf. Rom. 6:1).

How are we to make sense of this apparent contradiction? Since the Bible does not contradict itself, the problem is not with God's revelation, but with how we have conventionally defined sin. When the Bible talks about sin, the inspired authors almost always have in view *presumptuous* sin. A presumptuous—or willful—sin is the intentional, high-handed violation of the known will of God. Thus the commission of *presumptuous* sin, in general, is when someone knows what is right, yet still refuses—like an obstinate, rebellious child—to comply (cf. Jas. 4:17). The most critical ingredient to how the Bible most often uses the word *sin* is the element of human volition. Sin, as portrayed in the Bible, almost always involves the choice to either obey or disobey God's law as it is understood at the time. In the next few pages, notice how the Bible depicts sin.

THE BIBLE'S PREVAILING DESCRIPTION OF SIN

First Corinthians 13, often referred to as "the love chapter," is not technically a definition of love, but a description of it. Though the Bible often describes love, personifies loves using various rhetorical techniques, and presents Jesus as the embodiment of love, the Bible nowhere gives a concise *definition* of love. We must examine the context of each usage of the word *love* to better understand the biblical meaning.

Similarly, nowhere does the Bible give a succinct definition of sin. Because of how the *King James Version* inadequately renders 1 John 3:4 in our modern vernacular, many believe that John is giving an exhaustive definition of sin and how it is used typically in Scripture. The KJV verbiage "sin is the transgression of the law" leaves modern readers with the impression that *any* kind of violation of the law—regardless of whether it was

> *Sin, as portrayed in the Bible, almost always involves the choice to either obey or disobey God's law as it is understood at the time.*

committed presumptuously or in honest ignorance—is equally heinous to God in the life of a Christian. While there can be no sin without some sort of violation of the law (Rom. 5:13), this is not the complete picture of sin and there is considerably more to discover. The *English Standard Version* translates 1 John 3:4 in a more accurate way: "Everyone who makes a practice of sinning also practices lawlessness; sin is lawlessness." In the context, 1 John 3:1-4 is describing the man who has little concern for God's will as a *lawless man*. Thus, while we can't point to a single verse and say, "This is the exhaustive definition of sin," what we do have are almost countless *depictions* of sin.

> *Nowhere does the Bible give a succinct definition of sin.*

While space does not permit us to examine every passage that describes sin, we can examine a representative sampling of the Bible's portrayal of sin. From these passages, we can come to a better idea of the nature of sin and therefore the *kind* of sin from which Christians have been delivered from committing. As we survey some of these passages, pay attention to the golden thread weaving throughout each verse.

Genesis 3:6. In this verse, Adam and Eve commit the first human sin. Temptation was introduced by an outsider (Satan), and Eve's desire embraced that temptation, thus giving birth to sin (Jas. 1:14-15). She did not inadvertently eat the forbidden fruit; she *knew* she was violating God's command and chose to eat anyway (Gen. 2:16-17).

Genesis 4:6-7. In this context, Cain is deliberating how to respond to God's rejection of his sacrifice. God reminds him, "If you do not do well, sin is crouching at the door. Its desire it contrary to you, but you must rule over it." Sin is personified as a dangerous predator waiting for an opportunity to seize Cain's life. It all depends on Cain's choice—will he continue to disregard God's law, or will he repent and "do well"?

Exodus 9:12. Here we find one of many references to God hardening Pharaoh's heart (Exo. 7:3, 13; 10:20; 14:8). In reality, God only hardened Pharaoh's heart in the sense that His demand (to free the Israelites from slavery) went against the monarch's selfish interests (cf. Exo. 4:21). The Bible likewise tells us that Pharaoh hardened his own heart (Exo. 8:15, 32; 9:34). God punished Pharaoh for insubordination to a revealed divine command, which pushed Pharaoh deeper into rebellion. This account highlights the fact that as we create sin (when our desire yields to temptation, thus conceiving sin), repentance becomes increasingly difficult for us and thus it becomes easier for us to become even more rebellious. It is when we refuse to repent that we are storing up for ourselves God's wrath (Rom. 2:5; Rev. 16:9, 11)

1 Kings 15:5. The inspired author makes a very interesting observation regarding David. He says, "David did what was right in the eyes of the Lord and did not turn aside from anything that He commanded him all the days of his life." Then he parenthetically adds, "…except in the matter of Uriah the Hittite." To "turn aside" from God's commandments is sin. What makes this passage so puzzling is the obvious evidence that David certainly *did* sin against God's law several other times. David sinned when he took a census of the nation of Israel (1 Chron. 21:4-8), even after his commander (1 Chron. 21:3) and Scripture (Exo. 30:12) warned about the danger of doing so. David also sinned by accumulating many wives,[2] which he was specifically warned against in Deuteronomy 17:17. We might also be justified in the belief that David sinned in his parenting style (cf. 2 Sam. 13:14-29; 18:14-15). So why does the Bible say that David only "turned aside" from God's commandments in regards to murdering Uriah the Hittite? We could say David's sin regarding Uriah was different than his other sins in that David *deliberately* sinned against God's straightforward law prohibiting murder (Exo. 20:13) and therefore rebelled against God's will with a high hand. David himself recognized he had deliberately and knowingly sinned against God in this matter (Psa. 51:3-4). We could make a strong case that David's other sins were committed with varying degrees of weakness or ignorance.

---

2 David's first wife was Michal, Saul's daughter (cf. 1 Sam. 18:17; 19:11). Saul later gave Michal to another man, but after David became king, Michal was restored back to him (2 Sam. 3:14). David's second wife was Abigail, the former wife of the wicked Nabal (cf. 1 Sam. 25:42). The Bible then lists wives #3-7, Ahinoam, Miaacah, Haggith, Abital, and Eglah (cf. 2 Sam. 3:2-5; 1 Chron. 3:1-3). According to 2 Samuel 5:13, David married more wives in Jerusalem, but does not say how many, let alone name them. The eighth wife to be named is Bathsheba—after David committed the fornication with her and murdered her husband, she became his wife (cf. 2 Sam. 11). How many wives did David have? More than eight—perhaps significantly more.

Psalm 19:12-13. David says there are two kinds of errors: "hidden faults" (vs. 12) and "presumptuous sins" (vs. 13).[3] "Hidden faults" is from the Hebrew word *sathar*, which in this context merely refers to actions that fall short of God's law yet are unknown ("secret") to the one who committed them. Scripture doesn't paint *sathar* in this context as sin in the high-handed sense, though it is nonetheless a violation of God's law (and thus still needs to be avoided to the best of my ability and repented of in hindsight). What is important to notice in this passage is the explicit distinction made between presumptuous (intentional) sins against God and unintentional shortcomings of God's law.

Isaiah 59:2. Sin separates us from God. There is something about sin that He cannot tolerate. Verses 3-8 characterize the nature of this sin we have committed—the kind of sins which has separated us from God—as being no mere accident. Both Isaiah and Solomon observe that the feet of sinners "rush into sin" (cf. Prov. 1:16; Isa. 59:7; cf. Jer. 8:6). They desire it, hence the implied distinction between hidden faults and presumptuous sins.

Romans 14:23. This verse is in the greater context of whether or not it is permissible to eat otherwise legitimate food in the presence of another Christian who is under the impression that that specific food is wrong to eat. By eating this food and encouraging the other Christian to follow suit, you would be causing the other Christian to violate his conscience and thus causing him to sin (even though the eating of the food is not wrong in and of itself). As it relates to our topic, sin is here presented not as the mere breaking of God's law, but the decision to go ahead and violate God's will as you understand it at the time.

Hebrews 10:26. Here we find an unavoidable distinction between a deliberate sin and a sin of ignorance. For deliberate sin, there no longer remains a sacrifice.

James 1:13-15. James describes the universal ingredients of sin. First, "each person is tempted when he is lured and enticed by his own de-

---

3 Sometimes the song "Purer in Heart, O God" is sung, which contains the phrase "keep me from secret sin," referring to the "hidden faults" in verse 12. This phrase is a mistranslation of *sathar*; "faults" is a more accurate translation.

sires" (vs. 14). *Desire*, in this context, is the decision to indulge, pervert, or exploit an otherwise natural desire in an illicit way (i.e. a way that is contrary to the expressed will of God). I can be tempted to eat a juicy steak, which is a natural desire, not in and of itself contrary to the will of God (and thus not true temptation). However, *temptation*—in the biblical sense of the word—is the devil's suggestion of doing or using something I know is contrary to God's will. Second, when you submit to this illicit desire, you commit sin (i.e. "when it has conceived gives birth to sin," vs. 15). Thus we see that committing willful sin involves a conscious, contemplated element or premediated thought.

James 4:17. Often this verse is quoted to caution against sins of omission, but that is rather beside the point. The context of this verse is an admonition to incorporate God's will into all our plans. We must not miss, however, an important implication about sin contained within this verse. Failure to do something I *should* have (or, we could add, doing something I *shouldn't* have) is *always* a sin (regardless of whether I "knew" the right thing to do). Missing the mark is missing the mark. Yet only when I "know" the right thing to do but choose to deviate from it does God call my action a sin in this verse. The *knowledge* of my action changes the degree of culpability—I'm not merely guilty of missing the mark but am now guilty of *willfully intending* to transgress the law of God. Here we see the implicit distinction between unintentionally missing the mark and deliberate sin.

1 John 1:7. The blood of Jesus cleanses Christians of "all sin" as long as they continue to purposefully choose from the heart to continue "walking in the light" of Jesus. What sin can you be guilty of while "walking in the light"? Certainly not highhanded or deliberate sins! The only sins I can commit while simultaneously being faithful to Christ are the sins I *inadvertently* commit, either ignorantly or out of momentary weakness. Deliberate sins—sins wherein I choose to submit to the devil's temptation—are sins that lead to death (cf. 1 John 5:16-17). "Walking in the light" does not mean making sure we do more "good" than we do "not good," where we feel our lives are generally freer of sin than they are guilty of sin. Instead, "walking in the light" signifies a persistent, heartfelt commitment to serving God faithfully to the best of our ability.

1 John 3:4. The emphasis of this verse (along with the context) is a contrast between man who is actively seeking God as opposed to the person who has no regard for God and His will. In other words, there is a night and day difference between the man who is resolved to follow God's law and the man who is lawless. The lawless man may not even be consciously doing evil, but his sin is a direct result of choosing to not seek God's will.

1 John 5:18. Those who "keep on sinning" (who willfully commit sin without regard for God's law) have not been "born of God." Similarly, Paul bluntly says that those who willfully sin cannot enjoy the benefit of God's grace (Rom. 6:1-2). If by the word *sin* we mean the legal sense of "missing the mark" of God's law, then sin surely is inevitable and this verse robs us of all hope. Yet this verse teaches that we do not have to keep on sinning, and therefore a different kind of sin is in view—presumptuous, deliberate sins.

Throughout all of these passages, be impressed with how the Bible describes sin. The golden thread weaving through these descriptions of sin (and with nearly every other reference to sin) is the emphasis of the *presumptuous* nature of sin—the child of God knows God's will and then chooses to violate it. The kind of sin that so vastly fills the real estate of Scripture is not the mere accidental or unintentional missing the mark of God's perfect ideal, but a rebellious heart defined primarily as the absence of a desire to please the Lord.

TWO KINDS OF SIN

After surveying the Bible's portrayal of sin, we can begin to see that there are two different kinds of sin in the Bible: (a) sins committed out of ignorance or weakness (Num. 15:27-29; Psa. 19:12), and (b) sins committed presumptuously against God or intentionally unconcerned about His will (Num. 15:30; Psa 19:13; Heb. 10:26; 2 Pet. 2:10). E.G. Sewell, writing with David Lipscomb, makes the observation,

There is a very great difference between willful sins and sins committed through the weakness of the flesh. In the one case we purposefully refuse to do the will of God; in the other we allow sudden impulses of the flesh to so overcome us that we yield to them, and do and say things that are wrong, not because we want to do the wrong, but simply through human weakness.[4]

This distinction between sins of ignorance or weakness and deliberate sins is irrelevant to a person outside of Christ. He is lost because of his sin, regardless of the *kind* of sin. He is outside the state of God's grace because of his sin, period. He has violated God's law, and whether he has done so ignorantly or pre-sumptuously in a given instance is a fruitless discussion.[5] But for the faithful child of God, this distinction is critical, for it determines whether there remains a sacrifice for sin (cf. Rom. 8:1-8; 1 John 1:7; 1 Cor. 2:14-15).

> *The kind of sin that so vastly fills the real estate of Scripture is not the mere accidental or unintentional missing the mark of God's perfect ideal, but a rebellious heart defined primarily as the absence of a desire to please the Lord.*

Humans were created to seek God and to discover God's will (Acts 17:24-31). Therefore, when a man fails to pursue God and take His will into account, he is committing a willful sin by virtue of how he has chosen to live his life—even if he maintains a generally virtuous lifestyle. God does not desire people to merely be so-called good, upstanding, moral individuals. God desires us to bring every thought captive for Him (2 Cor. 10:5). Everything we do should be done in the context of a life set ultimately on bringing God glory (1 Cor. 10:31; cf. Col. 3:17).

---

4 E.G. Sewell, *Questions Answered*, p. 601
5 Distinguishing between sins of ignorance and presumptuous sins in the life of the alien sinner is fruitless, *except when it comes to bringing the conviction of sin to the heart during the evangelism process.*

SIN DESCRIBED FROM TWO DIFFERENT PERSPECTIVES

To better understand the Bible's own classification of sins committed willfully or presumptuously and sins committed out of ignorance or weakness, it will help us to look at them from their proper vantage point: (a) from a purely *legal* perspective, and (b) from a primarily *willful*, or *presumptuous* perspective. By *legal* we mean from the perspective of violating God's law, regardless of whether the law was broken with intent. Breaking God's law is breaking God's law, which is sin in the legal sense. By *willful* we mean from the perspective of deliberate or premeditated intent. Breaking God's law and *willfully doing so* is especially emphasized throughout the Bible as sin. All sin is a violation of God's law (sin in a legal sense), but not all sin is high-handed rebellion towards God's will (sin in both a legal sense *and* a willful/presumptuous sense).

> *God does not desire people to merely be so-called good, upstanding, moral individuals. God desires us to bring every thought captive for Him (2 Cor. 10:5).*

SIN FROM A LEGAL PERSPECTIVE

The most frequently used Greek verb used to explain a sinful action in the New Testament is the word *hamartano*, traditionally defined as "missing the mark; to step out of bounds; to trespass." Thus, from a legal perspective, sin is to "miss the mark" or "step out of bounds" of God's law. To violate a command or principle of Scripture is sin, regardless of whether it was committed intentionally or unintentionally. It is a sin to be in an adulterous marriage (Matt. 5:31-32; 19:9; Mark 10:11-12); it is a sin to lie (Col. 3:9); it is a sin to offer worship to God in ways that are unauthorized (John 4:24; cf. Lev. 10:1-2); etc. Because sin is "to miss the mark" of God's law, it is even sinful (in the strictly legal sense) to believe a religious doctrine that is in violation of God's law (Matt. 15:9; Eph.

4:14; 1 Tim. 1:3-4; 4:1; 6:3-4; Heb. 5:12, 14).

Hamartano evokes the imagery of a father teaching his son how to use a bow and arrow. Such a boy could shoot and "miss the mark" for any number of reasons. A good father will respond to a missed shot based upon his assessment of why his son missed. A child who is doing his best to hit the mark but falls short is very different from a child who is either negligent or willfully aims away from the mark and misses in order to hurt his father. It is an awkward application of the word *sin* to describe a boy who misses his target because his hands were too weak or the target was too far away (though in this metaphor he nonetheless missed the mark and thus sinned in the legal sense). However, if he intentionally shoots at his father or deliberately refuses to follow his father's marksmanship advice, this is a clear example of sin.

We can easily think of circumstances where it is possible to sin in a legal sense without intending to sin. The world is full of otherwise good, sincere people who sin ignorantly or without temptation. Even faithful Christians can and will be guilty of sin, in this strictly legal sense (1 John 1:8). We aren't proud of it—we try to avoid it. But we unintentionally yet inevitably "miss the mark" from time to time. We may inadvertently allow a bad attitude to creep into the heart; we may hurt someone without intending to; we may miscommunicate something important; we may believe a religious concept that we don't yet realize is in error. However, as we become more sanctified and as we grow in the grace and knowledge of the Lord, we will theoretically sin in this way (in this legal sense) less and less throughout life.

> *A boy could shoot his bow and arrow and "miss the mark" for any number of reasons.*

It is rare, however, for the Bible to refer to sin in an exclusively legal sense (i.e. without *any* intent to commit sin). In the Old Testament, there is the scarce mention of "sins of ignorance," particularly in Leviticus and Numbers. In Numbers 15:27-30, we are told that if a person sinned ignorantly, he was to offer a sin offering. Incidentally, it should be noted he could only repent of a sin of ignorance when he realized his sin *in hindsight*. If he never realized his sin, he was not necessarily severed from God's grace. Implied is the reality that even otherwise faithful children of God sin unwillingly or ignorantly. David prayed, "Declare me innocent from *hidden faults* (Psa. 19:12, emp. added). "Hidden faults" and "sins of ignorance" refer to the same thing and are to be distinguished from sins committed intentionally. Unintentional lapses or error are still sins in the legal sense, but they are void of premeditated intent. In Leviticus 5:18, we find, "The priest shall make atonement for him for the mistake that he made unintentionally, and he shall be forgiven." The author of the book of Hebrews also had a clear understanding of sins of ignorance and atonement. We read about the high priest who offered a sacrifice "for him and for the unintentional [i.e. non-highhanded—BG] sins of the people" (Heb. 9:7). The reason why the high priest was to be taken from among men was so he could "deal gently with the ignorant and the wayward, since he himself is beset with weakness" (Heb. 5:2). The fact that God made provision for even unintentional sins demonstrates that all sins—including even sins of ignorance—are serious to God. Therefore, we must be careful not to adopt a dismissive approach to *any* instance of missing the mark.

Sins of ignorance—even the most mild forms of missing the mark we can imagine—are still sins in a legal sense, and thus not only have the potential of enormous consequences, but also can merit God's wrath in some circumstances. We should always fear the violation of God's law. Christians are promised atonement when they err, and they quickly repent whenever they realize in hindsight that they have erred. Since Christ's blood continually cleanses the Christian of sin[6] (1 John 1:7), the only kind of sin a Christian can be guilty of while continuing in a state of grace is an unintentional sin or sin committed in weakness without a premeditated, high-handed choice to do so.

We are told to confess our sins (even unintentional sins when known in hindsight) to receive forgiveness (1 John 1:9), and that we have an

---

6 This is elaborated more in chapter 7, where we shall discuss the Christian's assurance of salvation.

advocate with the Father when we sin in such a way (1 John 2:1). Every Christian has his low points since becoming a Christian. Surely, in our Christian walk, we have not always done the right thing, but—upon realizing we have erred—we must repent and resolve to do better. Our commitment to do better comes in varying degrees of success. Yet, despite how often we may miss the mark, our walk with the Lord must always be defined by our desire to be faithful (2 Cor. 10:5; 12:9).

SIN FROM A WILLFUL OR HIGH-HANDED PERSPECTIVE

However, the majority of the time Scripture uses *sin*, it is talking about willful, presumptuous sin. Willful (or presumptuous) sin always necessitates two ingredients: (a) knowledge or light, and (b) choice or motive. The degree of willful sin is dependent upon these two ingredients. When the Bible discusses sin—even when using general terms that refer to "missing the mark" or "going astray"—the context is almost always high-handed rebellion; man deviates from the right way because he *chooses to follow the wrong way*. As C. Ryder Smith observes, "The ultimate definition of sin in the Old Testament is *ethical*,[7] and that this definition obtains throughout the New."[8]

The Bible is full of warnings against willful, intentional sin—the type of sin that God fully expects us to avoid. As we learn the truth of God's word, we must comply in humble submission. "If we go on sinning deliberately after receiving the knowledge of the truth, there no longer remains a sacrifice for sins" (Heb. 10:26). Describing those who are not faithful to Christ, Peter says "they are presumptuous, self-willed" (2 Pet. 2:10, NKJV). While there may remain a sacrifice for unintentionally missing the mark of God's holiness, there is no such sacrifice for sins a Christian commits

> *When the Bible discusses sin, the context is almost always high-handed rebellion; man deviates from the right way because he chooses to follow the wrong way.*

---

7 Smith is using the word *ethical* the same way we are using the word *presumptuous*.
8 C. Ryder Smith, *The Bible Doctrine of Sin*, p. 2

deliberately. David, after his sin regarding Uriah and Bathsheba had been exposed, knew a sacrifice would not benefit a high-handed sinner such as himself. He prayed, "For you will not delight in sacrifice, or I would give it; you will not be pleased with a burnt offering" (Psa. 51:16). Instead, David realized the sacrifices the Lord wanted were a "broken spirit" and a "broken and contrite heart" (vs. 17).

The Greek word *hekousiōs,* translated "deliberately" in Hebrews 10:26, is the same word found in 1 Peter 5:2, where shepherds are charged to shepherd the flock of God "willingly" or "voluntarily." The word refers to something that has been considered then deliberately chosen. The author of Hebrews is not referring to the Christian who falls into a sin in which he doesn't really want to be (either in ignorance or weakness) and is then forgiven as a result of God's grace and mercy. Instead, this is in reference to the sin John describes as the "sin that leads to death" (1 John 5:16). It is the same sin that causes one to "fall away from the living God" (Heb. 3:12; cf. Heb. 6:4-6). There can be no reasonable expectation of atonement for this sin so long as one continues in this kind of sin.

It is not necessarily the name of the sin that determines whether it is a sin of ignorance or a presumptuous sin. Instead, it is primarily an *attitude* manifested toward God on the part of the Christian committing the sin that makes the difference.[9] The difference between the Pharisee and the tax collector in Luke 18:9-14 was attitude—thus it was the tax collector who found God's grace. This is what makes deliberate sin so serious for the Christian. It is not the mere violation of God's law that necessarily severs our fellowship from God, but the violation when we know the thing to be wrong and do not care. We find the birth of deliberate, presumptuous sin described in James 1:13-15. One's desire comes in contact with temptation and then decides to embrace that temptation. It is at this point that deliberate sin is conceived and brings forth spiritual death.

---

9 We should note, however, that there are some sins that are so egregious that it is unthinkable they could be committed in ignorance, especially by a child of God (cf. 1 Cor. 6:9-10; Gal. 5:19-21; 1 Tim. 1:9-10; 2 Tim. 3:2-5; etc.).

GOD IS THE ONE AGAINST WHOM WE SIN: MISSING THE MARK VS. BEING HELD ACCOUNTABLE

While the Bible exposes our sin (Rom. 7:7-9), our sin is principally against God (Psa. 51:3-4). Thus, just because a man has sinned in relation to God's law does not necessarily mean that God will hold him accountable for that action. For one to be found guilty of sin, God must *charge* sin against him. David writes, "Blessed is the man against whom the Lord counts no iniquity, and in whose spirit there is no deceit" (Psa. 32:2). In other words, there are some people—faithful followers of God—against whom God does not count their shortcomings, and there is a direct relationship between these people and the intention of their hearts. Paul writes, "Blessed is the man against whom the Lord will not count his sin" (Rom. 4:1-8). In this way, the question is not whether I *sin*, but whether I am *culpable*. One's degree of culpability is the degree to which God holds one accountable. God, not mankind, is the final arbiter of sin. We may err, but God is the one who must ultimately charge us with sin. Stephen thus accurately prayed, "Lord, do not hold this sin against them" (Acts 7:54). While Stephen's prayer did not exonerate them, his words help us see that God, and God alone, has the final say about an individual's guilt.

> *There are some people—faithful followers of God—against whom God does not count their shortcomings, and there is a direct relationship between these people and the intention of their hearts.*

Any human police officer or judge understands the difference between violations of the law and punishment for violating the law. For example, I was once pulled over by a police officer for driving 10 miles over the speed limit. I was not intentionally speeding—I thought I was complying with the posted speed limit. What I did not realize, however, is that I was driving in a school zone, which was 10 miles per hour slower during school hours. Obviously, I had violated the law. Yet the police officer, believing that I had not *intentionally* broken

> *God, not mankind,*
> *is the final arbiter*
> *of sin. We may err,*
> *but God is the one*
> *who must ultimately*
> *charge us with sin.*

the law, only charged me with driving 5 miles over the speed limit. Later, when I appeared for my court date, the judge examined my record and said, "I see that you did not mean to drive recklessly and have had no prior history of speeding, therefore I will not fine you for this ticket." I freely admit that I was guilty of speeding, and I am not proud of it. At the same time, both the police officer and the judge had the authority to determine culpability and modify the consequences.

Similarly, there is a difference between violating God's law and God holding you accountable for your violation. God takes into account one's knowledge of His will, ability to comply to His law, and maturity of faith before charging one with sin in His cosmic court. And unlike imperfect human police offers and judges (who sometimes miscalculate their justice and abuse their authority), God is the perfect, supreme Judge. He executes punishment perfectly. James describes God's wisdom in James 3:17 with the Greek word *epieikēs*, which is usually rendered "gentle" but is actually very difficult to translate. It describes wisdom in knowing when it is in reality cruel to apply the strict letter of the law. William Barclay comments that the person who is *epieikēs* "knows how to make allowances, when not to stand upon individual rights, and how to soften justice with mercy, and always remembers that there are greater things in the world than rules and regulations."[10] It is a great comfort to know that God—who alone can charge with sin—is *epieikēs*. We know that God doesn't always charge sins of ignorance to man's account (cf. 1 Kings 15:5; Jas. 4:17).[11]

---

10 William Barclay, *The Letters of James and Peter*, p. 110

11 It is God's attitude towards unintentional sins and sins of weakness that is our template for our attitude in loving our fellow man (cf. 1 Cor. 13:4-7).

TO ERR IS HUMAN; TO SIN IS PRINCIPALLY DESCRIBED AS REBELLING AGAINST GOD

Christians have been released from the penalty of all sin, and they have been freed from the slavery of deliberate, intentional sin. "Whoever makes a practice of sinning is of the devil" (1 John 3:8). For the Christian, high-handed sin is entirely avoidable. In the words of Harold Ockenga, "Whether one can live sinlessly or not depends upon one's definition of sin. If sin is a voluntary transgression of the law, we may be faultless. If sin involves ignorant transgression or involuntary lack of conformity, then we cannot live without sin."[12]

Christianity is all about the will—God's will becoming our will. But God communicates His will through His word. Therefore, it is only to the degree that we know His word that we can follow His will. However, Scripture portrays a God who does not always hold His faithful children accountable for what they do not yet know about His will so long as their desire—their will—is to learn His will and do His will.

Does this mean that ignorance is bliss? Did Jesus teach that "ignorance is bliss" in His parables when He taught, "But the one who did not *know*, and did what deserved a beating, will receive a light beating" (Luke 12:48, emp. added)? Certainly not! What Jesus did teach—and therefore what we must teach—is that God takes into account a man's

Christianity is all about the will— God's will becoming our will.

knowledge of God's will before he is held accountable for his sin. But to practice a sort of "ignorance is bliss" lifestyle is a sin in and of itself, because the Bible repeatedly commands us to grow in knowledge (cf. Hos. 4:6; 2 Tim. 2:15; 2 Pet. 1:5-8; 3:18). A mark of a true child of God is that he *loves* truth (2 Thess. 2:10)—he does not remain willfully ignorant of it. We must live lives defined by the pursuit of Christ's word (John 8:31-32), or otherwise we will fall into lawlessness (1 John 3:1-4).

---

12 Harold J. Ockenga, *The Church in God*, p. 226

From our human vantage point, it is sometimes difficult to know what one *could* and *should* know. However, God always knows when an accountable human is culpable for a particular sin. The important principle to understand here is that God knows the heart (1 Sam. 16:7; Acts 1:24). God knew the hearts of Adam and Eve and punished them after they ate the forbidden fruit (Gen. 3:16-19); He knew the heart of Lot's wife and punished her when she turned around (Gen. 19:26); He knew the hearts of Nadab and Abihu and punished them when they offered unauthorized fire in the tabernacle (Lev. 10:1-2); He knew the heart of the Israelite who gathered sticks on the Sabbath and punished him (Num. 15:32-36); He knew the heart of Uzzah and punished him when he held the ark of God in his hand (2 Sam. 6:7).

> *A mark of a true child of God is that he loves truth (2 Thess. 2:10)—he does not remain willfully ignorant of it.*

If the Lord expects you to live faithfully and thus be free of sin, then we understand that He expects us to live free of any deliberate transgression of the law. In this way, Christians are people who are no longer sinners,[13] and we should not refer to ourselves as such. If we "sin daily," as some are quick to claim, then we cannot be faithful Christians. We cannot sin daily, in a high-handed sense, and be saved. Jesus expects us to "sin no more" (John 5:14; cf. Rom. 6:12-13; 1 Cor. 15:34; Heb. 12:1; 1 Pet. 2:21-22; 1 John 2:1, 6), and He never requires of us that which is impossible.

Don't forget Christ's comforting invitation, "Come to me, all who labor and are heavy laden, and I will give you rest. Take my yoke upon you, and learn from me, for I am gentle and lowly in heart, and you will find rest for your souls. For my yoke is easy, and my burden is light" (Matt. 11:28-30). Jesus doesn't burden us with something that is impossible—and it is impossible to fully avoid all unintentional shortcomings of the letter of His law. He has freed us from the slavery of what we once

---

13 Paul referred to himself as the "chief of sinners" in 1 Timothy 1:15, but he was referring to the fact that he was at one point a great sinner before God invited Him to conversion.

were—"lawless and disobedient, for the ungodly and sinners" (1 Tim. 1:9). Take joy in the reality that if we don't *want* to sin we don't have to be charged with sin.

When we understand *sin* to be the transgression of God's law to which God holds us accountable, then throughout the New Testament we find faithful Christians being described as people who no longer sin in highhanded rebellion. *Christians inadvertently miss the mark of God's law from time to time, but Christians should never high-handedly choose to sin. Be impressed with the fact that the salvation Christ offers Christians is not only salvation from the penalty of sin, but also salvation from the do-*minion *of willful, deliberate sin.* This is in contrast to how we once lived, when we were slaves to deliberate sin (Eph. 2:1-3). *While a Christian will inevitably be guilty of sins of ignorance or weakness, a Christian can theoretically go a whole lifetime without willful sin.*

Understanding how the Bible emphasizes *human choice* in the subject of sin is a crucial key to overcoming mediocrity in the Christian walk. The God of Scripture is a loving Father who is not so concerned about the unconscious infractions of His children as much as He hates a complacent attitude toward His authority, glory, and preeminence. To reduce sin to the mere inevitable "lack of conformity to the law," that even the strongest Christians among us are often guilty of, is to shortchange the way *sin* is primarily described in the Bible. James S. Stewart writes:

> *Jesus doesn't burden us with something that is impossible— and it is impossible to fully avoid all unintentional shortcomings of the letter of His law.*

To be united to Christ means to be identified with Christ's attitude to sin. It means seeing sin with Jesus' eyes and opposing it with something of the same passion with which Jesus at Calvary opposed it. It means an assent of the whole man to the divine judgment proclaimed upon sin at the cross. It means, as the writer to the Hebrews saw, "resistance unto blood." It means, as Paul put it tersely, death. In face of all this, to find antinomianism in Paul is simply to caricature His gospel.[14]

CONCLUSION

When in hindsight we realize we have missed the mark of God's holiness (to whatever degree we may have done so in ignorance or weakness), we tremble before Him with a penitent spirit. We need to be so aware of our proclivity to miss the mark that we approach the throne of God with deep reverence, humility, and fear—much like the penitent tax collector in Luke 18:9-14. But our relationship with God is not so volatile that He severs His relationship with His children every time they stumble unintentionally with no intent to enter into rebellion. James S. Stewart again writes:

> We talk about breaking [God's] law; but that, after all, is only relatively true. In one sense you cannot break a law; you can only be broken by it. But you can break a heart, and that comes nearer the truth about sin as Jesus saw it. Sin is not hurting the moral order, for an impersonal order cannot suffer. [...] Sin according to Jesus is something more than the Shorter Catechism has put into its definition, "any want of conformity unto, or transgression of, the law of God." It is something more than a blundering running of our heads against the inexorable laws of the universe. It is another nail hammered into love's cross, a clenched fist thrust up into the face of God. It is a blow struck at a loving heart.[15]

We approach God generally with a humble spirit knowing we have likely "missed the mark" unknowingly (Isa. 6:5; Luke 18:9-14), and approach God specifically with a contrite heart when we realize our mistake in hindsight (1 Chron. 21:8; 2 Chron. 7:14; Prov. 28:13; Luke 15:17-24; 1 John 1:9). While the Bible does not emphasize sins of ignorance *per se*, it does give special attention to what you do with a sin of ignorance *in hindsight*. Do you repent and confess your sin, or do you hide and deny your sin? Sins of ignorance or accident or weakness will be committed by people who are otherwise walking with God. These are a different class of sins. They are not rebellious, intentional, wicked

---

14 James S. Stewart, *A Man in Christ*, p. 196
15 James S. Stewart, *The Life and Teaching of Jesus Christ*, p. 81

deeds. However, they can become such when we realize we have done wrong yet begin making excuses for them. Then sins done in ignorance become sins of rebellion.

It should be noted that no true Christian believes he or she can fully overcome sin by his own human willpower. Not only has God's grace afforded us a way to be forgiven of past sins, but it is our submission to God's grace which keeps us from sin in the present (cf. Acts 20:32). Knowing what we have studied about sin, Christians must avoid two false extremes about sin. On one hand, Christians must fight the idea that they must be sinlessly perfect (sin in a legal sense) to go to heaven. On the other hand, Christians must fight the idea that sin (in a presumptuous sense) is inevitable. Christians cannot continue in sin. If sin is deliberately chosen, it will result in a fearful expectation of judgment unless one repents (Rom. 6:16ff; 8:6-8; Gal. 5:19-21).

> *Understanding how the Bible emphasizes human choice in the subject of sin is a crucial key to overcoming mediocrity in the Christian walk.*

The message of the Bible is that it is possible to once again live a life pleasing to God. Both Enoch and Noah, who were humans like us, "walked with God" (Gen. 5:24; 6:9). If they could walk with God (even without the benefit of a complete Bible like we have today), certainly we can too. I have met many Christians who are walking with God, and I want to be one of them. "Walking with God" doesn't mean being sinlessly perfect in the legal sense of the word *sin* (because we cannot achieve that); it means being fully submissive to God. Unintended missteps do not have to represent your manner of life. The Bible's portrayal of sin, however, is just the opposite of submission to God—it is self-assertion, disobedience, a departure from God. It is this type of sin from which the Christian has been freed.

DISCUSSION QUESTIONS

1. Respond to the statement, "I can't help but sin—I'm only human."

2. List some passages where God clearly commands us to stop sinning.

3. Is it possible to sin without there being the breaking of God's law in some way? Explain your answer, taking into account Romans 5:13.

4. Among nearly every passage describing or portraying sin, what ingredient to they almost always share in common?

5. From what two perspectives is sin described in the Bible?

6. Consider James 4:17. Isn't it still technically sin in the legal sense when we fail to do the right thing, regardless of whether we knew the right thing? Does God hold us to a greater degree of culpability when we violate what we know is the right thing? Explain your answer.

7. Consider Hebrews 9:13-10:18. If a sacrifice involving the "blood of bulls and goats" was necessary for even sins committed in ignorance under the Law of Moses (cf. Num. 15:27-29), do we need a sacrifice for sins committed in ignorance today? If so, what blood is necessary to provide atonement?

8. Is ignorance bliss?

9. Explain the Greek word *epieikēs*, found in James 3:17. How does this word apply to God?

10. Are Christians sinners? In what sense?

CHAPTER 7

SWEET SERENITY

CHRISTIAN ASSURANCE

THERE are two extremes every Christian must avoid. The first extreme is the idea that salvation is a guarantee, regardless of what one believes or practices. Those who hold this view think that as long as someone is *generally* a good person and identifies as a Christian, then they are surely saved. Many in this group are willing to take liberties in matters where God has spoken, innovating in the Christian faith wherever they feel it is pragmatic to do so. Others in this group are apathetic about Christianity in general, demonstrating a lack of dedication in the work of the church, faithfulness to the Lord, and commitment to sanctification. This group is in denial about their salvation—feeling they are secure in Christ when that is the *last* thing they should feel. The Bible offers no comfort to nominal Christians (Rev. 3:15-16), no hope to those who rebel against the authority of Jesus (Heb. 10:26-31), and no forgiveness to those who practice sin (1 John 3:8). This chapter is not for this group.

The second extreme is the belief that—while it does matter what one believes or practices—salvation can never be guaranteed. There are countless Christians who fill our church pews each week who are living like they are saved but are still *insecure* about their salvation. We are sympathetic to these Christians. After all, as we try our best to live faithful, sanctified lives to God, it is only natural for us to be keenly aware of our shortcomings. If we are not careful, however, we can be so conscious of our imperfections that we lose confidence in the promise that Christ actually *wants* to save us.

The enigma of Christianity is that while we can be free of presumptuous sins, we are still going to miss the mark of absolute perfection. It is in this sense John writes to Christians, "If we say we have no sin, we deceive ourselves, and the truth is not in us" (1 John 1:8). Because we still sin from time to time,[1] we will inevitably be seized with insecurity if we base our hope on our own estimation of self-righteousness.

No one can be happy when he has a terrible feeling of insecurity. If someone is insecure, there will only be anxiety, worry, and—eventually—disillusionment. Both research and personal experience has led me to believe that many have left the church because of the bogus idea that "we cannot know that we are saved."[2] That's not the Christianity of the Bible. Insecurity causes Christians to serve God largely out of fear. While there is a sense in which Christians should always serve God out of *reverential* fear,[3] no child should have to fear his Father like German citizens once feared Hitler. God isn't a ruthless dictator. Paul says, "For God gave us a spirit not of fear but of power and love and self-control" (2 Tim. 1:7).

> *The enigma of Christianity is that while we can be free of presumptuous sins, we are still going to miss the mark of absolute perfection.*

Never mind perfection. New Testament Christianity is not for robots. Jesus lived a perfect, sinless life in part because He knew we *wouldn't*. While Christians need to have a healthy concern about the possibility of losing our salvation, it is never a good thing when people who should be secure in their salvation *aren't* and are robbed of the joy of the Christian life. Paul writes, "Rejoice in the Lord always; again I will say, rejoice" (Phil. 4:4). If Paul's words are difficult for you to relate to, this chapter is for you.

---

1 Christians sin from time to time, at least in the legal sense of the word sin. See chapter 6 for a discussion on legal vs. willful sins.
2 Flavil R. Yeakley, Jr., *Why They Left*, p. 70
3 Chapter 9

IS ASSURANCE POSSIBLE?

What does the Bible say about eternal assurance? Is it even possible to have assurance? If so, how? Take a look at the apostle Paul's confidence in his salvation: "I know whom I have believed, and I am convinced that He is able to guard until that day what has been entrusted to me" (2 Tim. 1:12). Can you echo his words? Or do you say, "I don't know. I think I'm saved; I hope I'm saved." That's not how Paul talked!

Out of the 105 verses contained in the book of 1 John, the word *know* is found 21 times in the English Standard Version. Pay attention to some of those verses:

> Whoever keeps His word, in Him truly the love of God is perfected. By this we may *know* that we are in Him. (1 John 2:5)

> Beloved, we are God's children now, and what we will be has not yet appeared; but we *know* that when He appears we shall be like Him. (1 John 3:2)

> We *know* that we have passed out of death into life, because we love the brothers. (1 John 3:14)

> By this we shall *know* that we are of the truth and reassure our heart before Him. (1 John 3:19)

> By this we *know* that we abide in Him and He in us. (1 John 4:13)

> I write these things to you who believe in the name of the Son of God, that you may *know* that you have eternal life. (1 John 5:13)

To know is to be confident of something as fact. If you were to die unexpectedly at any given moment, can you *know* you will be saved? If the Bible is true, then absolutely!

This chapter is only for *faithful* Christians. I am not writing to the person who has not yet obeyed the gospel—the non-Christian. The alien sinner has no relationship with God (Rom. 6:23) and has no divine mediator to speak on his behalf (Rom. 6:17-18; 2 Tim. 2:10). Furthermore, the last person I have in mind as I write this chapter is the *unfaithful* child of God. Unless those who are unfaithful turn from their unfaithfulness, there is no hope for them. "If we go on sinning deliberately," thus trampling underfoot the Son of God, there is nothing but vengeance in store for us (Heb. 10:26-31). Let these words sink deep within us: "For if, after they have escaped the defilements of the world through the knowledge of our Lord and Savior Jesus Christ, they are again entangled in them and overcome, the last state has become worse for them than the first" (2 Pet. 2:20). If you are a nominal Christian—the kind of Christian whose church attendance is irregular, who cares little about what you watch, how you dress, where you go, how you treat others, what you believe, or how you speak, who exercises little discernment in what one believes or teaches—this chapter is not for you.

Concerning our subject at hand, let's now look at a few views of **apostasy**.[4]

IMPOSSIBILITY OF APOSTASY

ONCE SAVED, ALWAYS SAVED?

There is a popular idea within Christendom, probably held by many of your own religious friends, called **perseverance of the saints**. It is more commonly known as "once saved, always saved," or "once in grace, always in grace." This is the idea that once one becomes a so-called "believer," it is literally *impossible* for that person to be guilty of apostasy and lose his salvation. At the moment he believes he becomes a Christian, he is "eternally secure." There is *nothing* he can do to lose his salvation.

This is the logical conclusion of Calvinism. If we are supposedly "totally depraved" (we are so evil that we cannot personally choose to follow God), "unconditionally elected" (God chooses who He will save personally), "irresistibly bestowed with grace" (we cannot resist salvation), then our free moral agency is not a factor. Just as one cannot *accept* salvation, one cannot *cast it aside*. *The Westminster Confession* summarizes the "of-

---

4 **Apostasy** means "falling away."

ficial teaching" of this doctrine: "They whom God hath accepted in His beloved, effectually called and sanctified by His Spirit, *can neither totally nor finally fall away from the state of grace*; but shall certainly persevere therein to the end, and be eternally saved"[5] (emp. added).

Those who hold to Calvinism believe that Christians will be eternally saved without *any* condition on their part. To support this teaching, they cite several go-to passages which emphasize God's own faithfulness in keeping His promises and protecting His children from various enemies: "No one will snatch them out of My hand" (John 10:27-29); "He who began a good work in you will bring it to completion at the day of Jesus Christ" (Phil. 1:6); "The calling of God [is] irrevocable" (Rom. 11:29); "I am convinced that He is able to guard until that day" (2 Tim. 1:12); "By God's power [we] are being guarded through faith for a salvation" (1 Pet. 1:5); "[Nothing] will be able to separate us from the love of God in Christ Jesus our Lord" (Rom. 8:31-39).

Without a doubt, these passages are true. In them we find reassurance that if we belong to God, He is going to keep His covenant with us. God truly wants Christians to be saved, and He will protect us from all outside forces that try to draw us away from Him. But no passage, including the ones just read, teaches that our security in Christ is unconditional. *God will never cast us aside, but we can cast Him aside.*

The Bible, as we shall see, teaches that God will not force anyone to be saved. Christians can voluntarily discard their own salvation. As Jack Cottrell summarizes, "God Himself will never leave us and will never initiate the severing of our saved relationship with Him, but He will not prevent us from leaving Him if that is our choice."[6]

God will never cast us aside, but we can cast Him aside.

The foolishness of "once saved, always saved" is seen in the self-identifying Christian who now feels he can commit *any* sin, such as theft or

---

5 *The Westminster Confession of Faith*, p. 89
6 Jack Cottrell, *The Faith Once for All*, p. 376

murder, without losing his salvation. James Buswell, a Calvinist himself, points out the problem with this teaching:

> I have heard several pseudo-Calvinistic speakers in Christian college chapel exercises say, "Dear young people, there are two ways to go to heaven: the spiritual way and the carnal way. It is so much better to take the spiritual way!" I knew a certain young person who believed this false doctrine and said to the Dean, "I am a Christian, but I do not mind sitting in the bleachers. I choose to go to heaven the carnal way!"[7]

Thus, more conscientious Calvinists like Buswell, realizing the absurdity of a Christian who actively practices sin without fear of losing his soul, would argue that if someone continues in sin, he wasn't truly saved to begin with. However, the Bible teaches us that there were several followers of Christ who were genuinely saved at one time, but lost or jeopardized their salvation: Simon (Acts 8:14-24), Hymenaeus and Alexander (1 Tim. 1:19-20), and Judas (Matt. 10:1-2; John 17:12; Acts 1:25), among others. Sadly, there are former Christians[8] today who have forfeited their salvation.

THE SECURITY OF THE CHRISTIAN IS CONDITIONAL

Though we have demonstrated that Calvinism is wrong, we can still have assurance of our eternal security. But our assurance is not based on the doctrine of "once saved, always saved." Instead, assurance is conditional on our faith: "If you practice these qualities, you will never fall" (2 Pet. 1:10). This "if" is emphasized *throughout* the New Testament (1 Cor. 15:2; Heb. 3:7-15; Col. 1:23; 1 John 1:7; etc.).

The Bible repeatedly warns that we can choose to walk away from our salvation. We can "make shipwreck" of it (1 Tim. 1:19); "depart" from it (1 Tim. 4:1); "abandon" it (1 Tim. 5:12); "swerve" from it (2 Tim. 2:18). Hebrews warns Christians, "Take care, brothers, lest there be in any of you an evil, unbelieving heart, leading you to fall away from the living

---

7 James Buswell, *A Systematic Theology of the Christian Religion, Vol. 2*, p. 146
8 If the definition of a Christian is *one who follows Christ*, then a *non-following follower of Christ* (i.e. a follower of Christ who is no longer following Christ) is an oxymoron. They are erring, unfaithful Christians. In this sense, one can be a former Christian.

God" (Heb. 3:12). In fact, nearly half of the entire book of Hebrews is a warning to Christians against forfeiting their salvation.[9]

It is possible for a child of God to fall from grace. The Bible says, "You are severed from Christ, you who would be justified by the law; you have fallen away from grace" (Gal. 5:4). To Christians, Paul says, "Therefore let anyone who thinks that he stands take heed lest he fall" (1 Cor. 10:12). "For it would have been better for them never to have known the way of righteousness than after knowing it to turn back from the holy commandment delivered to them" (2 Pet. 2:21).

In contrast to Calvinism, the Bible teaches that a child of God who lives in sin—who continues in the practice of sin, who walks after the flesh instead of the Spirit—*will not receive forgiveness as long as he knowingly continues in sin* (Rom. 6:1-2; 8:1-4; Gal. 5:19-21; Rev. 21:8). A person like that is not a faithful Christian, and we can offer no hope to that person other than a heartfelt plea to repent.

> *Nearly half of the entire book of Hebrews is a warning to Christians against forfeiting their salvation.*

But pay close attention: Just because a Christian *can* fall from grace does not necessarily mean a Christian *will* fall from grace.

PROBABILITY OF APOSTASY

There are many otherwise godly, righteous Christians who live in constant fear that they will be lost. They only know a blanket definition of sin, defined as falling short of God's standard of perfection in *any* way (making no distinction between sins of ignorance and presumptuous sins), which they surmise they have committed several times in a given day (I know I have yet to live a perfect day myself). And because they were perhaps taught that every sin must be specifically confessed before it can be forgiven, they believe they cannot be sure of heaven until they

---

9 There are five warning passages in Hebrews: 2:1-4; 3:7–4:13; 5:11–6:20; 10:26-39; 12:18-29.

have prayed for forgiveness. I am convinced the only hope some people have is to be lucky enough to die shortly after confession—before they could accidentally commit another sin. They think perhaps they go from "saved" to "lost," "saved" to lost," several times a day. Perhaps others hope to die with a piece of the Lord's Supper still in their mouths. Beyond dying under an extraordinary circumstance like these, they think one's eternal destination is anyone's guess.

Dear Christian, look to heaven where you will see "a great multitude that no one could number" (Rev. 7:9). Tell me that this multitude of people never committed sins of ignorance or weakness; tell me that each person of that multitude happened to die with a prayer of forgiveness on their lips. In reality, they are *real* human beings; saved not because *they* were perfect, but because the *Son of Man* was perfect. If even the great Bible figures of faith in Hebrews 11 were guilty of sins of weakness and ignorance, what makes you think God expects us to reach sinless perfection before we can enter heaven?

In our refutation of "once saved, always saved," many have sacrificed the idea that Christians can have any security at all. They have adopted a nearly opposite belief from the "impossibility of apostasy," namely the *probability* of apostasy. However, the Bible plainly teaches that eternal security is an unshakable reality for all faithful Christians. While Christians can't behave immorally or rebelliously and still have fellowship God, a cursory reading of John 10:27-29 demonstrates that *faithful* Christians have no fear of being lost. Jesus said: "My sheep hear my voice, and I know them, and they follow me. I give them eternal life, and they will never perish, and no one will snatch them out of my hand. My Father, who has given them to me, is greater than all, and no one is able to snatch them out of the Father's hand."

Just because a Christian <u>can</u> fall from grace does not necessarily mean a Christian <u>will</u> fall from grace.

How dishonest is it for us to sing songs like, "Blessed Assurance" if we doubt what Jesus said. It is just as wrong to sing an untruth as it is to speak an untruth. As long as we are with Christ, no one can snatch us out of His hand; nothing can rob us of our salvation. Can you *decide* to walk away from a saving relationship with God? Yes. But you don't have to walk away from God's loving embrace.

Paul says, "For I know whom I have believed, and I am convinced that He is able to guard until that day what has been entrusted to me" (2 Tim. 1:12). Do you have confidence like Paul? Many Christians I know would reply, "I don't know. I think I'm saved, but I'm not sure." How sad! This isn't how Paul talked. He said, "I *know* whom I have believed, and I am convinced that He is able to guard until that day what has been entrusted to me."

POSSIBILITY OF APOSTASY: ONLY IF YOU STOP WALKING

Apostasy is neither impossible nor does it have to be probable. Instead, apostasy is *only a possibility*—a choice God allows us to make. If we want to continue being saved from sin, listen to what the apostle John says: "If we say we have fellowship with Him while we walk in darkness, we lie and do not practice the truth. But *if we walk in the light, as He is in the light*, we have fellowship with one another, and the blood of Jesus His Son cleanses us from all sin" (1 John 1:6-7, emp. added).

Find comfort in the reality that you don't have to be sinlessly perfect to go to heaven[10]—you just have to keep "walking in the light." Cecil May Jr. comments:

> Since in that promise, walking in the light and being cleansed of sin both happen at the same time, *walking in the light cannot mean never sinning*. Repentance, confession, and prayer for forgiveness of known sins is an important part of walking in the light. However, this promise and others in Scripture, tell us, if we are Christians, if our heart is right, and if our walk and lifestyle is in harmony with the will of God, He does not wait until we have confessed and prayed to forgive.[11] (emp. added)

---

10 See chapter 6
11 Cecil R. May, Jr., *Bible Questions and Answers*, p. 297

The Bible acknowledges that the child of God—who "walks in the light" (1 John 1:7) and who "walks not after the flesh but after the Spirit" (Rom. 8:4)—still sometimes misses the mark of God's will—even while he is faithful. Of course, God does not approve of the Christian's shortcomings, but the Christian's life is a *life* of faithfulness and God approves of it. The great paradox of Christianity is this: How can God possibly approve of someone while they still sometimes sin inadvertently, either due to ignorance or weakness? Because of the power of Christ's blood, God forgives and does not charge His faithful children with sin (Psa. 32:2; Rom. 4:7-8). Wayne Jackson adds, "The Lord's cleansing blood continues to function on their behalf as they struggle with sin in their Christian lives."[12]

The apostle John reminds Christians, "If we say we have no sin, we deceive ourselves, and the truth is not in us" (1 John 1:8). In almost the same breath, he tells those same Christians, "My little children, I am writing these things to you so that you may not sin. But if anyone does sin, we have an advocate with the Father, Jesus Christ the righteous" (1 John 2:1). Yes, sometimes we sin, and every reader of this book will admit it. But we hate it when we sin—we try not to sin—and we don't *continue* in sin when we realize we are guilty! The message of assurance is this: God's faithful children don't have to worry about their relationship with God being interrupted after every sin they commit in ignorance or weakness. In the words of Guy N. Woods, "1 John 1:7-8 teaches us that sins involving frailties, weaknesses, unintentional lapses are continuously cleansed as we 'walk in the light' of God's truth."[13] Woods then adds:

> *God does not approve of the Christian's shortcomings, but the Christian's life is a life of faithfulness and God approves of it.*

---

12 Wayne Jackson, "The Cleansing Fountain," *ChristianCourier.com*
13 Guy N. Woods, *Questions and Answers Vol. II*, p. 187

Perfection in the flesh is unattainable (1 John 1:8, 10), and the acceptable relation we are able to enjoy with the Father, the Son, and the Holy Spirit results from the appropriation of the plan which they have provided to keep us justified. If we keep on walking in the light, the blood of Jesus Christ keeps on cleansing us from sin (1 John 1:7). This is a state of grace—not of human perfection—and we should be ever more thankful that in spite of our imperfections we may through grace enjoy His approval.[14]

Walking in the light does not demand perfection; it does not require a perfect understanding of everything in the Bible; it does not call for a trust in oneself that he has not sinned today. Walking in the light means putting your trust in God, to study to show yourself approved, to submit in obedience as you learn along the way. We will fall short of perfection—God simply requires that we "make every effort" (2 Pet. 1:5).

Just as the source of light is the sun, the source of purity, perfection, and holiness is God Himself. Isaiah says, "Come, let us walk in the light of the Lord" (Isa. 2:5). God is light, and we are flawed humans. A human cannot walk on the sun, but we can walk in its light. Likewise, we will never achieve God's level of purity, perfection, and holiness, but we can still walk in His light. God does not ask us to do the impossible. Solomon observes, "Surely there is not a righteous man on earth who does good and never sins" (Ecc. 7:20). Thankfully, the Bible only teaches us to *strive* for sinless perfection (cf. Prov. 4:23; Heb. 11:6; Phil. 3:13; 2 Pet. 3:14). It never teaches we must *attain* sinless perfection before we can enjoy continuous fellowship with God.

> *God is light, and we are flawed humans. A human cannot walk on the sun, but we can walk in its light.*

CONDITIONAL ASSURANCE

If we want the assurance of God's forgiveness, there are some conditions Christians must continue to meet.

---

14 p. 188

First, our forgiveness is conditioned upon a forgiving spirit towards our fellow man (cf. Matt. 6:12-15; 7:2). There is a very real sense in which you get to decide the degree of scrutiny by which you will be judged by God. In His sermon on the mount, Jesus made it clear that there is a direct link to our judgment of others and God's judgment of us (cf. Matt. 18:21-35). If we want God to be inclined to overlook our sins when we unintentionally stumble, then we must possess the same spirit towards our fellow man. The child of God can only expect a harsh Day of Judgment when he harbors resentment towards others and holds them to an unrealistic standard. There is no hope for the child of God who refuses to forgive those who will accept forgiveness.

Second, our forgiveness is conditioned upon confessing sin—even the likelihood of sins of which we have committed unaware (Luke 18:13; Psa. 19:12; cf. 1 John 1:9). There is no hope for Christian who will not confess and pray like the tax collector, "God, be merciful to me, a sinner!" Or like David, who prayed, "Declare me innocent from hidden faults."[15] There should be no such thing as a proud Christian. We must confess the sins we know about, while simultaneously possessing a deep awareness that there is probably much we don't know. Surely I hold some beliefs about Bible doctrine that are inaccurate; surely I have not been an efficient steward of the time, energy, wealth, and opportunities with which God has blessed me; surely I have not distanced myself from temptation like I should have; surely I have forgotten prior obligations and commitments; surely my temperament as a parent and spouse has not always been stellar; etc. Upon recognizing these realities, I pray, "Father, please forgive me. Help me to do better." We should recognize that even at our most exemplary level of compliance to God's will, we are still unprofitable servants (Luke 17:10).

> *There is a very real sense in which you get to decide the degree of scrutiny by which you will be judged by God.*

---

15 Sometimes this is called the "second law of pardon." The "first law of pardon" is what is discussed in chapter 4, which we entitled "The Master Plan." The first law of pardon is what the sinner must do to be saved; the second law of pardon is what a Christian must do when he realizes his sin. He must repent, confess, and pray. The second law of pardon is just as important for the Christian as the first law of pardon is for the non-Christian.

Furthermore, we must always repent, confess, and ask for forgiveness of *known* sin. This is what Peter commanded Simon, the sorcerer-turned-Christian, when his sin was exposed after the fact (Acts 8:22). The Israelites, upon recognizing in hindsight they had erred, were allowed to make a sacrifice and live (Num. 15:29-31). Repentance involves a genuine commitment to not committing the same sin again. Just as a Christian must "pray without ceasing" (a figure of speech referring to a prayerful attitude, cf. 1 Thess. 5:17), a Christian must have a humble, penitent spirit without ceasing—so that, by God's grace, his sin will not be charged against him (Rom. 4:7-8).

Third, our forgiveness is conditioned upon our pursuit of faithfulness (Rev. 2:10). Skeptics about what the Bible says about the continuous cleansing blood of Jesus argue that this puts a premium on ignorance. Does God offer a blanket forgiveness of all sins committed in ignorance for every human being? Surely not. But He does forgive (or does not charge) unintentional sins committed to those who "walk in the light" because John promised the blood of Jesus cleanses us from "all" sin (1 John 1:7). The condition, however, is "walking in the light."

Can one "walk in the light" while being content with ignorance? Absolutely not (Heb. 5:11–6:2; 1 Pet. 2:1-3). Can one "walk in the light" while being unconcerned with personal holiness? Absolutely not (John 17:17; 2 Cor. 7:1; Heb. 12:14; 1 Pet. 1:14-16; 1 John 3:6-10). Can one "walk in the light" while being a nominal Christian? Absolutely not (Rom. 12:11; 1 Cor. 15:58; 2 Thess. 3:11-12; 2 Tim. 2:15; Jas. 1:22; 4:17).

"TO WHOM THE LORD WILL NOT COUNT HIS SIN"

The beauty of Christianity is seen in the relationship that between a child and his heavenly Father. A human father does not sever the relationship he has with his child based upon the slightest infraction. Perhaps we have seen firsthand *bad* fathers who are quick to punish in an overly harsh way. Not only is this parenting approach cruel and unforgiving, but it is apt to produce emotionally damaged children. Instead, when a child *misses the mark* in some way, a good father first takes into account the child's *knowledge* of the father's will in the matter, *intention*, and level of *maturity* before deciding how to react appropriately. It is when a child is *careless* or *rebellious* that a good father proceeds with stronger disciplinary measures. If this is true with good human fathers, how much more true is it with our perfect heavenly Father (cf. Matt. 7:9)? Are we to think that human fathers are capable of being more loving than God?

As seen in chapter 6 of this book, to commit sin is different than being charged with that sin. And like a good human father, our heavenly Father does not always charge His children with sin. Again, remember the words of the David, "Blessed is the man against whom the Lord counts no iniquity" (Psa. 32:2). Who is that man? That man is the faithful child of God. Oh how blessed is that man! V.P. Black comments here:

> The man of whom God will not mark up his mistakes, his blunders, his short-comings is this faithful, dedicated child of God who is walking in the light, giving his best to the master, doing his very best to serve God. However, even at his very best he is going to stumble; he is going to fall; he is going to make mistakes, but John says the blood of Jesus Christ will keep his life clean before God.[16]

Have you ever considered the number of issues that are questionable—things that some faithful Christians consider to be sin, but others do not? If two of the wisest, most intelligent preachers each made a list of things they thought were sinful—making their lists as thorough and comprehensive as they could—their lists would be similar but not identical. Things that are explicitly called sins like anxiety or worry (cf. Matt. 6:25-34), pride, envy, greed, waste of anything over which God has made us stewards, prejudice, etc. would obviously make both lists. However, both preachers may disagree over the point at which someone becomes guilty of one of those sins.

At what point does the content of a movie become sinful to watch? At what point does the Lord remove the "candlestick" of a church that neglects to appoint elders or fails to withdraw from impenitent members? At what point does clothing become immodest? The list goes on.

---

16 V.P Black, *Back to Basics*, p. 169

I do not raise these examples to espouse moral relativism, because the Bible speaks very clearly about these things. The point is this: While something is either sinful or it isn't, we don't always know *when* we are guilty of sin. To which our Father says, "You don't have to know everything. Keep your eyes on Jesus and His New Testament, repent when you realize you've done wrong, and I will keep you saved."

We could quibble about questions like, "What sins can a Christian commit and not be lost?" or, "Is this or that matter a salvation issue?"[17] No human can always know 100% of the time where God draws the line. But our concern is not merely avoiding what is wrong, but pursuing what is right. Those who "walk in the light" endeavor to avoid all sin, however miniscule human wisdom perceives some sins to be. While God does not wink at sin, in His sovereign will He says, "I will be gracious to whom I will be gracious, and will show mercy on whom I will show mercy" (Exo. 33:19).

Remember, "Blessed is the man against whom the Lord will not count His sin" (Rom. 4:6-8). There is a difference between committing sin and having that sin charged against you. Does God charge sin to everyone? No, because Paul says there is someone "against whom the Lord will not count His sin." Who is that person? The one who keeps "walking in [His] light." It is when we become indifferent in our fight against sin and our walk towards holiness that we cease being in His light.

Our concern is not merely avoiding what is wrong, but pursuing what is right.

"NOT A RESULT OF WORKS, SO THAT NO ONE MAY BOAST"

Don't ever forget the basis of our salvation: "For by grace you have been saved through faith. And this is not your own doing; it is the gift of

---

17   See appendix for a biblical critique of the phrase "salvation issue."

> *Our salvation is based upon Christ's meritorious work, not our meritorious work.*

God, not a result of works, so that no one may boast" (Eph. 2:8-9). If your basis of security is based upon how effectively you feel have followed God's commandments this past week, you are building your assurance on the wrong foundation. Faithful Christians always put a premium on obedience, but we put our trust in the Lord's promises. V.P. Black writes, "It's true that a person must believe in Christ, repent of his sin, and be baptized [...] in Christ and live the Christian life to the very best of his ability. But let me state to you, my friends, when an individual does this, he is still saved by the grace of God. Man cannot merit salvation."[18]

Our salvation is based upon Christ's meritorious work, not our meritorious work. Have you ever wondered how Jesus is going to present the church to the Father "holy and without blemish" (cf. Eph. 5:25-27)? The church is comprised of people who are full of blemishes.[19] Yet He will purify them by His cleansing blood. Isaiah writes, "'Come now, let us reason together,' says the Lord: 'though your sins are like scarlet, they shall be as white as snow; though they are red like crimson, they shall become like wool'" (Isa. 1:18).

Peter tells us that Christians are guarded by God's power "through faith" (1 Pet. 1:5). When we live according to God's promise and plan in Jesus Christ, our relationship to God is unbreakable. To be justified by faith is to be justified by our trust in the all-sufficient blood of Jesus. Or, putting chapters 3 and 5 into view, we are justified by the blood of Christ, not by attaining a certain level of sanctification. It is when we start living for the world that we start putting our trust in something else.

---

18 V.P Black, *Back to Basics*, p. 166
19 Albeit blemished people *who are not content with their blemishes.*

CONCLUSION

Hold these words close to your heart: "Submit yourselves therefore to God. Resist the devil, and he will flee from you. Draw near to God, and He will draw near to you" (Jas. 4:7-8). Our hope is not based primarily upon how well we happen to practice God's law externally (as important as that is). Otherwise, the brand new Christian who is still a babe in Christ—who surely will unknowingly err more often than a mature Christian—has less of a chance of salvation than the man who has been a Christian for 50 years. Paul said that his desire was to simply "be found in [Christ], not having a righteousness of my own that comes from the law, but that which comes through faith in Christ, the righteousness from God that depends on faith" (Phil. 3:9).

I know of a man on his deathbed whose last words were, "I hope I was good enough." His son, a well-known preacher at the time, was disillusioned by these words, contributing to his eventual departure from the faith. Today he remains an infamous apostate, speaking venomous words against the church of Jesus Christ. His example is a testament to the fact that we need to understand the nature of Christ's continuously cleansing blood; otherwise our misunderstanding will serve as a catalyst for our own departure from the faith.

Don't ever ask if you are good enough to go to heaven. The answer to that question will always be, "Of course not!" But as unworthy of heaven as you and I are, *we can still go there.* We didn't earn heaven ourselves. Heaven is offered to us by the grace, mercy, and love of God. "For by grace you have been saved through faith. And this is not your own doing; it is the gift of God, not a result of works, so that no one may boast" (Eph. 2:8-9). Do you believe these words?

> *Don't ever ask if you are good enough to go to heaven. The answer to that question will always be, "Of course not!"*

God does not automatically forgive everyone. There is no such thing as *unconditional* salvation. But nonetheless, by God's grace, He offered us a way to obtain salvation and a plan by which we could live in a saved condition. His offer of pardon is a gift, which can be had if we will only accept His gift through simple, honest faith—which we receive at obedience and we keep through faithfulness.

This lesson is not for unfaithful or nominal Christians; God offers no assurance to those people. Only those who are faithful, dedicated children of God should find comfort in the security of Christ's blood. Christians should be people of faith, confidence, and joy in serving a God who is capable of keeping His children saved.

DISCUSSION QUESTIONS

1. What are two extremes Christians must avoid regarding the assurance of their salvation?

2. What does insecurity eventually do to a Christian's faith?

3. What is the Calvinistic doctrine of **perseverance of the saints**? What are some of the extreme yet necessary implications of this teaching?

4. Can a Christian lose his salvation?

5. How would you define the doctrine we have coined the "probability of apostasy"?

6. Do Christians have to be sinlessly perfect to go to heaven? Explain your answer.

7. Do you have to specifically know every sin you have committed in order to be saved? Explain your answer.

8. What are the conditions of Christian assurance?

9. What is the difference between falling short of God's and being charged with that sin?

10. Comment on the statement, "God's grace is the basis of our salvation." What qualifiers would you give?

CHAPTER 8

SAVED IN CHILDBEARING

THE PRINCIPLE OF AUTHORITY IS PRINCIPAL

ONE of the most difficult to understand texts in the Bible is the last sentence of 1 Timothy 2:12-15, where Paul instructs Timothy (the preacher at the Ephesian church):

> I do not permit a woman to teach or to exercise authority over a man; rather, she is to remain quiet. For Adam was formed first, then Eve; and Adam was not deceived, but the woman was deceived and became a transgressor. *Yet she will be saved through childbearing*—if they continue in faith and love and holiness, with self-control. (emp. added)

How can a woman "be saved through childbearing"? What makes this verse so complicated is that *it seems to say what it cannot possibly mean.* How ridiculous (and contradictory to the rest of Scripture) is the notion that a woman can live a life of total rebellion towards God without any fear of being lost so long as she gives birth to a child? Nowhere else does the Bible teach that salvation can be attained by procreation. In fact, Paul himself seemed to teach just the opposite when he advised some people not to marry (1 Cor. 7:1, 8, 38). What the Bible clearly teaches is that men and women, though different in many ways, are spiritual equals. Both bear the image of God (Gen. 1:27); both are saved only through Jesus (Gal. 3:26-28); both are saved by faith and obedience to the gospel (Rom. 1:16-17).

1 TIMOTHY 2:15: A TEST CASE
IN BIBLICAL AUTHORITY

So what does Paul mean when he says that a woman "will be saved through childbearing"? Some argue that "saved" refers to physical safety. If this is true, then this can be nothing more than a proverb, since most of us have known of Christian women who have perished during childbirth. Furthermore, if Paul is referring to physical safety, not only would this be an unusual comment contextually ("if they continue in faith and love and holiness, with self-control"), but also an unusual usage of the Greek word translated "saved," *sōzō*. Elsewhere in the New Testament, *sōzō* more commonly refers to *spiritual* salvation.

Others argue that Paul is referring to Eve, who is mentioned in the same text. Just as one woman—Eve—introduced sin into the world, another woman—namely Mary—introduced redemption. The weakness with this argument, however, is that our salvation was not achieved when Mary bore Jesus (as significant as that day was), but rather when Christ was crucified and resurrected for the sins of the world (1 Cor. 15:1-4). If Paul had in mind Mary's childbirth, "he could have hardly chosen a more obscure or ambiguous way of saying it," as Donald Guthrie observes.[1]

Some argue that "they" in verse 15 refers to the offspring of a woman, thus interpreting "childbearing" as meaning more specifically "childrearing." In other words, "She will be saved—or be shown to be saved—if she rears children who grow to be faithful to the Lord." If this were what Paul meant, then the salvation of a woman depends in part on the faithfulness of her children, which also cannot be true (cf. Eze. 18:20). Furthermore, the Greek word Paul used, *teknogonias*, is a very specific word and means exactly what it is translated to mean: *childbearing*. Elsewhere in the letter, Paul uses another word, *teknotropheō* (1 Tim. 5:10), which specifically refers to the nurturing and training of children.[2] If he meant "childrearing," why didn't he use that word?

---

1 Donald Guthrie, *Pastoral Epistles: An Introduction and Commentary*, p. 92
2 Clyde Woods, "How Can Women Be Saved By Childbearing?," *FHU 2018 Lectures*, p. 425

The most widely accepted explanation of 1 Timothy 2:15 seems to be that "childbearing" is a figure of speech,[3] representative of "the general scope of activities in which a Christian woman should be involved."[4] It seems most of the Christian women Paul is concerned about in this text are married, so he can mention the bearing of children to designate an *attitude* which embraces their appropriate female roles generally.

Throughout the letter of 1 Timothy, we learn about some of the false teachings that had infiltrated the Ephesian church. Some were forbidding marriage (4:3), requiring abstinence from otherwise good foods (4:3), teaching "irreverent, silly myths" (4:7), encouraging inattention to the needs of one's offspring (5:8), and claiming knowledge of things about which they were ignorant (6:20). (Does some of this sound familiar today?) *Many of the Christian women in Ephesus had been swayed by some of these ideas, which evidently included the disparagement of marriage and submission to a husband, bearing children, and prioritizing family life.* (Again, does this not echo the message of today's feminist movement?) Douglass Moo argues, "False teachers were claiming that women could really experience what God had for them *only* if they abandoned the home and became actively involved in teaching and leadership roles in this church."[5] In response to those who were encouraging women to discard their special role in the home, Paul writes:

> Women should adorn themselves in respectable apparel, with modesty and self-control, not with braided hair and gold or pearls or costly attire, but with what is proper for women who profess godliness— with good works. Let a woman learn quietly

> *Many of the Christian women in Ephesus had been swayed by certain teachings that disparaged marriage and submission to a husband, bearing children, and prioritizing family life.*

---

3 Or, more precisely, a **synecdoche**. C. Michael Moss comments: "Christian women are not saved through teaching and asserting authority, but by attention to their traditional role. 'Childbearing' serves as a figure of speech to illustrate Paul's argument that women need not behave as men but rather fulfill their divinely appointed role to find salvation" (*The College Press NIV Commentary: 1, 2 Timothy & Titus*, p. 64). See also Ann L. Bowman, "Women in Ministry," *Two Views on Women in Ministry*, p. 290.
4 Douglas Moo, "1 Timothy 2:11-15: Meaning and Significance," *Trinity Journal* 1.1 NS (1980), p. 72
5 Douglas Moo, "What Does It Mean not to Teach or Have Authority over Men?" *Recovering Biblical Manhood & Womanhood*, p. 192

with all submissiveness. I do not permit a woman to teach or to exercise authority over a man; rather, she is to remain quiet. For Adam was formed first, then Eve; and Adam was not deceived, but the woman was deceived and became a transgressor. (1 Tim. 2:9-14)[6]

In my opinion, many more people will populate heaven based on the efforts of godly mothers than through the efforts of preachers. God custom-made women for their critical role.

In other words, God intends for men to assume the leadership roles in the church and the home (cf. 1 Tim. 2:8; 1 Cor. 14:34-35; Col. 3:18), and He intends for women to fulfill the vital role of keepers and nurturers of the home (1 Tim. 5:14; Titus 2:3-5). Men are charged with the responsibility of leading the Lord's church. Thus, the New Testament only authorizes *men* to serve as elders or wear an official title as deacon (1 Tim. 3; Titus 1). Only men can lead in the mixed-gender worship assemblies (1 Tim. 2:8). Instead of pursuing leadership roles, Christian women are to be "adorned with good works rather than with outward, seductive trappings, learning quietly and submissively, refraining from taking positions of authority over men, giving attention to those roles to which God has especially called women."[7]

Thus, the phrase "she shall be saved through childbearing" does not mean that a woman must have children to be saved. C. Michael Moss comments, "It is simply a call to realize that a woman's salvation is fulfilled within the role which she has been granted by God."[8] In my opinion, many more people will populate heaven based on the efforts of godly mothers than through the efforts of preachers. God custom-made women for their critical role. *What 1 Timothy 2:15 tells us is that it is going*

---

6 To anyone in either the 1ˢᵗ century or the 21ˢᵗ century who believes that God's laws regulating gender role distinctions are no longer relevant to Christians, Paul points back to the beginning of time—to Adam and Eve. The woman's role of submission was not based upon what was culturally expected in Ephesus at the time, but about creation and the fall of man (vs. 13).

7 Douglas Moo, "What Does It Mean not to Teach or Have Authority over Men?", *Recovering Biblical Manhood & Womanhood*, p. 192

8 C. Michael Moss, *The College Press NIV Commentary: 1, 2 Timothy & Titus*, p. 64. Douglass Moo adds: "We think it is preferable to view verse 15 as designating the circumstances in which Christian women will experience (work out; cf. Phil. 2:12) their salvation—in maintaining as priorities those key roles that Paul, in keeping with Scripture elsewhere, highlights: being faithful, helpful wives, raising children to love and reverence God, managing the household (cf. 1 Tim. 5:14; Titus 2:3-5)." ("What Does It Mean not to Teach or Have Authority over Men?", *Recovering Biblical Manhood & Womanhood*, p. 192).

to be awfully difficult to get to heaven when we adopt a libertarian attitude towards God's law regarding submission and gender roles.

OUR SALVATION IS TIED TO OUR SUBMISSION TO GOD'S AUTHORITY

Therefore, 1 Timothy 2:15—like many other passages—links the principle of submission to salvation. To usurp God's authority is to reject the salvation He offers. When God speaks, we bow in humble submission. None of us has the right to walk up to God's throne and say, "Scoot over, I'd like to sit down." This is precisely what Eve tried to do. Her sin was not the mere disobedience of God's law; it was even more sinister at heart. *She desired to make herself equal with God* (cf. Gen. 3:5-6). Thus Paul pointed all the way back to the consequence of Eve's sin, not the cultural expectations of Ephesian society in that day, when he reiterated God's law regarding gender roles (1 Tim. 2:13-14). *An attitude of discontent with our divinely appointed roles in life is the precursor to rebellion.*

Today, however, any semblance of submission in the home or in the church is apt to bring ridicule from the world. We live in a culture that is markedly against the idea of yielding to anything, especially on the basis of gender. The influence of radical feminism has engulfed our generation, explaining why many professing Christians are now against the idea of male-only leadership in the church. Now, perhaps more than ever before, it is critical for Christians to have a clear understanding of the Bible's doctrine of submission.

"Wives, submit to your own husbands, as to the Lord" (Eph. 5:22). This yielding is an action of the will, where a wife deliberately decides to subordinate her role to that of her husband. In this submission she becomes his helpmeet (Gen. 2:18, KJV). She submits out of the realization that the husband occupies the same role in the home as Christ occupies in the church—that of *headship*. There is a direct link between the attitude of submission a woman has for her husband and her attitude of submission she has for the Lord. If she views one relationship of submission with contempt, she will eventually view the other the same way. *You can't have both a high view of Scripture and a low view of submission.*

The principle of submission is not restricted to women, however. The husband must provide a type of submission as well. "Husbands, love your wives, as Christ loved the church and gave Himself up for her" (Eph. 5:21-25). The submission is not to the wife, but to how the Holy Spirit has defined the husband's role. Male leadership is not possible without submission to the Lord. The husband must protect his wife, provide for her, and give "himself up for her" even as Christ gave Himself up for the church. To whatever extent this role is not deliberately and voluntarily accepted, to that extent the relationship will be impaired.

You can't have both a high view of Scripture and a low view of submission.

Every human being must find himself in God's hierarchy of delegated authority. Paul writes, "I want you to understand that the head of every man is Christ, the head of a wife is her husband, and the head of Christ is God" (1 Cor. 11:3). No human is an authority in and of himself; we all ultimately report to God. When we submitted to the Lord's command to be baptized (cf. Matt. 28:19-20), we made a commitment to accept all future commands as well. Christians are people who submit to their Lord without argument.

You can't be a disciple of Christ if you do not voluntarily submit to His authority. "If anyone would come after me, let him deny himself and take up his cross daily and follow me" (Luke 9:23). Paul commands, "Have this mind among yourselves." In other words, we are to adopt the attitude of Jesus, "who, though He was in the form of God, did not count equality with God a thing to be grasped, but emptied Himself.... He humbled Himself by becoming obedient to the point of death, even death on a cross" (Phil. 2:5-8). Jesus said, "I have come down from heaven, not to do my own will but the will of Him who sent me" (John 6:38).

WHAT DO WE MEAN BY AUTHORITY?

All human relationships fit into a framework of authority and compliance. For example, the relationship between parents and children is based upon a child's submission to his parents (Eph. 6:1-2). The relationship between citizens and their government is based upon civil government's right to regulate behavior (Rom. 13:1-7; Titus 3:1; 1 Pet. 2:13-17). Most social organizations and institutions, such as businesses or the military (cf. Matt. 8:9; 1 Pet. 2:18-20), have a structure of authority that gives some members the right to direct the behavior of others. The church of the New Testament, though comprised of a priesthood of believers (1 Pet. 2:5), is governed by elders (1 Thess. 5:12-13; 1 Tim. 3:1-9; Titus 1:5-9; Heb. 13:7, 17; 1 Pet. 5:1-5). In marriage, the wife is told by the Spirit to submit to the headship of her husband (Eph. 5:22-23; Col. 3:18-19; 1 Pet. 3:1-7). But no human—whether in the context of home, government, military, business, or church—has absolute authority. Any authority a human may have has been delegated by God, who is sovereign over all. Therefore, any *abuse* of that authority will be met with God's wrath.

We may define *authority* as the *right* (Matt. 8:9: 28:19), *power* (Mark 1:27; Acts 8:19; 1 Cor. 7:37), and *responsibility* (2 Cor. 10:8; 13:10) *to direct someone else*. Only God perfectly yields all three of these aspects of authority in an infinite way. Among humans, each aspect of authority is limited and varies from one human relationship to another. For example, concerning the *power to direct someone else*, God has entrusted government with the sword (Rom. 13:4); parents with the rod (Prov. 13:24); businesses with the ability to fire an employee (Luke 16:2); elders with the ability to lead the church in disciplining a member (Matt. 18:15-17; 1 Cor. 5:1-13). One's *right* is the *extent to which one can direct someone*. For example, parents have the right to be involved in the most minute aspects of their child's life, telling him to make his bed and close his mouth when he eats. The government, on the other hand, hasn't been granted such an extensive right.

The *right* and *power* to direct someone else should be exercised in the context of *responsibility*, especially among Christians. Authority should be seen in view of servanthood: "You know that the rulers of the Gentiles lord it over them, and their great ones exercise authority over them. It shall not be so among you. But whoever would be great among you must be your servant" (Matt. 20:25-26). Christians understand that authority is something that should be cautiously borne, not eagerly flexed. Authority is a sacred duty that is exercised for the good of other people. A church withdraws fellowship from an impenitent member as a last resort, not as an act of vengeance. A parent spanks his children out of affection, not as an impulse of his temper. A husband doesn't domineer over his wife; he make lovingly makes decisions based upon her best interest. An employer shows mercy to his employee; he doesn't exploit his superior position.

As it relates to the authority of husbands, their authority is their leadership and headship. Husbands are not authorized to subjugate their wives. Instead, wives *are* to submit (subject) *themselves* to their husbands. Ephesians 5:25-27 is the model for both husbands and wives. Christ works to promote the holiness of His bride by suffering for her, not by coercing her to suffer for Him. If the husband loves his wife "as Christ loves the church," her smallest request will be an easy task that he will gladly undertake. Mutual love requires mutual sacrifice.

> *Christ works to promote the holiness of His bride by suffering for her, not by coercing her to suffer for Him.*

JESUS IS MORE THAN OUR SAVIOR— HE IS OUR LORD

No one can adequately obey the gospel if they do not first understand this principle of authority. The essence of true Christianity is our absolute submission to the will of Christ in everything we say, do, and think (Col. 1:18). "Submit yourselves therefore to God" (Jas. 4:7). This is the very definition of being a Christian and it is demonstrated when one takes great care to learn and keep God's laws.

Jesus stated clearly that the Father had given Him all authority in heaven and on earth (Matt. 28:18; cf. John 17:2). Because of His humble submission to the Father, "God has highly exalted Him and bestowed on Him the name that is above every name, so that at the name of Jesus every knee should bow, in heaven and on earth and under the earth, and every tongue confess that Jesus Christ is Lord, to the glory of God the Father" (Phil. 2:9-11). God has put all things under Jesus' feet and made Him as head over all things among the church (Eph. 1:22-23).

The truth is that there is no faith in Christ as Savior without submission to Him as Lord. From the beginning, Jesus was preached as "both Lord and Christ" (Acts 2:36), and those who heard the message were called on to "repent" (2:38). Inherent in repentance is a change of heart toward God. Where sin has reigned in rebellion, faith must rule in submissive obedience. If we will not confess Jesus as Lord, we cannot know Him as our Savior (Rom. 10:9). And no man has believed in Jesus as Lord who has not determined in his heart "to observe all things" He has commanded (Matt. 28:20).

Many assume they can find salvation on their own. Our society is rotten to the core with people who have no intention of being bound to the laws of man, let alone the law of God. Why should I submit to a rule that inconveniences me? Why shouldn't I lie if it gets me what I want? Why shouldn't I take drugs if it makes me feel good? Yet the Bible teaches otherwise. Solomon recognized, "There is a way that seems right to a man, but its end is the way to death" (Prov. 14:12). Still, many live as though they are "equals" with God—as if their private judgment is as good as the Lord's instruction. Jeremiah, however, recognized the futility of mankind's judgment: "I know, O Lord, that the way of man is not in himself, that it is not in man who walks to direct his steps" (Jer. 10:23).

Salvation can only be found when we submit to God's authority. The song lyrics "I did it my way" make for a terrible slogan for the Christian life. We must set out to always do things *His* way. Heartfelt submission to God's authority is the dividing line between those who are saved, and those who are lost. Many have cast God aside, thinking His laws are counter-intuitive and impractical by the standard of man's own wisdom. They have stopped their ears from listening to Him, especially in regards to matters where they disagree with Scripture. As Zephaniah described Judah, "She listens to no voice; she accepts no correction. She does not trust in the Lord; she does not draw near to her God" (Zeph. 3:2)

Would Abraham have been known as "the friend of God" if he had lived in rebellion to the Lord's will (Heb. 11:8, 17; Jas. 2:23)? Would Noah have been saved from the flood if he had disobeyed God's command to build the ark (Gen. 7:5; Heb. 11:7)? Would the walls of Jericho have collapsed if the children of Israel had disobeyed the Lord's command to march around the city for seven days (Josh. 6:20; Heb. 11:30)? Would Naaman have been cured of his leprosy had he refused to obey the Lord's command to dip in the Jordan River seven times (2 Kings 5:14)? What then makes people think they can be saved from their sins if they refuse to submit to the last will and testament of the Lord? "And being made perfect, He became the source of eternal salvation to all who *obey* Him" (Heb. 5:9). Jesus Christ, the "author" and "captain" of our salvation states the conditions upon which men are saved (Heb. 2:10). We must obey Him (Matt. 28:18; 17:5).

> *Heartfelt submission to God's authority is the dividing line between those who are saved, and those who are lost.*

THE AUTHORITY OF GOD FOUND IN THE BIBLE

Jesus promised the apostles, "The Helper, the Holy Spirit, whom the Father will send in my name, He will teach you all things and bring to your remembrance all that I have said to you" (John 14:26). He told them that the Holy Spirit would guide them into "all the truth" as communicated by the mouth of Christ (John 16:13).

Thus the apostles and the prophets who wrote the books of the New Testament spoke with the authority of Jesus, since they were guided by the Spirit sent from Jesus (2 Pet. 1:20-21). The apostle Paul acknowledged the authority of his inspired words when he wrote, "If anyone thinks that he is a prophet, or spiritual, he should acknowledge that the things I am writing to you are a command of the Lord" (1 Cor. 14:37). In other words, when the Lord speaks through the words of Paul, such as we find happening in letters like 1 Corinthians or 1 Timothy, the matters addressed should be settled. The same is true with any prophet or apostle of God. Jesus has spoken. For all who would call Jesus "Lord," we submit to His instruction. How dare we refer to Jesus as "Lord," but then refuse to submit to what He commanded through the apostle's words? "Why do you call me 'Lord, Lord,' and not do what I tell you?" (Luke 6:46).

"All Scripture is breathed out by God and profitable for teaching, for reproof, for correction, and for training in righteousness, that the man of God may be complete, equipped for every good work" (2 Tim. 3:16-17). Scripture is our eternal standard that teaches, reproves, corrects, and trains us. It can accomplish these things only because it has inspired authority in our lives. When it teaches, we listen; when it reproves, we heed the warning; when it corrects, we penitently straighten our thinking and behavior; when it trains, we joyfully try to do better.

FALSE STANDARDS OF AUTHORITY

If we have not resolved to submit entirely to the authority of God's word, we will inevitably turn to another authority. Consider some common false standards of authority:

DENOMINATIONS

A "denomination," here used in a theological sense, is a religious sub-group or sect of Christendom. Every denomination is founded on the heritage and theological identity of its human founder.[9] There are virtually thousands of denominations within Christendom, each with their

---

9   For example, the Lutheran church traces its roots to Martin Luther; the Presbyterian church attributes much of its heritage to John Calvin and various man-written documents, such as the *Westminster Confession of Faith*; many flavors of the Baptist church trace their roots back to John Smyth; *ad nauseum*.

own traditions and distinct points of doctrine, and are more or less distinct from one another. Because Jesus only started one church (cf. Matt. 16:18), any other church that has been started since then has been started, by implication, by a fallible man. You, the reader—if you wanted to—could start your own denomination.

The major problem with denominationalism, however, is it is the *division* of self-identifying Christians—something that is unpleasing to God (John 17:20-21; 1 Cor. 1:10). How can we intentionally divide if God wants us to be united (1 Cor. 1:10; 1 Pet. 3:8)? Equally problematic is the reality that for a denomination to maintain its identity, it must base itself on something in addition to the Bible, such as a man-made creed or written confession of faith. However, if the Bible is true, *the only authority in deciding matters of faith and religion is Scripture* (cf. John 17:20-21; Rom. 16:17-18; 1 Cor. 4:6; 2 Tim. 1:13). We have no command from God authorizing a man-made creed to rise to the level of His word. As helpful as man-written works can be, they are only true to the degree that they are in accordance with Scripture. For instance, if anything I have written in this book is contrary to God's will, then it is wrong and should not be defended.

We need to appreciate the freedom that accompanies being bound only by the New Testament. A Christian, released from the bondage of a denomination, does not need to know what some theologian 100, 200, or 500 years ago taught. You do not need to know the various religious confessions, councils, creeds that have been enforced among the countless groups of Christendom. All you need to know are the Scriptures.

> *If anything I have written in this book is contrary to God's will, then it is wrong and should not be defended.*

In our refutation of denominationalism, we must be careful that we do not allow denominationalism to influence what we understand the Bible to teach. For example, we rightfully argue against the denominational teaching of "once saved, always saved" or "unconditional grace." Such doctrines are in error (cf. Gal. 5:4; 2 Pet. 2:20-22). However, if we are not careful, we can combat this error to the degree that we miss what the Bible does say about assurance—whether out of neglect or fear of being misunderstood (Rom. 8:1, 4, 36-39; 1 John 1:7). God forbid we allow what others are saying to cause us to adopt a primarily *reactionary* religion.

TRADITIONS

It is common for Christians (including elders and preachers) to struggle with adequately distinguishing between what is authorized in God's word and what is merely a tradition. We are in dangerous territory when we allow our past way of doing things to become the standard by which we judge what we do or the standard by which we judge the faithfulness of others in what they do (Matt. 15:1-3, 8-9). Instead, we should always examine the status quo in light of the Scriptures (Mark 7:1-13). At one time, Christians required circumcision of new converts because it was the status quo (Acts 15:1). At one time, partaking the Lord's Supper during a common meal was the status quo in Corinth (1 Cor. 11:17-22). But just because "we've always done it that way" doesn't mean we should continue doing it that way.

What is the only standard that actually matters? Truth (John 17:17; Psa. 119:160; Prov. 23:23). We need to remember the words of Jesus: "You search the Scriptures because you think that in them you have eternal life; and it is they that bear witness about Me, yet you refuse to come to Me that you may have life" (John 5:39-40). If we want to truly be God's people, we need to be able to differentiate clearly between what is Scriptural and what is just traditional.

INNOVATIONS

We need to be as creative as possible in spreading the message of the gospel. We are commanded to take the news about Jesus and His kingdom to the ends of the earth (Matt. 28:19-20), and Jesus has allowed a great deal of freedom in how we choose to market His message. But we must always remember to never allow our method to alter the message. We can be "up-to-date" in our presentation without thinking that the faith once for all delivered to the saints is "out-of-date." We can do whatever is most effective or pragmatic in reaching the greatest number of people, so long as we continue to submit entirely to the authority of God's word (1 Cor. 9:20-23).

OUR SPIRITUAL OR BLOOD ANCESTORS

We appreciate the legacy of faith demonstrated by many of our ancestors. Yet many have refused to submit to the authority of the New Testament because doing so would require them to deny the religion of their parents. But we cannot allow the opinion of a spouse, a parent, or a friend to trump our obedience to God's word. So long as the beliefs of our family members are our authority, we cannot be followers of Jesus (Matt. 10:37; Luke 14:26).

Furthermore, we must not be married to the erroneous—and often conflicting—views of some of the great leaders of the church in the past. It is sometimes helpful to know the teachings of Augustine, Luther, Calvin, Wesley, Campbell, Lipscomb, or McGarvey, but we must continually recognize that they were just human beings like us. We may pride ourselves in being part of a movement that aims to "speak where the Bible speaks and be silent where the Bible is silent." But never lose sight of that goal by focusing too much on the people of our past. We commend the contributions many have made in the "Restoration Movement." But they were just people trying to use the Bible properly. What they said or did should not be our authority for what is right. Sometimes they got it wrong. Only the Bible is our authority.

EMOTIONS

Phrases like "I feel like…," "I want…," or "I think this is how…" are foreign to the Bible. Living in submission to God requires a humble heart that is willing to push aside personal desires (Matt. 16:24; Rom. 15:2-3). In fact, we are to be driven by what God wants, not what we want.

CONCLUSION

It is the crime of all crimes to rebel against the authority of the King of kings and Lord of lords. Where God has spoken, the heart of the Christian must be one of humble submission to His word. Before Jesus, let every knee bow, and let every tongue confess that He is Lord (Phil. 2:9).

Jesus submitted to the authority of the Father. "I have come down from heaven," He said, "not to do my own will but the will of Him who sent me" (John 6:38). It is no surprise, therefore, to hear Him pray, "Father… not my will, but yours, be done" (Luke 22:42). To be saved means to live by that same authority.

DISCUSSION QUESTIONS

1. How would you explain the meaning of 1 Timothy 2:13-15 to someone?

2. How is the degradation or blurring of gender roles in the home and the church an example of theological liberalism? (See footnote 5 in chapter 3 for a definition of liberalism.)

3. Does the Bible teach that husbands are to force or coerce their wives into subjection, or does the Bible teach that a woman should voluntarily submit to the leadership of her husband?

4. Is it possible to have a high view of biblical authority while simultaneously holding a low view of the concept of different gender roles?

5. What is *authority*?

6. In what way, or to what extent, is the practice of Christianity hampered by a reluctance to submit to the authority of Jesus?

7. Do we have to fully understand all of God's commands before we obey them? Explain your answer.

8. How does Jesus exercise His authority among Christians today?

9. What are some false standards of authority? Can you think of any examples that were not listed in this chapter?

10. As it relates to submission, how do faithful Christians demonstrate their faith in Jesus?

CHAPTER 9

FORGIVEN SO WE CAN FEAR

THE FEAR OF GOD

"THE fear of God is the soul of godliness," wrote John Murray.[1] The way in which both the Old and New Testaments repeatedly emphasize the fear of God makes such a statement impossible to deny. Only those who fear God are eligible to walk with Him. For that reason, I have selected the fear of God as our final study in this book.

It used to be that if someone was called a "God-fearing man," people knew exactly what that meant. While the idea that God should be feared is something that has largely been lost in popular religious thought, it should not be true among God's children. Instead of minimizing the fear of God in our lives, Christians should "*be zealous* for the fear of the Lord all the day" (Prov. 23:17, NKJV, emp. added). Only in the context of godly fear can we realize the joy of being a follower of Christ. Whenever you remove the fear of God from Christianity, all that remains will be a rotting carcass of cold religion, counterfeit piety, and complacent morality.

As we begin our study, let us consider how jam-packed the Bible is with references to the fear of God.

SURVEY OF THE FEAR OF GOD IN THE BIBLE

Open any concordance (such as *Strong's* or *Young's*) and be impressed with how often explicit references to the fear of God are found. A ca-

---

1   John Murray, *Principles of Conduct*, p. 229

sual examination of every occurrence of the word *fear* in the English Standard Version revealed that there are between 225 and 250 direct references to the fear of God found across more than half the books of the Bible. If you add to this number all the times where the fear of God is exemplified, the number of occurrences would surely double or triple. As we briefly survey the Bible's references to the fear of God, notice how impossible it should be for a child of God to remain apathetic about a theme so thoroughly central to Scripture.

THE PENTATEUCH

In Genesis 31:42, Jacob says to Laban, "If the God of my father, the God of Abraham and the *Fear of Isaac*, had not been on my side, surely now you would have sent me away empty-handed" (emp. added). Throughout the Scriptures, God is called by several names: Alpha and Omega (Rev. 1:8); I Am (Exo. 3:14); King of Kings (1 Tim. 6:15; Rev. 19:16) Great Shepherd (Heb. 13:20); Rock (Deut. 32:4); Ancient of Days (Dan. 7:9); etc. And here, in Genesis 31:42, God is called the "Fear of Isaac." If, in our pursuit of God and our knowledge of Him, we do not come to fear God like Isaac feared Him, we do not know the God of the Bible.

> *We cannot remain apathetic about a theme so thoroughly central to Scripture.*

In Exodus 20, we find Moses receiving the commandments from God. Surrounding Mount Sinai is a frightful scene: thunder, lightning, and "the sound of the trumpet and the mountain smoking" (vs. 18). The Israelites are so overwhelmed by their close proximity to God that they fear for their lives (vs. 19). Moses then says, "Do not fear, for God has come to test you, *that the fear of Him* may be before you, that you may not sin" (vs. 20, emp. added). In other words, this incredible moment was not merely intended to cause terror, but to cultivate a true fear of God that would lead His people to live righteously. Do not miss the direct correlation between fearing God and avoiding sin.

Later, when Moses communicated God's commandments to the

Israelites, he shared with them God's words regarding their faithfulness: "Oh, that they had such a heart as this always, to *fear me* and to keep all my commandments, that it might go well with them and with their descendants forever" (Deut. 5:29, emp. added). The only way God could guarantee that the nation of Israel would flourish is if they would continue in the fear of Him by keeping His commandments.

THE BOOK OF JOB

Our survey moves from God's dealings with His covenant people to His dealings with an individual saint. Job was a man who "feared God and turned away from evil" (Job 1:1). This phrase is uttered again when God boasted in His relationship with him: "Have you considered my servant Job, that there is none like him on the earth, a blameless and upright man, who fears God and turns away from evil?" (vs. 8). Satan answered the Lord, saying, "Does Job fear God for no reason?" (vs. 9). Satan accused Job of being faithful to the Lord only because he was blessed by God, not because of any true devotion to Him. However, the book of Job confirms that Job truly did love God from the heart. As it concerns our study, however, we see the unavoidable truth that the essence of true religion is the fear of God.

THE PSALMS

More than a quarter of the Psalms contain direct references to fearing God. Psalm 2 is a Messianic psalm describing God's plan to send His Son to the earth to demonstrate grace and execute judgment. After announcing this plan, David writes, "Now therefore, O kings, be wise; be warned, O rulers of the earth. Serve the Lord with fear, and rejoice with trembling" (Psa. 2:10-11).

In other words, God says, "Knowing what my Son is going to do with the authority I have given Him, the only appropriate response is to obey Him in the context of godly fear." We must not neglect this critical implication: If our view of Christ does not compel us to submit to Him in godly fear, then we do not have the right view of Christ.

Next, we come to Psalm 25, which is the intimate prayer of a man who has submitted himself entirely to the Lord. He begs God for mercy and exalts God's revealed law. Then he adds, "The friendship of the Lord is for those who fear Him" (vs. 14). The word translated "friendship" refers to a company of people sitting together, sharing intimate conversation. The only way to have a close relationship with God is by cultivating a deep-seated fear of Him.

In Psalm 130 we find a rather peculiar reference to the fear of God. The psalmist sings to the Lord, "With you there is forgiveness, that you may be feared" (vs. 4). God's forgiveness, when properly understood, elicits *fear*. We will examine this verse again in our study, but for now, do not ignore the link between forgiveness and fear. We serve a God whose kindness is intended to bring about repentance (Rom. 2:4) and whose forgiveness is extended to bring about fear. Similarly, Psalm 103 tells us that God reserves His compassion "to those who fear Him" (vs. 13). What I need, more than anything else, is God's compassion. Otherwise, I do not stand a chance (cf. Psa. 130:3).

THE WRITINGS OF SOLOMON

Proverbs 1 needs to be a familiar chapter to every child of God. In the first six verses, Solomon explains that the purpose of this book is to give us wisdom and instruction. Then, starting with verse 7, he explains how we are to attain knowledge and wisdom: "The fear of the Lord is the beginning of knowledge; fools despise wisdom and instruction." The fear of God is not just like learning simple arithmetic, such as $2 + 2 = 4$, with the goal of eventually practicing more advanced mathematics, such as trigonometry and calculus. Instead, the fear of God is likened to the numerical system as a whole. A mathematician never matures beyond the numerical system; he will forever use the same fundamentals he knew since preschool. Similarly, the fear of God is the most fundamental element of knowledge. It is not just the *beginning* of knowledge, but also the *foundation* or *framework* of knowledge he will gain throughout the course of life. Without the fear of God, there is no true wisdom.

We move now to the book of Ecclesiastes, which is the memoir of a man who has attempted to find meaning and satisfaction in life in every possible way. He tried money, art, power, and sex, yet each road ultimately led to disappointment. He eventually came to the conclusion found in the last chapter: "The end of the matter; all has been heard. Fear God and keep His commandments, for this is the whole duty of man" (Ecc. 12:13). This is not a complete summary of God's plan for mankind, as Solomon left out God's plan for our redemption. However, he clearly identifies the chief attribute that should characterize our existence: the fear of God. Even keeping God's commandments is a rather pointless endeavor if they are not kept by a heart that primarily fears God.

We serve a God whose kindness is intended to bring about repentance (Rom. 2:4) and whose forgiveness is extended to bring about fear.

THE PROPHETS

Isaiah 11 is a messianic prophecy about the Christ being of the blood-line of the tribe of Jesse:

> There shall come forth a shoot from the stump of Jesse,
> And a branch from his roots shall bear fruit.
> And the Spirit of the Lord shall rest upon him,
> The Spirit of wisdom and understanding,
> The Spirit of counsel and might,
> The Spirit of knowledge and the *fear of the Lord*. (vs. 1-2, emp. added)

From these two verses, we see that that the Spirit would rest upon the Messiah, as we now know happened at His baptism in Matthew 3. The Spirit would come not only as the Spirit of power, wisdom, knowledge, and miracles, but also as the Spirit of "the fear of the Lord." Verse 3 gives special emphasis regarding the Spirit's involvement in the ministry of Christ: "His delight shall be *in the fear of the Lord*" (emp. added). Isaiah tells us that one of the primary characteristics of the Messiah would be His deep fear of the Lord. This should put to bed all harebrained ideas that the fear of God is somehow incompatible with enjoying a relationship with God. No one had a closer relationship with God than Jesus (cf. John 10:30). It was in the context of the "Spirit of the fear of the Lord" that God said, "This is my beloved Son, with whom I am well pleased" (Matt. 3:17).

In Jeremiah 3:8, the Lord is grieving over the fact that Judah did not listen to His instruction and instead embraced idolatry. Judah "did not fear, but she too went and played the whore." Apostasy is the result of an absence of godly fear. In Jeremiah 32, Jeremiah prophesies about a new covenant for God's people. We now know this covenant would be communicated and enacted by the death and resurrection of His Son (cf. Heb. 8-10). Notice how God describes this new covenant:

> They shall be my people, and I will be their God. I will give them one heart and one way, that they may fear me forever, for their own good and the good of their children after them. I will make with them an everlasting covenant, that I will not turn away from doing good to them. And I will put the *fear of me in their hearts*, that they may not turn from me. (Jer. 32:38-40, emp. added)

In other words, God says, "The reason why I am going to enter into a new covenant with my people is so I can instill within them a heart full of fear so that they will not turn from me again." If you identify as a Christian—believing yourself to be a direct beneficiary of this new covenant—yet do not live in the fear of God, then you are in reality a stranger to this covenant. You have not been saved from your sins, and you are still under the wrath of God.

THE GOSPELS

At this point, some may object by saying the fear of God was only intended for those living during the dark, distant days of the Old Testament. "Today," some say, "God doesn't want Christians to experience any kind of fear." This, we shall see, is a gross misunderstanding of God's will.

Upon learning that she was going to give birth to the Christ, Mary uttered a song of praise recorded in Luke 1:46-55. She said, "He who is mighty has done great things for me, and holy is His name. And His mercy is for those who fear Him from generation to generation" (Luke 1:49-50). Not only did God's saints fear Him in the Old Testament dispensation, but His people would continue to fear Him throughout the days of His new covenant. God intends to show mercy to those who fear Him.

Jesus told His disciples, "Do not fear those who kill the body but cannot kill the soul. Rather fear Him who can destroy both soul and body in hell" (Matt. 10:28). Jesus did not come to suppress the fear of God, but to encourage it. Those in sin should fear falling into the hands of the living God (Heb. 10:31). It should drive any sane individual to terror, and—even more importantly—to repentance. The fear of God is intended to prevent us from sin. John Murray says, "The essence of sin may be said to be the negation of God's fear."[2] The worst of sinners are those who fear God the least.

THE ACTS OF THE APOSTLES

During the early days of the church of Christ, at a time when it was experiencing phenomenal growth, we read, "So the church throughout all Judea and Galilee and Samaria had peace and was being built up. And walking in the fear of the Lord and in the comfort of the Holy Spirit, it multiplied" (Acts 9:31). Perhaps we have been conditioned to think that when we are comforted by the Holy Spirit we do not have to fear God. On the contrary, the same Spirit that rested upon Christ—the Spirit of whom the Isaiah described as "the Spirit of the fear of the Lord" (Isa. 11:2)—rested upon His church, instilling the fear of Him. The more Christ's church is characterized by the Spirit, the more His church will know the fear of God.

> *The fear of God is intended to prevent us from sin.*

---

2 John Murray, *Principles of Conduct*, p. 237

In 2 Corinthians 5:11, Paul says, "Knowing the fear of the Lord, we persuade others." Aware of the fact that his whole life and ministry will come under God's scrutiny, he dedicates his life to persuading men to obey the gospel. In 2 Corinthians 7:1, he writes, "Let us cleanse ourselves from every defilement of body and spirit, bringing holiness to completion in the fear of God." A Christian does not primarily put to death the remaining sin in his life as a result of his joy, happiness, and peace in Christ (as true as this is). Instead, Christian becomes sanctified as a result his fear of the Lord.

In Ephesians 5:21, we are told to submit "to one another in the fear of Christ" (NASB). It is in the context of our fear of Christ that we are to strengthen the husband/wife relationship (Eph. 5:22-33), the parent/child relationship (Eph. 6:1-4), and the master/slave relationship (Eph. 6:5-9). No human relationship can reach its fullest potential without the fear of the Lord.

> *No human relationship can reach its fullest potential without the fear of the Lord.*

In his letter to the Philippians, Paul commands Christians to work out their own "salvation with fear and trembling" (Phil. 2:12-13). Only in the context of "fear and trembling" can we find assurance in our salvation. Those who boast in self-righteousness—thinking their practice of Christianity has made them good enough to merit heaven—are working out their salvation in an illegitimate way. Those who approach Christianity with a whimsical spirit or an arrogant attitude are working out their salvation in a reckless way. Only in the context of godly fear before our Creator can we find the proper footing for salvation.

The Hebrews author commended Noah for building the ark "in reverent fear" (Heb. 11:7). When Moses received the tablets of the law of God, He said, "I tremble with fear" (Heb. 12:21).

The apostle Peter tells Christians to conduct themselves before God "with fear" (1 Pet. 1:17). This begs the question, knowing that we have been saved by God's grace through the sacrifice of His Son, doesn't this disarm us of any fear of God? On the contrary, knowing we are "not redeemed with perishable things like silver or gold" (vs. 18), our fear of God should increase. In other words, knowing that we were redeemed at such an incredible, terrifying price, we should be overcome with fear.

REVELATION

Perhaps the most interesting fact about the fear of God lies not in the reality of hell, but in the reality of heaven. We think that the fear of God is reserved for those who have sinned. Yet even the angelic host, who have never known sin, are overwhelmed with awe and reverence before God's holiness. And the saints in heaven, as they are worshiping God, sing, "Who will not fear, O Lord, and glorify your name?" (Rev. 15:4). Even when Christians have been translated to the presence of God and thus have been purified of whatever sin remained in their earthly bodies, they will still fear God. A similar scene is found in Revelation 19:4-5: "And the twenty-four elders and the four living creatures fell down and worshiped God who was seated on the throne, saying, 'Amen. Hallelujah!' And from the throne came a voice saying, 'Praise our God, all you His servants, you who fear Him, small and great.'" How are the saints in heaven described? They are called the ones "who fear Him."

SUMMARY

We have only examined a fraction of the biblical references to the fear of God. Yet it does not matter how many verses we could quote; the observation remains the same: if you do not know the fear of God, you do not know saving faith. We should not be afraid to make such a serious conclusion. If the Spirit of Christ was one that feared God (Isaiah 11:3), then to be without the fear of God is to be without the Spirit of Christ. We also know that to be without the Spirit of Christ is to be without Christ and His saving blood (Rom. 8:9).

> *If you do not know the fear of God, you do not know saving faith.*

To be called a man "who fears God" is one of the most important things that could be said about you. Not only should "the fear of God" be in our vocabulary, it should be our goal in life (Ecc. 12:13). If someone were to ask your closest friend, "What is the one thing that characterizes [your name here]?" Would they be able to say, "He fears God"? This is a reputation that can't be bought or faked for long; it must be consistently and genuinely lived. Nehemiah referred to Hananiah as a more "God-fearing man than many" (Neh. 7:2). Whatever faithfulness and wisdom he had to be a governor was surely due in large part to the fact that he feared "more than many."

WHAT IS THE FEAR OF GOD?

It is one thing to be impressed with how often the Bible speaks of the fear of God. It is quite another thing to *understand* that fear. Even if every page of the Bible were about the fear of God, without a solid grasp of godly fear we would still be ignorant.

TWO WAYS IN WHICH FEAR IS USED

First, *fear* is used to describe the emotion of terror, dread, or alarm. This is what typically comes to mind today when we hear the word *fear*. It is what a small boy feels when a large, vicious dog starts running towards him, or what a wife feels the moment she is informed that her husband has been involved in an accident. When the Israelites were told to dispossess the peoples in the land of Canaan, God assured them, "I will begin to put the dread and *fear* of you on the peoples who are under the whole heaven, who shall hear the report of you and shall tremble and be in anguish because of you" (Deut. 2:25, emp. added). In Acts 5:11, upon hearing that God had killed Ananias and Sapphira because of their lie to the Holy Spirit, we read, "Great *fear* came upon the whole church and upon all who heard of these things" (emp. added).

Second, *fear* is used to describe the emotion of awe, profound reverence, deep respect, or wonder. This second meaning of the word *fear* is markedly different than the first usage. God commanded each Israelite child to "revere his mother and his father" (Lev. 19:3). The Hebrew word *yare'*, in this verse rendered as *revere*, is a common word in the Old Testament and is literally translated *fear*. Is God commanding children to look at their parents with terror, much like they would a vicious dog foaming at the mouth? Absolutely not, but He does want children to *fear* their parents. In other words, not only should children see their parents as taller, older, and wiser, they should also see their parents as bearers of God's delegated authority to rule over them. By virtue of their position of authority, parents should be respected and honored.

Fearing God involves both aspects. When you visit the Grand Canyon, for example, you are overwhelmed with the commanding majesty and grandeur of such a magnificent sight. It is hard not to feel small and insignificant in comparison to such a colossal expanse. At that moment, you are experiencing the second aspect of fear—you are in awe and wonder of the powerful scene before your eyes. And if you were to look down over the edge of the Grand Canyon, you may experience the first aspect of fear as well—terror at the thought of plunging to your death. According to one source, there have been over 600 recorded deaths at the Grand Canyon since 1870, some of which were the result of "overly zealous photographic endeavors."[3] You should feel a healthy fear while peering over the edge, considering that many have acted foolishly and died. The same is true of God. There is a legitimate sense in which fearing God means being afraid of His holiness and justice, and there is the sense in which fearing God means being gripped with profound reverence, honor, and wonder. Our fearful terror of God motivates us to repent of sin, and our fearful reverence of God motivates us to draw near to Him and submit to Him in loving obedience.

Growing up, I had a good relationship with my dad (and still do). My love and respect for him was without limits. But when he told me to be

---

3 Katheryn Venegas, *Natural Wonders of the World*, p. 34

home by curfew, I made sure I was home by curfew. Why? Because I feared him—and not just in the sense that I honored him, but primarily in the sense that I didn't want to face his wrath. I had great respect, but also great dread of his punishment. Likewise, Christians serve God primarily because we love Him, but there should also be a sense in which we serve Him because we know it is a fearful thing to fall into the hands of the living God (Heb. 10:31).

THE DREAD AND TERROR OF GOD

When Adam and Eve heard God's voice calling in the Garden after they ate the forbidden fruit, Adam said, "I heard the sound of you in the garden, and I was afraid, because I was naked, and I hid myself" (Gen. 3:10). Adam was not overcome with reverence, but with dread. Is this kind of fear what God wants from us? Is it right for a person to tremble with terror before God? In the words of John Murray, "It is the essence of impiety not to be afraid of God when there is reason to be afraid of God."[4] What if Adam, instead of hiding from God, swaggered up to Him and said, "Hey God, what's up?" Not only would this be brazenly irreverent, but it would also demonstrate that Adam was out of touch with the gravity of his sin. However, to Adam's credit, he remembered God's warning, "In the day that you eat of the tree you shall surely die" (Gen. 2:17) and thus knew that anything less than fearful dread would have been extreme stupidity.

Picture a man leisurely walking on a railroad track, seemingly indifferent about the fast-moving train only a few hundred yards away barreling towards him. Instead of jumping out of the way, he's just whistling a familiar tune as he moseys down the track. What would you think of this man? Either he's blind, deaf, and totally oblivious to the fact that he is about to die a tragic death, or he is mentally ill. The fact that he has no fear of what is about to happen to him means he is totally out of touch with reality. Similarly, the person who knows he is guilty of sin but is not overcome with a fearful dread of God's wrath is

---

4 John Murray, *Principles of Conduct*, p. 233

either spiritually blind or spiritually crazy. He does not understand the holiness or justice of God, nor is he aware of the gravity of his sin and subsequently his impending destruction. Whenever Scripture exposes our sin, the only sane response is terror of God's judgment followed by the urgent call for repentance.

Should faithful Christians feel dread and terror of God? Yes, because one cannot understand God's holiness without understanding His fierce hatred of all sin. One does not understand God without knowing His need to punish all sin. The deep awareness that "it is a fearful thing to fall into the hands of the living God" (Heb. 10:31) should discourage us from sin. Jesus told His followers to "fear Him who, after He has killed, has authority to cast into hell" (Luke 12:5). This is not a cowering fear, prompting us to run from God, but a preventative fear—a fear that is ever conscious of God's holiness and judgment. Consider the words of the psalmist, "My flesh trembles for fear of you, and I am afraid of your judgments" (Psa. 119:120). When we know the God as revealed in Scripture—the God whose glory and majesty we love—we tremble at the thought of what He will do to those in judgment.

But haven't Christians been forgiven of sin? What is left for us to fear? Consider Psalm 130:3, where the psalmist acknowledges that if God were to directly deal with his sin in strict justice, he wouldn't stand a chance. "If you, O Lord, should mark iniquities, O Lord, who could stand?" How can we then enjoy God's presence and hope for communion with God in heaven? Read verse 4: "But with you there is forgiveness, *that you may be feared*" (emp. added). God forgives His children for the purpose of instilling godly fear. If the alien sinner should fear God, the child of God should fear God *more*. Christians understand better than anyone else the length to which God is willing to go in order to punish sin. The terrifying display of God's holiness in the destruction of Sodom and Gomorrah—cities that went up "like the smoke of a

> *Whenever Scripture exposes our sin, the only sane response is terror of God's judgment followed by the urgent call for repentance.*

> *God's grace and mercy should instill a type of fear that surpasses all the terror we may feel at the expectation of temporal destruction.*

furnace" (Gen. 19:28)—is dwarfed by the fearful display of God's holiness that occurred in Gethsemane and Calvary. For that reason, Christians understand better than anyone else how exceedingly precious their salvation is. God's grace and mercy should instill a type of fear that surpasses all the terror we may feel at the expectation of temporal destruction.

Peter writes to Christians, "If you call on Him as Father who judges impartially according to each one's deeds, conduct yourselves *with fear* throughout the time of your exile" (1 Pet. 1:17, emp. added). Never forget that we serve a God who judges mankind impartially. Paul's wrote the warning, "The wages of sin is death" (Rom. 6:23) to *Christians*. We should be confident in our salvation, but we should not be overconfident to the degree that we become careless and arrogant before our Creator. Instead, there should be a measure of holy dread of God for the rest of our days (cf. Heb. 4:1).

THE VENERATION AND AWE OF GOD

When the Bible says, "The fear of the Lord is the beginning of knowledge" (Prov. 1:7), it is not emphasizing the dread and terror we should have of God, but rather it is emphasizing the worship, awe, and reverence that should characterize our devotion. While God's children should always have a measure of holy dread towards God's justice, the dominant kind of fear that should define God's saints is their fearful reverence of Him.

Consider Moses, when the angel of the Lord appeared to him in the burning bush as he was tending the flock of his father-in-law. Upon realizing it was God was speaking to him through the **theophany**[5] of the burning bush, Moses "hid his face, for he was afraid to look at God" (Exo. 3:6). Moses was afraid of God, but was it the kind of fear that

---

5 A **theophany** is a visual representation of the immediate presence of God.

made him want to flee from God? No, because in their conversation God communicated His love for the Israelites and His plan to save them (vs. 7-8). Instead of running from God because of his sin, as was the case of Adam, Moses possessed a true reverence for God and talked with Him face to face. He covered his face, not out of shame, but because he was in the immediate presence of the holy God.

Next, consider Isaiah 6, where Isaiah shares his vision of the throne-room of God. Above God's throne were the angelic hosts—the seraphim—crying to one another, "Holy, holy, holy is the Lord of hosts" (vs. 3). Because they were in the presence of God, they were covering their faces (vs. 2). Though they are angels who have never committed sin, they still veil their faces before God. This is not primarily terror as a result of God's justice, but fearful reverence being in the presence of the holy God. Isaiah, on the other hand, was not only overwhelmed with reverence, but also with terror because of his guilt of sin (vs. 5). Upon being forgiven of sin (vs. 6-7), Isaiah confidently approaches God in loving submission.

Finally, consider Peter. Before he became a disciple of Jesus, he was a professional fisherman. After seeing Jesus's miracle, Peter realized He was in the presence of the Lord and fell down at His feet, saying, "Depart from me, for I am a sinful man, O Lord" (Luke 5:8). Jesus responded, "Do not be afraid; from now on you will be catching men" (vs. 10). The next verse says, "When they had brought their boats to land, they left everything and followed Him." First, Peter tells Jesus to depart because he is a sinful man. Then he "leaves everything" to follow Jesus. How do we make sense of this? Upon realizing that only God could perform the miracle he had just witnessed, he was overcome with reverential awe and dread, similar to that of Isaiah. He was so aware of his sin that he was overcome with dread being in the presence of the Lord. At the same time, he longed to be in God's presence to the degree that he was willing to leave everything to be with Christ. This is the kind of fear that we are to have of God.

NECESSARY INGREDIENTS TO FEARING GOD

If we are to grow in godly fear, consider three essential ingredients for growing in our fear of God. We must know who God is, know we are in His presence, and know our responsibilities as His children.

KNOWING WHO GOD IS

Consider Revelation 15:4 again, which we cited earlier in this chapter. The context is the scene of the saints in heaven who have overcome the world and the devil's influence. Now they are in the presence of God, and verses 3-4 record their praise:

> And they sing the song of Moses, the servant of God, and the song of the Lamb, saying,
> "Great and amazing are your deeds,
>> O Lord God the Almighty!
> Just and true are your ways,
>> O King of the nations!
> Who will not fear, O Lord,
>> and glorify your name?
> For you alone are holy.
>> All nations will come and worship you,
> for your righteous acts have been revealed."

As they worship God for who He is—great, just, true, holy, righteous—they rhetorically ask, "Who will not fear you?" In other words, anyone who sees God for who He is cannot help but fear Him. This is why it is of great importance to think accurately about the character of God. When we allow popular culture to shape our view of God, we will not know the God of the Bible. And if we don't know God as He has revealed Himself, then we will not fear Him.

One of the biggest problems in mainstream Christendom today is that many of its adherents have censored out what they deem to be the "inconvenient" attributes of God—His justice, holiness, jealousy, wrath, and omnipotence. Many are so busy shaping God after their own flimsy concepts of love, mercy, and grace that they no longer know His more intimidating and breathtaking characteristics. Therefore, they cannot fear Him because they do not know Him.

What more powerfully illustrates God's unwavering justice than the sight of Jesus on the cross? God is so holy and so pure that He would forsake His only begotten Son, about whom He said, "This is my beloved Son, with whom I am well pleased" (Matt. 3:17). The blood-stained cross demonstrates God's inflexible justice and fiery hatred of sin even more than it demonstrates His incredible love and mercy. When we view the sacrifice of Christ as we should, we cannot help but "serve the Lord with fear, and rejoice with trembling" (Psa. 2:11).

KNOWING GOD'S PRESENCE

In Psalm 139, David describes the omniscience of God. "You have searched me and known me, you know my sitting down and rising up" (vs. 1-2). "You are acquainted with all my ways. Even before a word is on my tongue, behold, O Lord, you know it altogether" (vs. 3-4). But what kind of omniscience is this? Does God see and hear everything only from a distance, way up in heaven? No, God is much closer than that. David says, "You hem me in, behind and before, and lay your hand upon me" (vs. 5). God knows everything about David, not because He is watching from afar, but because His hand is upon him. David goes on to say:

> Such knowledge is too wonderful for me;
>   it is high; I cannot attain it.
> Where shall I go from your Spirit?
>   Or where shall I flee from your presence?
> If I ascend to heaven, you are there!
>   If I make my bed in Sheol, you are there! (vs. 6-8)

David is not saying he cannot escape God's omniscience, knowledge, or watchful eye. More precisely, David is saying He cannot escape God's *presence*. God is not just *aware* of David, He is *there with* David. And what effect did that have on David? So long as he knew he was in God's presence, David wanted to rid himself of sin and evil. He wrote,

Search me, O God, and know my heart! Try me and know my thoughts! And see if there be any grievous way in me, and lead me in the way everlasting (vs. 23-24).

Fearing God is inseparable from the all-pervasive sense that God is present. When we know God is near, we cannot bear the thought of grieving Him and walking in a way that is contrary to His will. This is why the Bible tells us that the fear of the Lord is to turn away from evil (Job 28:28; Prov. 3:7). How many times have you been tempted to do something wrong, but the mere presence of someone else discouraged you from committing that sin? It is easier for a child to obey when he knows a parent is watching. When you are having a disagreement with your spouse, it is easier for both of you to speak with kindness to one another when another person is in the room. A boy is much less willing to cheat at school when he knows his teacher is right behind him.

Pay close attention: You can love sound doctrine, you can refute false teaching, and you can recite every fact about God to be known, but unless you live with an awareness of God's presence, none of these admirable qualities will change how you live.

Consider Joseph who one day found himself alone with Potiphar's wife. Long before this day, she had been making sexual advances towards him. But on this particular day, she actually grabbed Joseph and begged him to have an affair with her. There is no reason for us to think he was not a normal man with a normal sex drive, and there is also no reason for us to think Potiphar's wife was unattractive—in fact, we have every reason to think this aristocratic woman was probably very beautiful. Yet Joseph emphatically denied her and said, "How then can I do this great wickedness and sin against God?" (Gen. 39:9). It was because Joseph was deeply aware of God's presence that he wouldn't allow himself to succumb to whatever temptation he felt from Mrs. Potiphar.

If God's presence is a deterrent to sin, the inverse is surely just as true. The first step towards sin is the abandonment of our awareness of God's presence. How many sins could be prevented if we knew God was so near that He could lay His hand on our shoulder?

Pay close attention: You can love sound doctrine, you can refute false teaching, and you can recite every fact about God to be known, but unless you live with an awareness of God's presence, none of these admirable qualities will change how you live. This explains why there are some Christians who—though they may have only a basic understanding of the Bible—are deeply aware of God's presence and thus live holier, more faithful lives than other Christians who—though they may be very knowledgeable about the Bible—are very worldly in their manner of life. I know some very worldly preachers who have been preaching for decades, and I know some very godly Christians who were baptized only a few months ago.

Hophni and Phinehas grew up in the household of their father the high priest; they lead the tabernacle worship; they knew the Law of Moses like the back of their hand. But they were still "worthless men" who "did not know the Lord" (1 Sam. 2:12). They had no awareness of the presence of the Lord.

The key to living in the fear of God is the recognition that He is not far from us (Acts 17:27). Paul said, "In Him we live and move and have our being" (vs. 28). Paul is not espousing pantheism with these words, but he is reminding us that we live in the presence of God—an awareness which should cause us to fear Him.

KNOWING OUR RESPONSIBILITIES BEFORE GOD

Consider Jesus again, about whom Scripture says, "His delight shall be in the fear of the Lord" (Isa. 11:3). Jesus lived in the fear of the Lord. The most extreme example of His delight is seen in the garden of Gethsemane, where He petitioned His Lord, "Father, if you are willing, remove this cup from me." Yet, this same Jesus taught that following God means denying one's own life (Luke 14:26). Thus, He then said to the Father, "Nevertheless, not my will, but yours, be done" (Luke 22:42). Jesus was unquestioningly submissive to God, to the point of death (Phil. 2:8). How is this an example of fearful obedience? The author of Hebrews, commenting on this fateful prayer in the garden, writes:

> ...who, in the days of His flesh, when He had offered up prayers and supplications, with vehement cries and tears to Him who was able to save Him from death, and was heard because of His *godly fear*, though He was a Son, yet He learned obedience by the things which He suffered. (Heb. 5:7-8, NKJV, emp. added)

Jesus models for us perfect obedience in the fear of God. The Bible, likewise, joins the concept of obedience with the command to fear God. Notice, for example, Deuteronomy 10:12-13, where Moses summarizes what God desires:

> And now, Israel, what does the Lord your God require of you, but to *fear* the Lord your God, to walk in all His ways, to love Him, to serve the Lord your God with all your heart and with all your soul, and to keep the commandments and statutes of the Lord, which I am commanding you today for your good? (emp. added)

When we know God is near, we cannot bear the thought of grieving Him and walking in a way that is contrary to His will.

In the New Testament, Paul says something similar: "Therefore, my beloved, as you have always obeyed, so now, not only as in my presence but much more in my absence, work out your own salvation with *fear* and trembling" (Phil. 2:12, emp. added).

There is nothing more important than your relationship with the Lord. And with any important relationship comes obligation. The message of the Bible may be summarized this way: The glorious, most holy God of the universe created you and redeemed you with His own blood. Not only do you owe Him your existence, but you also owe Him heartfelt allegiance of undivided love, trusting obedience, and unshakable faith.

We obey the secular governing authorities (Rom. 13:1); we obey the shepherds of the church (Heb. 13:17); we obey our superiors (1 Pet. 2:18); we submit to our equals (Eph. 5:21)—all because God tells us to do so. And if our obedience to someone else requires us to disobey God, then we must first and foremost choose to obey God (Acts 5:29). We refuse to lie or engage in dishonest business (Eph. 4:25); we flee sexual sin (1 Cor. 6:18; 2 Tim. 2:22); we do not take part in sinful recreation (1 Pet. 4:4); we guard what entertains us (1 Cor. 15:33)—all because of our supreme obligation to God and His promise to supply the necessary grace to overcome temptation. If we are ever disobedient to God, it is first and foremost because we do not fear Him (Rom. 3:18).

CONCLUSION

John reminds us that anything that we ask according to God's will, He hears us (1 John 5:14-15). There should be no doubt in our minds that it is God's will for us to grow in the grace of the fear of Him. Let us ask for godly fear, the soul of true religion. God has given us a model prayer for this fear in Psalm 86:11, where David prays, "Teach me your way, O Lord, that I may walk in your truth; unite my heart to fear your name."

Only those who are humble, contrite, and tremble at God's word will receive His blessings (Isa. 66:2). Fearing God is the foundation for all knowledge and wisdom (Prov. 1:7; 9:10). God's desire for all of mankind can be summarized in fearing Him and keeping His commandments (Ecc. 12:13-14). Though fear indicates a sense of reverential awe that leads to obedience, there should also be a sense of terror of His justice that would cause us to tremble. Christians—God's people—are His temple, bought with the blood of Jesus (1 Cor. 3:16; 6:19-20). We have not come to Mount Sinai, as did the Israelites who were overcome with fear, but we have come to Mount Zion and the city of the living God, the heavenly Jerusalem, to myriads of angels, to the general assembly of the saints destined for heaven. Above all, we live in the awareness that we are in God's presence (Heb. 12:22-24). If the sights and sounds of Mount Sinai were so impressive to the Israelites, how much more should we be impressed who have come to something even greater?

DISCUSSION QUESTIONS

1. What immediately comes to mind when someone is referred to as a "God-fearing man"?

2. How does God's forgiveness produce fear?

3. How does the fear of God prevent us from sinning?

4. Do we put to death sin in our lives primarily because of the happiness we experience in Christ, or primarily because of the fear of God? Explain your answer.

5. How is every legitimate human relationship enhanced by the fear of God?

6. Did Adam and Eve react appropriately to God's presence in the Garden after they sinned? Explain your answer.

7. In what way should Christians fear God even more than the alien sinner?

8. How does fear drive us towards God, instead of away from Him?

9. What are the ingredients of godly fear?

10. How is the fear of the Lord the beginning of knowledge and wisdom?

WHAT'S A "SALVATION ISSUE"?

THE question about whether something is a "salvation issue" gets thrown around occasionally among some circles. "Is using instrumental music in worship is a salvation issue?" "Is what you wear to worship a salvation issue?" "Is church attendance a salvation issue?" Used this way, the phrase "salvation issue" (a term coined by man and not found in the Bible) is employed to describe an issue that Christians must get right in order to go to heaven.

Perhaps we should reassess whether it is even healthy for man to make a theoretical distinction of what is a salvation issue as opposed to a non-salvation issue. After all, it doesn't matter what I, or any other human, thinks is a salvation issue. Are we willing to embrace a pseudo-Christianity that categorizes certain commands or teachings of God as being either important or non-important?

IF THERE WERE SUCH A THING AS "SALVATION ISSUES" VS. "NON-SALVATION ISSUES..."

...WHO GETS TO DECIDE?

In the course of my research, it seemed that the phrase "salvation issue" began being popularly used only a generation ago in the context of justifying those who failed to believe what the Bible taught on a given issue. The ecumenical movement of the '80s and '90s was fueled by the false concept of a so-called "core gospel." The reasoning went something like this: "You can be wrong about a host of different biblical issues so long as you believe the truth about Jesus or salvation." Hence, some key issues were made to be "salvation issues—matters in which there was no room for disagreement (e.g. Jesus is the Son of God, or Jesus was resurrected from the grave)—while all other issues could be "given to interpretation" and thus minimized as "not a matter of fellowship."

With that being said, what issues can I label as being "inconsequential" to my salvation? No one has the right to walk up to God's throne and tell Him to scoot over. If I disobey God regarding any issue He has addressed in His word (either explicitly or implicitly), I am guilty of sin. Sin, in the legal sense of the word,[1] is the violation of God's law on any given issue, regardless of how petty it may be (Rom. 5:13; 1 Tim. 1:3-4; 1 John 5:17). All sins —from "big" to "little"—have the power to damn my soul (Rom. 6:23).

Do we dare compartmentalize issues regarding matters such as sexuality and marriage, worship, gender roles in the church, baptism, and denominationalism as either "essential" or "non-essential" matters? Which of these am I willing to be wrong about?

...WHAT IS THE LEAST I HAVE TO DO TO BE PLEASING TO GOD?

One of the dangers of categorizing things as salvation issues is that it fosters a sort of "checklist" mentality when it comes to Christianity. ("As long as I'm good on *these things* over here, I don't have to worry about *those things* over there.") Yet Christianity has never been a merit-based system. It is a system of salvation granted to us only by the grace of God (Eph. 2:8-9). While God's gift of salvation has some conditions (such as belief and submission, cf. Mark 16:15-16), a saving relationship with God is foundationally based upon our obedient love for Him. Someone who is deeply in love with God never tries to categorize His will into important issues and non-important issues. Jesus rebuked the ancient scribes and Pharisees for forgetting the basis from which their obedience was to spring (cf. Matt. 23:23-24).

---

1 See chapter 6

When I take matters on which God has spoken and relegate them to mere matters of opinion or non-essentials, I have sacrificed the conviction that God's word can be known and understood. God has never spoken out of both sides of His mouth on an issue. There is no biblical teaching about which all interpretations are equally valid.

If I don't get everything right in my understanding of the Bible, it isn't because God could not adequately communicate His word—it's because of *me*. The human heart itself is the most common limitation in understanding God's word. The heart that does not recognize or desire truth is the most common and pervasive pitfall in biblical interpretation.

We need to be levelheaded about this question. The first order of business is to get our baseline right: God, and God alone, gets to decide what is a salvation issue.

ONE MUST BE A CHRISTIAN

Of course, the Bible teaches (in no uncertain terms) that there are things one must believe and do in order to be saved by God's grace, despite the sincerity of someone to the contrary.

- I must have faith in God and His reward for the faithful (Heb. 11:6; cf. Rev. 2:10).
- I must repent of my sins, entering into a covenant with God to conform to the identity of His Son (Luke 13:3; Acts 3:19; Gal. 2:20).
- I must have at least a basic, though no-less fervent, understanding of what it means to yield to the Lordship of Christ (Matt. 28:20; Acts 2:36; 10:36; Rom. 10:9-10; Jude 4; Rev. 17:14).
- I must be baptized for the express purpose of (a) receiving forgiveness of sins (Acts 2:38; Gal. 3:26-27; 1 Pet. 3:21)

and (b) being added by Jesus to His church (Acts 2:47; cf. Col. 1:13).

➤ And, I would argue, I must have at least a rudimentary concept of the kingdom of God, since it was so central to the preaching of the gospel during the beginning of the church (Acts 8:12; 19:8; 20:25; 28:23, 31; cf. Col. 1:13).

In other words, sincerity is not enough. There will be plenty of people—a heartbreaking number—who honestly believed they were Christians but did not satisfy the requirements of salvation so clearly stated by the New Testament (Matt. 7:21-23). There are simply some things a person must get right from the beginning in order to be saved.

ALL CHRISTIANS ARE ON A LEARNING CURVE

When someone becomes a Christian, do they have to understand everything about instrumental music, denominationalism, modesty and other moral matters, the Lord's Supper, the church's organization, the division between the Old and New Testaments, etc.? As important as these issues are, certainly not immediately!

Once someone has become a Christian, he/she begins a lifelong period of growth. We must remember that all Christians have varying degrees of spiritual maturity—some growing faster than others. (Much of the speed of this development is based upon desire [1 Pet. 2:2].)

We need to be patient with Christians if they have not yet attained a coherent knowledge of the truth (cf. Rom. 14:1; 15:1; 1 Cor. 8:9). Someone may hold to an incorrect biblical position for the time being, but still be searching for the truth. I know there are many topics in the Bible that I am still trying to better understand.

Not only are we to teach our fellow Christians the truth, but we are to do it with "complete patience" (2 Tim. 4:2). The apostle Paul, knowing Christians mature at different rates of speed, wrote:

We urge you, brothers, admonish the idle, encourage the fainthearted, help the weak, be patient with them all. (1 Thess. 5:14)

…With all humility and gentleness, with patience, bearing with one another in love, eager to maintain the unity of the Spirit in the bond of peace. (Eph. 4:2-3)

Put on then, as God's chosen ones, holy and beloved, compassionate hearts, kindness, humility, meekness, and patience, bearing with one another and, if one has a complaint against another, forgiving each other; as the Lord has forgiven you, so you also must forgive. (Col. 3:12-13)

Some Christians used to be members of various denominations, and many will likely have some theological baggage to overcome. Someone who grew up being a Catholic, Mormon, Jehovah's Witness, Methodist, Baptist, etc., will likely be disadvantaged in adapting to pre-denominational Christianity. They will have to "unlearn" several of the false beliefs they had previously been taught.

Other Christians grew up being taught a postmodern worldview, and thus will have some philosophical baggage to overcome. The truth claims of the Bible will run counter to the relative truth that culture has taught them through the years. Yet other Christians grew up in an abusive household, or suffer from learning disabilities, and thus will have some psychological or emotional baggage to overcome.

We are under obligation to contend for the faith if false religion is being taught (Jude 3). Yet, at the same time, those who harshly insist their brethren immediately drop what is deemed to be a wrong belief, without being willing to first patiently teach them, are often a cancer in the church.

The often-abused example is given of the late brothers Gus Nichols and Guy N. Woods who, a generation or two ago, publicly disagreed about the nature of the indwelling of the Holy Spirit, yet still maintained fellowship with one another (with Woods holding the position that the Spirit dwells within the heart representatively, and Nichols holding the position that the Spirit dwells within the heart literally and personally). Let us not make the mistake of thinking that both positions were equally valid and thus of no consequence. Though Nichols and Woods honestly disagreed on this topic, I hold that both men are presently in glory. And we can assume both of these great men of God died *saved*—not because their disagreement about the indwelling of the Spirit was or wasn't a salvation issue—but because the blood of Jesus cleansed them of the issues about which they were still honestly mistaken and hadn't yet worked out (1 John 1:7).

So long as a person is still breathing on this earth, he/she must always be in pursuit of the truth (2 Thess. 2:12). It is when a Christian *rejects* God's word about something that an issue—any issue—can become a salvation issue.

GOD OFTEN GRANTS A PERIOD OF GRACE

God is often merciful and gives us a period of grace. Consider the "seven churches of Asia" in Revelation 2–3. Jesus critiqued each congregation, telling them what they needed to change if they still wanted to be saved. To the Ephesian church of Christ, for example, He said:

> Remember therefore from where you have fallen; repent, and do the works you did at first. If not, I will come to you and remove your lampstand from its place, unless you repent. (Rev. 2:5)

By the phrase "remove your lampstand," I suppose God still considered the names of those Christians still written in the Book of Life (cf. Rev. 3:5), but He was placing them on probation. They were guilty of sin—and all sin is a salvation issue. But by His grace He gave them a period to repent.

When does God's grace period end? To the Thyatira church, Jesus said:

> I have this against you, that you tolerate that woman Jezebel, who calls herself a prophetess and is teaching and seducing my servants to practice sexual immorality and to eat food sacrificed to idols. I gave her time to repent, but she refuses to repent of her sexual immorality. Behold, I will throw her onto a sickbed, and those who commit

adultery with her I will throw into great tribulation, unless they repent of her works. (Rev. 2:20-22)

Did Jezebel get to decide when God's grace period ended? Perhaps her preacher tried to comfort her by saying, "Yes, sexual deviancy is a frowned upon at this church, but it isn't a salvation issue."

Only God, in His sovereignty, gets to decide how far His grace will extend. We are not promised an opportunity to repent always (Acts 5:1-11). But when we refuse to obey the words of Christ, any issue can become a salvation issue (2 Thess. 1:8).

CONCLUSION

Before entering into Christ, all sins are salvation issues (Rom. 6:23; 3:23). After the gospel has been obeyed, Christians must "walk according to the Spirit" (Rom. 8:1-2); otherwise any sin—however seemingly small—can once again become a salvation issue.

One of the beautiful things about Christianity is that I don't have to get everything right—I just have to "walk in the light" (1 John 1:7). I simply must continually *try* to get everything right. It is when I become dispassionate about serving God—willing to categorize His commands as "salvation issues" or "non-salvation issues"—that I harbor an attitude that is not consistent with the Christian faith. I cannot afford to stop pursuing the truth of His word.

I might not get everything right concerning the various teachings of the Bible (in fact, I'm confident I won't). I might be honestly mistaken when it comes to issues like church attendance, modesty, gambling, the indwelling nature of the Holy Spirit, the "end times," the proper use of church funds, etc. This doesn't mean the truth can't be known, nor does it mean there is "room for disagreement." But there is, however, room in the church for greater patience with those who are honestly mistaken on these issues—but are still searching for the truth. I might be the one who is honestly mistaken about a given issue. (And if someone is publicly teaching something that he/she is honestly mistaken about, we should gently explain the truth "more accurately" to them [Acts 18:25-26].)

I must continually strive to better understand the gospel of Christ, because *anything* can become a salvation issue when I stop seeking the truth and obeying God. By God's grace, He will let my lampstand burn long enough for me to come to a better knowledge of the truth. And even at my best, at the end of the day, I will just be an "unprofitable servant" (Luke 17:10). Thank God for His grace.

BIBLIOGRAPHY

Attenborough, David. "Humans Are Plague on Earth." *The Telegraph*. 22 Jan 2013. Accessed 31 Oct 2017. <http://www.telegraph.co.uk/news/earth-news/9815862/Humans-are-plague-on-Earth-Attenborough.html>.

Arndt, William F., et al. *A Greek-English Lexicon of the New Testament and Other Early Christian Literature*, 3rd ed. University of Chicago Press: Chicago, Illinois, 2000.

Baker, William R. *College Press NIV Commentary: 2 Corinthians*. College Press Publishing Company: Joplin, Missouri, 1999.

Bell, Rob. *Love Wins*. HarperCollins Publishers: New York, New York, 2011.

Black, V.P. *Back to Basics*. Williams Printing Company: Nashville, Tennessee, 1979.

Bonhoeffer, Dietrich. *The Cost of Discipleship*. Touchstone Books: New York, New York, 1995.

Bowman, Ann L. "Women in Ministry," Edited by Stanley N. Gundry. *Two Views on Women in Ministry*. Zondervan Publishing House: Grand Rapids, Michigan, 2001.

Boyd, James William. *System of Salvation*. Williams Publishing Company: Nashville, Tennessee, 1990.

Brents, T.W. *The Gospel Plan of Salvation*. McQuiddy Printing Company: Nashville, Tennessee, 1911.

Burke, Denny. "PCUSA Rejects Popular Hymn 'In Christ Alone.'" *DennyBurk.com*. 29 July 2013. <http://www.dennyburk.com/presbyterian-church-u-s-a-rejects-popular-hymn-in-christ-alone-because-of-wrath/>. Accessed 13 Mar 2018.

Buswell, James Oliver. *A Systematic Theology of the Christian Religion*, in 2 Volumes. Zondervan Publishing House: Grand Rapids, Michigan, 1973.

Chafer, Lewis Sperry. *Systematic Theology*. Dallas Seminary Press: Dallas, Texas, 1947.

Calvin, John. *Institutes of the Christian Religion*. Hendrickson Publishers: Peabody, Massachusetts, 2009.

Cottrell, Jack. *His Truth*. Wipf & Stock Publishers: Eugene, Oregon, 2001.

–––. *The Faith Once for All*. College Press: Joplin, Missouri, 2004.

Diagnostic and Statistical Manual of Mental Disorders, Fifth Edition. American Psychiatric Association: Arlington, Virginia, 2013.

Encyclopedia of Philosophy, Volume Seven. The Macmillan Company: New York, New York, 1967.

Encyclopedia of Psychology. American Psychological Association, Oxford University Press: Washington, D.C., 2000.

Everest, Harvey W. "Repentance." *The Old Faith Restated*. Edited by J.H. Garrison. Christian Publishing Company: St. Louis, Missouri, 1891.

Freud, Ernst L. *Letters of Sigmund Freud, 1873-1939*. London: Hogarth Press, 1961.

Geisler, Norman. *Christian Ethics*. Baker Book House: Grand Rapids, Michigan, 1994.

–––. *Systematic Theology: In One Volume*. Baker Publishing Group: Grand Rapids, Michigan, 2011.

Grudem, Wayne. *Bible Doctrine*. Zondervan: Grand Rapids, Michigan, 1999.

Guthrie, Donald. *Pastoral Epistles: An Introduction and Commentary*. InterVarsity

Press: Downers Grove, Illinois, 1990.

Hodge, Charles B., Jr. *The Agony and Glory of the Cross*. Truth for Today: Searcy, Arkansas, 2007.

Jackson, Wayne. "Jehovah's Righteous Branch." *ChristianCourier.com*. Accessed 25 April 2018. <https://www.christiancourier.com/articles/1119-jehovahs-righteous-branch>.

---. "The Cleansing Fountain." *ChristianCourier.com*. Accessed 6 May 2018. <https://www.christiancourier.com/articles/870-1-john-1-7-the-cleansing-fountain>.

---. "What Must I Know to Be Saved?" *ChristianCourier.com*. Accessed 13 April 2018. <https://www.christiancourier.com/articles/1568-what-must-i-know-to-be-saved>.

Lamar, J.S. *The Old Faith Restated*. Edited by J.H. Garrison. Christian Publishing Company: St. Louis, Missouri, 1891.

Lewin, Roger. *Complexity: Life at the Edge of Chaos*. University of Chicago Press: Chicago, Illinois, 1999.

Lipscomb, David. *Salvation from Sin*. McQuiddy Printing Company: Nashville, Tennessee, 1913.

Luther, Martin. *Babylonian Captivity of the Church*. World Library Foundation. Translated by A.T.W. Steinhauser. Accessed 11 April 2018. <http://uploads.worldlibrary.org/uploads/pdf/20110830030704babylonian_captivity.pdf>. 1520.

Marshall, Jeremy. "'In Christ Alone': Why I Won't Sing THAT Line." Slouching Towards Emmaus. 7 Feb 2014. <https://neoprimitive.wordpress.com/2014/02/07/in-christ-alone-why-i-wont-sing-it/>. Accessed 13 Mar 2018.

May, Cecil, Jr. *Bible Questions and Answers*. Faulkner University: Montgomery, Alabama, 2012.

McClish. Dub. "The Holy Spirit, Sanctification, and Sinless Perfection." Ed. Wendell Winkler. *What Do You Know About the Holy Spirit?*. Winkler Publications: Hurst, Texas, 1980.

McGarvey, J.W. *Sermons*. The Standard Publishing Company: Cincinnati, Ohio, 1893.

McGlothlin, W. J. *Baptist Confessions of Faith*. American Baptist Publication Society: Philadelphia; Boston; Chicago; St. Louis; Toronto, 1911.

Menninger, Karl. *Whatever Became of Sin?*. Hawthorn Books: New York, New York, 1973.

Merriam-Webster, Inc. *Merriam-Webster's Collegiate Dictionary*. 2003

Metzger, Bruce M. *A Textual Commentary on the Greek New Testament*. 2nd Edition. United States Bible Societies: New York, New York, 2002.

Moo, Douglas. "1 Timothy 2:11-15: Meaning and Significance," *Trinity Journal* 1.1 NS (1980).

---. "What Does It Mean Not to Teach or Have Authority Over Men?" Edited by John Piper and Wayne Grudem. *Recovering Biblical Manhood and Womanhood*. Crossway Books: Wheaton, Illinois, 1991.

Moss, C. Michael. *The College Press NIV Commentary: 1, 2 Timothy and Titus*. College Press Publishing Company: Joplin, Missouri, 1994.

Müller, Michael. *God the Teacher of Mankind; or, Popular Catholic Theology: The Apostles' Creed*. B. Herder: St. Louis, Missouri, 1888.

Murray, John. *Principles of Conduct*. Eerdmans Publishing Company: Grand Rapids,

Michigan, 1977.

Ockenga, Harold J. *The Church in God: Expository Values in Thessalonians*. Fleming H. Revell Company: Westwood, New Jersey, 1956.

Rall, Franklin Harris, Steele Daniel. "Sanctification." Ed. James Orr, et al. *The International Standard Bible Encyclopaedia*. The Howard-Severance Company: Chicago, Illinois, 1915.

Reese, Gareth. *A Critical and Exegetical Commentary on Paul's Epistle to the Romans*. Scripture Exposition Books: Moberly, Missouri, 1996.

Renn, Stephen D. *Expository Dictionary of Bible Words*. Hendrickson Publishers: Peabody, Massachusetts, 2005.

Schreiner, Thomas R. *Four Views: The Nature of the Atonement*. InterVarsity Press: Downers Grove, Illinois, 2006.

Sewell, E.G., and David Lipscomb. *Questions Answered*. Edited by M.C. Kurfees. McQuiddy Printing Company: Nashville, Tennessee, 1952.

"Shorter Catechism." *The Constitution of the Presbyterian Church (U.S.A.), Part 1: Book of Confessions*. The Office of the General Assembly: Louisville, Kentucky, 2014.

Simpson, George Gaylord. *The Meaning of Evolution*. Mentor: New York, New York, 1956.

Singer, Peter. *Practical Ethics*. 2nd ed. Cambridge University Press: Cambridge, Massachusetts, 1993.

Smith, C. Ryder. *The Bible Doctrine of Salvation*. The Epworth Press: London, England, 1946.

–––. *The Bible Doctrine of Sin*. Epworth Press: London, England, 1953.

Smith, F. LaGard. *Troubling Questions for Calvinists*. Cotswold Publishing: Lynchburg, Virgina, 2007.

Stewart, James S. *The Life and Teaching of Jesus Christ*. Abingdon Press: Nashville, Tennessee, 2000.

–––. *A Man in Christ: The Vital Elements of St. Paul's Religion*. Hodder and Stoughton Limited: London, England, 1951.

Stocker, Abby. "'Wrath of God' Keeps Popular Worship Song Out of 10,000-Plus Churches." *Christianity Today*. 1 Aug 2013. Accessed 27 Feb. 2018.

Stott, John W. *The Cross of Christ*. InterVarsity Press: Downers Grove, Illinois, 1986.

Swanson, James. *Dictionary of Biblical Languages with Semantic Domains: Greek (New Testament)*. Logos Research Systems, Inc., 1997.

Tertullian. "Against Marcion," Book I. *The Writings of Tertullian*, Part Second. *The Ante-Nicene Fathers*, Book 3. Edited by Alexander Roberts, James Donaldson. Hendrickson Publishers: Peabody, Massachusetts, 2012.

Thomas, J.D. *Romans*. R.B. Sweet Company: Austin, Texas, 1965.

Venegas, Katheryn. *Natural Wonders of the World*. University Publications: New York, New York, 2016.

Westminster Confession of Faith, The. Westminster Assembly. William S. Young: Philadelphia, Pennsylvania, 1851.

Wilkes, L.B. *Designs of Christian Baptism*. Guide Printing & Publishing Company: Louisville, Kentucky, 1895.

Woods, Clyde. "How Can Women Be Saved By Childbearing?" *Freed-Hardeman Uni-*

versity 2018 Lectures. Freed-Hardeman University: Henderson, Tennessee, 2018.

Woods, Guy N. *Questions and Answers, Volume II*. Gospel Advocate Company: Nashville, Tennessee, 1986.

Yeakley, Flavil R., Jr. *Why They Left*. Gospel Advocate Company: Nashville, Tennessee, 2012.

TOPICAL INDEX

48, 59, 182
Gareth Reese 34
gender 157
gender roles 155, 192
George Gaylord Simp-
son 1
Gnosticism 9, 22
God
asiety of 11
attributes of 40, 46
authority of 157
commandments of 89
deity of 40
family of 102
fear of 134, 169
ingredients in 184
two kinds 178
fellowship with x, 51
forgiveness of 108
gift of x
government of 55
grace of 150
holiness of 14, 23, 29,
40, 44, 62, 143, 182
image of 12, 101, 153
immutability of 40
invitation of 70
judgement of 67
justice of 46, 185
law of 103, 113-114
likeness of 102
love of 46, 64, 184
mercy of 48
names of 170
perfection of 44
power of 100
presence of 185
relationship with 172
revelation of 23, 97
reverence of 182
righteousness of 40
sovereignty of 2, 29, 35,
55, 147
submission to 33
vengeance of 44
will of 23, 118, 189

wrath of 43, 45, 62, 63,
67, 99, 115, 174
good works 87
gospel
faith and obedience to
153
offensive to the world
44
Gospels, the 174
government 159
grace x, 63, 107-108, 150,
198
cheap 93
fall from 139
period of 196
Grand Canyon 179
guilt of Adam's Sin 38
Gus Nichols 195
Guy N. Woods 142, 195

H

Hadean realm 3, 5
hamartano 120, 121
headship 157, 160, 161
heart 8, 97, 149
human 7, 114
rebellious 118
heaven 191
hekousiōs 124
hell 15, 48, 62
heretic 45
Hinduism 22
hobbies 104
holiness 29, 53, 145
Holy Spirit 8, 80, 84, 97,
105, 139, 158, 162,
175, 197
gift of 80, 84
indwelling of the 195
homosexuality 75
hope 106
Hophni & Phinehas 187
human 111
body 10
cognitive ability 9
sexuality 10

consciousness 15
accountability 30
choice 35, 41, 50, 71,
112, 123, 129, 137-
138
conscience 23, 27
cruelty 22
error 127
fallibility 40
heart 29, 114
ignorance 28
limitations 40
physical dimension 4
pride 33
rebellion 31
reconciliation 22
spirit 37
spiritual dimension 6
unbelief 138
volition 113, 138
willpower 131
human creeds 164
human dignity 2
humanity, creation of 35,
40
human relationships 176
Hymenaeus & Alexander
138
hypocrisy 169

I

idolatry 76, 112
ignorance 28, 100, 105,
114, 145
is bliss 127
immersion 81, 85
immorality 105
impenitence 160
imputed righteousness 58
In Christ Alone 43
infanticide 10
inherited sin 35
innovations 165
instrumental music in
worship 191, 194
inward self 9

SCRIPTURE INDEX

Old Testament